Building Classic ARTS & CRAFTS FURNITURE

Shop Drawings for 33 Traditional Charles Limbert Projects

by

MICHAEL CROW

POPULAR WOODWORKING BOOKS
CINCINNATI, OHIO
www.popularwoodworking.com

TABLE OF CONTENTS

DINING ROOM

STUDY

BEDROOM

INTRODUCTION

THE ARTS AND CRAFTS MOVEMENT

The Arts and Crafts movement has its roots in the writings of John Ruskin, and grows out of the work of William Morris in response to the industrialization and excessive ornamentation characteristic of late Victorian culture. In *The Stones of Venice*, Ruskin argued that industrialization dehumanized society and suggested a return to handwork would solve the problem. Inspired by Ruskin, Morris founded a decorative arts firm with the intent of creating goods by hand. Operating under a number of names, the company produced stained glass, metalwork, textiles, and wallpaper as well as furniture. In addition to shaping the decorative style of the time, Morris had a tremendous influence on society, inspiring cultural foundations, schools and politics.

In the United States, the Arts and Crafts movement found its greatest champion in Gustav Stickley. Stickley began by selling furniture — heavy, rectilinear forms that emphasized joinery as ornamentation, the integrity of simple materials and the importance of handwork in its construction. His designs caught the imagination of the time and inspired numerous imitators, but he didn't limit himself to furniture. He ventured into architecture, construction, social reform, and, most influentially, into publishing. From 1901 to 1917, he edited *The Craftsman*, a magazine dedicated to promoting the ideals of the Arts and Crafts movement. The magazine featured articles on an array of subjects including urban planning, art, history, architecture and travel. Many issues featured architectural drawings of Craftsman-styled homes and measured drawings for Craftsman furniture. Though diverse, the content served, as Stickley noted, the "interest of Better Art, Better Work, and a Better and More Reasonable Way of Living."

Stickley, though, was either unwilling or unable to adapt to changing taste and to a country at war. Financially overextended, he filed for bankruptcy in 1915 and shuttered *The Craftsman* in 1917. At the height of his popularity, he inspired numerous imitators content to produce cheap knock-offs of his designs as well as a few makers who would put their own stamp on the Arts and Crafts movement. Gustav's brothers, Leopold and John George, built furniture that matched their brother's for design and quality, but unlike Gustav, they were able to adapt to the changing market. In Pasadena, the Greene brothers designed homes and furnishings for a wealthy clientele. These "ultimate bungalows" show what can be achieved when talented designers are granted great control and great resources. Inspired by a meeting with William Morris, Elbert Hubbard founded the Roycroft Shop, publishing the magazine *The Philistine* and the Little Journeys book series. Eventually the Roycrofters produced copper and leather handicrafts as well as furniture. In Grand Rapids, Charles Limbert marketed furniture using the language of the Arts and Crafts movement, but with their cutouts, curves, and slanting sides, his best pieces were markedly different from Craftsman furniture and Stickley's many imitators.

CHARLES POTTER LIMBERT (1854-1923)

A *New York Times* article announcing a 1995 exhibit of Limbert furniture suggested, "If Stickley was Hertz, Then Limbert Was Avis." The comparison may seem apt at first glance, since both Limbert and Stickley were some of the most prominent makers of the American Arts & Crafts movement, but Stickley, despite his more recognizable name and reputation as the father of the Arts & Crafts movement in the United States, was ultimately less successful than Limbert, ending his career in bankruptcy. Limbert, less well known than Stickley today, was an innovator at least as interested in the practice of business as he was in perpetuating the ideals of the Arts and Crafts movement.

Charles P. Limbert, courtesy of the Archives, Grand Rapids Public Library, Grand Rapids, Michigan.

Limbert was born in Logansville, Pennsylvania, and grew up in Akron, Ohio. After a brief detour in the carriage trade, he followed his father into furniture sales. He began as a traveling salesman, working for different companies in the Midwest including Monk & Roberts and the John A. Colby Company. During this period, he met Philip Klingman, another salesman. The two agreed to represent each other's wares, reducing the size of their territories. The agreement marks the beginning of an extended partnership and shows Limbert's willingness to experiment with how he did business.

In 1889, Klingman and Limbert settled in Grand Rapids. By this time the city had established itself as a national center for furniture construction and sales. Home to numerous makers, it also hosted a semi-annual trade show. Leasing the Blodgett Building, the two men sublet the floors they didn't use to out-of-town manufacturers. It was not just a novel solution for using unneeded space; it was also, as The Grand Rapids Press later described, the "origin of the furniture exposition building." Real estate was not their primary pursuit; they established the Klingman & Limbert Chair Company. But their Victorian-styled furniture failed to find a customer base, and the venture proved short-lived, dissolving in 1892.

The failure of the Klingman & Limbert Chair Company freed Limbert to pursue his own goals. He founded the Charles P. Limbert furniture company in 1894 and spent the rest of the decade building it. During this period he was also president of the Heald Furniture Company and continued to sell the goods of other makers, including the outdoor furniture of the Old Hickory Company, a brand he would continue to sell even after his own company's success. By the turn of the century, his reputation as a furniture salesman was well established — the April 1901 *Grand Rapids Furniture Record* called him the "furniture commission man." That skill earned him several prominent contracts, including the Patlind Hotel in Grand Rapids, the Grand Canyon Hotel, the Mission Inn (Riverside, CA), and the Old Faithful Inn in Yellowstone National Park.

The company's growing success prompted Limbert to move his factory to nearby Holland in 1906. Limbert's marketing materials would make much of the Holland connection, using the Dutch revival then sweeping the country to increase interest in his "Dutch Arts & Crafts furniture." Limbert's *Booklet 119* boasted the city was "an environment more conducive to artistic effort and a higher quality of craftsmanship." Artistic considerations aside, the new factory was three times the size of the original building and featured modern machinery and easy railway access. Even this expanded space would prove inadequate as the company expanded. It doubled in size through a series of additions over the course of just a few years.

All this capacity supported an expanding product line pushed through a national distribution network. Limbert did not sell directly to customers, instead building relationships with a network of merchants across the country. Re-sellers could count on sponsored national campaigns that included streetcar signs and ads in *The Craftsman*. They would also receive signs customized with their names for display in storefront windows, color portfolios for in-store use and black-and-white booklets they could send home with interested customers.

Even the best advertising couldn't prevent changing taste. As interest in Arts and Crafts furniture faded,

BLODGETT BUILDING

GRAND RAPIDS, MICHIGAN

The Pioneer and Leader

Exclusive Furniture Exhibition Building

FIFTY-SEVENTH SEMI-ANNUAL DISPLAY

EXHIBITORS

Charles P. Limbert Co.	Holland, Mich.
Grand Rapids Bookcase & Chair Co.	Hastings, Mich.
Rockford Chair & Furn. Co.	Rockford, Ill.
Stow & Davis Furn. Co.	Grand Rapids, Mich.
Grand Ledge Chair Co.	Grand Ledge, Mich.
Binghamton Chair Co.	Binghamton, N. Y.
Overton Company	Grand Rapids, Mich.
John Widdicomb Co.	Grand Rapids, Mich.
Lauzon Furn. Co.	Grand Rapids, Mich.
Maher Bros. Co.	Medina, N. Y.
Banta Furn. Co.	Goshen, Ind.
Gunn Furniture Co.	Grand Rapids, Mich.
C. H. Campbell Furniture Co.	Shelbyville, Ind.

Limbert and Klingman first leased the Blodgett Building in 1895. It remained Limbert's showroom for decades, even after construction of the Holland factory.

The Holland factory before the 1912 expansion. Image courtesy of the Holland Historical Trust.

Limbert shifted production to meet those tastes and successfully weathered the storms that would sink Stickley. Though later catalogs still featured some of Limbert's most distinctive Arts and Crafts pieces, they shared the page with a variety of styles, including Chinese, Italian, Queen Anne and William and Mary.

In 1921 Limbert suffered a stroke while traveling in Hawaii. He would never recover fully, and declining health prompted him to sell his shares in the company in September of 1922. He was dead less than a year later, leaving an estate of roughly $500,000 (worth about $6.5 million in 2011 dollars) to his sister and sole heir, Clara. The company that bore his name survived Limbert's death, but it could not survive the economic austerity imposed by World War II, closing in 1944.

LIMBERT FURNITURE DESIGN

While relatively little is known about Limbert's personal life (he raised chickens and was an avid gardener), the output of his professional career is well-documented in surviving marketing materials and the furniture itself. In the prefaces to his booklets and in *The Grand Rapids Furniture Record*, Limbert traced the roots of Mission furniture from the Spanish west, back to Spain's commercial ties with Holland. The Spanish, reliant on Holland for commercial goods, took their familiarity with Dutch furniture with them to the Southwest, interpret-

The Limbert Furniture Co. adapted to changing taste by expanding their furniture line beyond Arts and Crafts. The Italian pieces from this 1916 advertisement (left) featured prominently in the January 1917 exposition, as did their other period styles.

Limbert's Holland Dutch Arts & Crafts Furniture

Salesroom: First Floor Blodgett Bldg., Since 1889

Our January Exhibition of Dutch Arts & Crafts Furniture will include over seventy-five new patterns which have been added to our present well known, large and comprehensive line.

Buyers who are interested in Arts & Crafts Furniture will find our line the most complete and desirable that is made.

Goods that are priced right, sound in construction and practical—made and finished so they do not need the attention of a cabinetmaker when they are unpacked, nor must they be followed up by a repair man when sold.

Nothing has been produced up to the present time which gives equal value for the price, or which affords the dealer so quick a "turn-over" and such large profits as does Limbert's Holland Dutch Arts & Crafts.

CHARLES P. LIMBERT COMPANY

**BLODGETT BUILDING,
47-51 OTTAWA ST.,
GRAND RAPIDS, MICH.**

**FACTORY AND
EXECUTIVE OFFICES
HOLLAND, MICH.**

SALESMEN
**M. D. BLUM — AL KLINGMAN
A. L. BRACKETT — L. A. JAMES
R. W. HERRICK — D. B. K. VAN RAALTE**

ing those forms through the materials and tools available to them in the New World. This purported lineage is another attempt, like Limbert's description of the Dutch heritage of his workers, to associate his company and products with the values associated with Holland and its people during the Dutch Revival. From paint to household cleaners to furniture, Dutch stood for traditional values, hard work, and cleanliness. But the influences on Limbert's style are rather more expansive than a single country. He made several trips to Europe, buying furniture and researching furniture manufacturing and sales techniques. This broad exposure finds expression in much of the company's output.

Limbert is often dismissed as a copyist of more capable designers. And the debt some of his pieces owe to other makers is obvious, but he was more than a mere imitator. Rather, at his best, he was a capable synthesist, combining diverse elements from European, American, and Japanese design into striking (and sometimes strikingly modern) forms. The sources for his inspiration are wide ranging. His earliest Arts and Craft line shows a debt to the architect Charles Voysey, Dutch folk forms, and Art Nouveau. The later line shows Limbert's familiarity with the Craftsman furniture produced by Gustav Stickley, the Prairie style of Frank Lloyd Wright, and the work of Charles Rennie Mackintosh and the Vienna Secessionists.

The 1903 catalog captures Limbert's first full line, and is, from its typography to its pen-and-ink illustrations, carefully orchestrated to evoke a sense of traditional handwork. That sensibility carries into the design of the furniture as well. This is Limbert at his most rustic, with many of the pieces almost crude in design and construction. Heavy joinery and heart-shaped cutouts abound. Limbert was not yet calling his furniture "Holland Dutch Arts and Crafts," but many of the pieces in the 1903 catalog would not seem out of place in the Dutch countryside. Evident, too, in the overhanging

A living room furnished by Limbert. From an ad in the December 1916 *Grand Rapids Furniture Record.*

A Library in Limbert's Holland Dutch Arts and Crafts

Many of the booklets contained color plates illustrating rooms furnished by the Limbert Company. Rendered here is a library, complete with desk, rocker, Morris chair, magazine stand, and bookcase. Image Courtesy, The Winterthur Library: Printed Book and Periodical Collection.

The overhanging top and sloping sides of many Limbert pieces evoke the *torii*.

tops and flaring sides of several pieces is a visual allusion to the Japanese *torii*, or temple gate.

By the time the 1905 catalog was published, Limbert appears to have controlled his more whimsical impulses as he enters what will be the peak of his creative output. A few pieces (some Art Nouveau-influenced bookcases, the No. 602 Cellarette, the No. 416 China Cabinet) carryover from the 1903 catalog, but much of the line shows a Mission influence. The exposed joinery, rectilinear forms and visual mass of this furniture would not be out of place in the offerings of the many manufacturers responding to the increasing popularity of Craftsman furniture. Some of these designs match or exceed Stickley's.

As proficient as Limbert was in the Mission vernacular, much of his best work falls into a broader category of Arts and Crafts. Sharing the pages of the 1905 catalog with Mission-influenced work are some of Limbert's best pieces, those fusing American and European sensibilities. Alloyed in this furniture are the Arts and Crafts emphasis on honest materials and minimal ornamentation with Mackintosh's use of negative and positive space and the tapered sides of the Vienna Secessionists. The resulting designs are greater than the sum of their parts, yielding unique forms that brought the best of diverse influences together and made them available to the mass market. These designs are also often curiously timeless. Visual rhythm, canted sides and acute angles make the No. 81 hall chair a striking design. In fumed quartersawn oak, it's at home in a room with other Arts and Crafts furniture. In teak or maple, the chair would not be out of place amidst mid-Century or Dutch modern. Paint it silver or red and the same chair is at home in the most atomic of ranch houses.

Changing tastes prompted Limbert to move away from the Arts and Crafts style to a variety of period reproductions. The adaptation saved the company, but at the cost of Limbert's unique contribution to the history of furniture. The company's period reproductions lack the impact of Limbert's earlier designs, and it is those earlier designs that cement Limbert's legacy as a guiding light of the Arts and Crafts movement in America.

A reproduction of the No. 81 Hall Chair.

LIMBERT FURNITURE CONSTRUCTION

Limbert's booklets linger on descriptions of materials and construction techniques used to produce the company's furniture and emphasize the level of handwork required to produce each item. If you believe the marketing hyperbole, it seems individual cabinetmakers produced each piece by hand using only the best construction techniques. The company actually used an array of joinery techniques from plugged screws to dowels, to pinned mortise and tenons.

putting them on. The front posts have a tenon cut on them and are mortised through the arms, then a pin is driven through the arm into the post. It is obvious that such construction is as strong as is possible to make and at the same time is a crafty looking and ornamental feature.

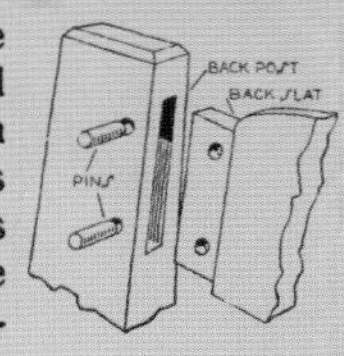

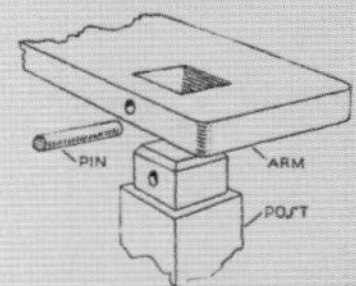

There are other structural devices which are ornamental as well as strong, for example those shown in the two following sketches. In the one the stretcher of a table is represented mortised through the leg and left projecting on the opposite side. The other sketch shows a table stretcher mortised through the leg and a key driven through the end, both are examples of good construction.

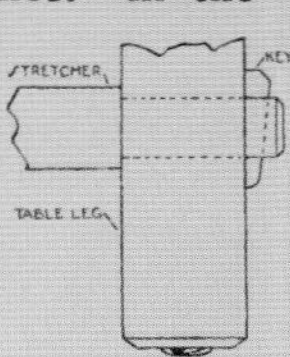

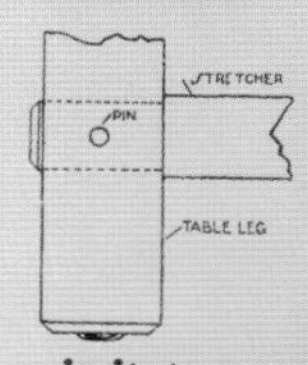

All seating pieces have perfect fitting corner blocks, which are glued and screwed in to add to their strength. Throughout our construction will always be found the soundest devices known to the cabinet-maker's art. Our construction is what it appears to be. We use no subterfuges to imitate sound structural devices.

All our rocking chairs are provided with rockers that are cut straight with the grain of the wood and bent in large bending presses. This eliminates the danger of breaking that is common with rockers which are cut on a curve that partly crosses the grain.

The quaint designs which have developed into what is now known as "Flanders Furniture," illustrations of

18

The booklets emphasized the craft involved in building Limbert furniture. This page details variations on the mortise and tenon. Image Courtesy, The Winterthur Library: Printed Book and Periodical Collection.

Many of the pieces from the 1903 catalog were assembled using plugged screws, either to allow for shipping the items flat with assembly at their destination, or to minimize production costs. The Mission pieces tended to be well built, often featuring pinned mortise and tenons, tusked tenons, splined miter joints, and either tongue-and-groove or splined slab sides and tops. Backs were of three-ply material and attached with screws through elongated holes. Dust panels separated drawers, and silver draws featured removable leather pads. The modest dowel freed Limbert to experiment with splayed sides and cutouts, yielding some of his most striking designs. The outdoor furniture tended to use less-desirable flatsawn wood and was often bolted together.

The company began by offering furniture in ash or oak, but eventually most furniture was only available in white oak. The oak was quarter sawn, then air dried before use. Quartersawn oak (first cut into pie shaped wedges, then those wedges cut

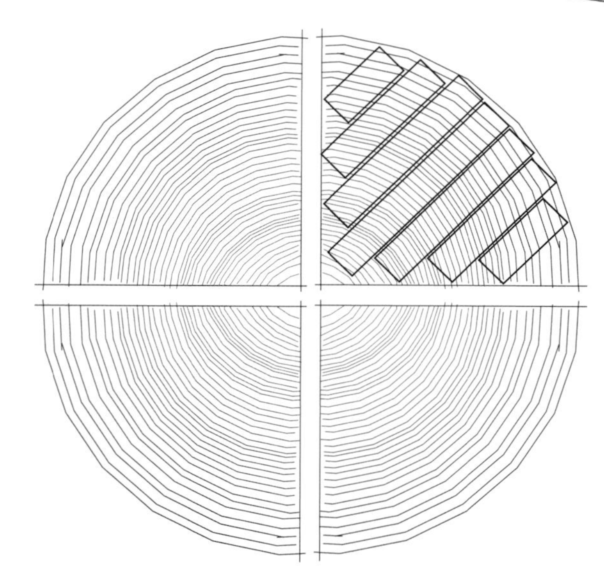

To produce boards with vertical grain, a log is cut into quarters, then sawn into planks.

into boards so that the tree's annular rings are turned into vertical grain), also shows attractive grain and ray flecks. The process yields less lumber per log, so it is more costly than flatsawn wood, but produces more stable and more attractive lumber. Customers could buy unfinished furniture, select from a number of finishes from golden to dark brown or have furniture stained to match the interiors of their homes. A fumed finish, where the oak was sealed in airtight containers and exposed to ammonia fumes to darken it, was the most popular finish according to *Booklet 119*, but at least some pieces were sprayed with a natural resin varnish.

As it did for many local makers, the Grand Rapids Brass Company supplied the hardware used in Limbert furniture. Hammered copper pyramid pulls, knobs and rings all had their place, and drawers often had mortised locks.

UPHOLSTERY

Customers could choose to have their purchases upholstered in Morocco, a goat skin, or in top grain Steer hide. The company also offered a selection of tapestry fabrics chosen

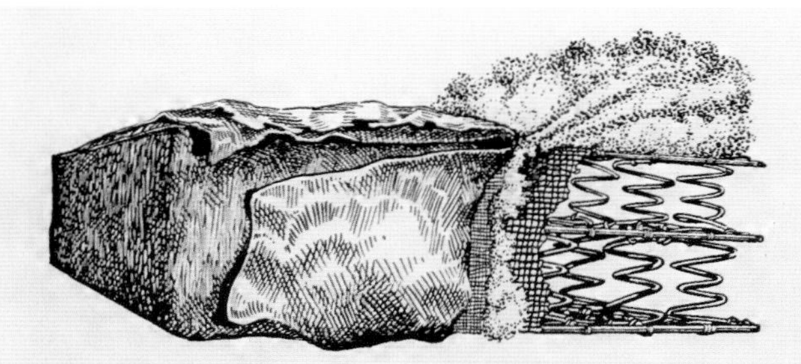

Construction of our Double-Deck Spring Cushions

The company's marketing materials boasted about the double layer of springs used in its cushions. Image Courtesy, The Winterthur Library: Printed Book and Periodical Collection.

THE GROTE-RANKIN CO.

Comp. Furnishers of Homes, Steamboats and Hotels.

Arts and Crafts Furniture

For the Living Room and Den

Wherever furniture built on the Arts and Crafts or Mission order is known, the furniture made by the Charles P. Limbert Co. is recognized as the best the country produces in its line. Therefore, we feel that in offering Limbert Arts and Crafts furniture to the people of Seattle, we are giving them the best that money and American skill are capable of creating.

The frames of this furniture are made of carefully selected white oak, finished in a beautiful brown color that no other manufacturer of furniture has ever been able to equal. Some pieces are upholstered in leather and some come with loose leather cushions—the only covering used being soft, pliable goatskin, the handsomest and most durable leather to be had.

This combination of the best of materials, assembled by the highest class of workmanship, produces the very best of the Mission furniture on the market today. We welcome comparison of Limbert's Arts and Crafts furniture with any other similar kind.

And the line is very moderately priced. Chairs are on display, from $6.00 up; rockers, from $9.75 up; settees, from $15.00 up; davenports, from $31.00 up, and center and library tables, from $9.75 up, and many other pieces, such as magazine racks, stools, seats, etc., at a wide range of prices.

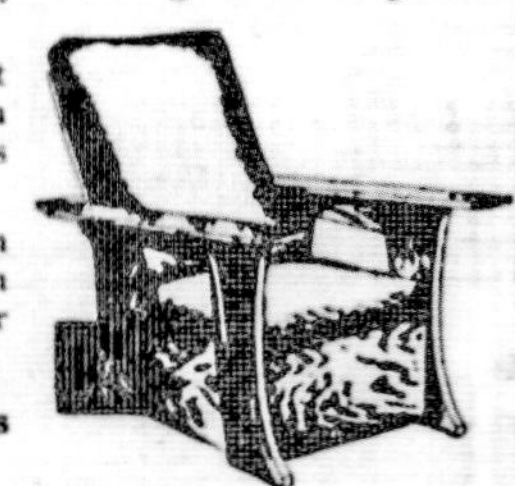

The Grote-Rankin Store Is the Exclusive Seattle Agency for Limbert's Arts and Crafts Furniture.

A 1908 ad from The Seattle Star emphasizes that Limbert furniture was available in a "wide range of prices."

to complement the fumed oak finish. Options were much more limited for outdoor furniture: cushions were available in green denim.

Depending on the piece slats, webbing, or springs supported loose spring cushions featuring a double layer of springs with a soft upper deck and more supportive lower deck. The spring layers were covered in burlap, padded, and upholstered in muslin before receiving their leather covers.

PRICE

The Limbert Furniture Company produced two kinds of marketing materials. Booklets, generally intended for customers, did not contain pricing information; catalogs, meant for re-sellers, did. From the catalogs, it is not clear whether the price is the manufacturer's suggested retail price or the wholesale price offered to the re-seller. Where these original prices are available, they have been included in the descriptions accompanying the drawings.

Limbert furniture sold at a number of price points targeted to a range of customers. A simple magazine stand like the No. 353 cost only $4.50 in 1905. The more elaborate No. 322, with its triple bays and leaded-glass doors cost $54.00. Adjusted for inflation, the No. 353 would have cost about $110 and the No. 322 $1,300 in 2011 dollars. Inflation-adjusted prices don't tell the whole story. Consider that the average worker in the United States made about $500 in 1905. An accountant could earn $2,000, a mechanical engineer $5,000. The $200 No. 848 sofa required almost half a year's average income to purchase, and an accountant would need to crunch the numbers before deciding to buy an item that cost more than a month's pay.

ABOUT THE DRAWINGS

In 50 years of business, the Limbert Furniture Company produced a staggering variety of designs in many different styles. In selecting the pieces to include here, I've chosen from the best of the company's Arts and Crafts output (roughly 1903-1917) while trying to include furniture suitable for all around the home. I've also avoided including previously published works. See the section on Further Reading at the back of the book for more information on those pieces.

With rare exception, these drawings are based on measurements extrapolated from known dimensions using catalog and auction photos. With dimensions in hand, I then created three-dimensional models of the pieces before generating the 2D views and parts lists presented here. Such an approach carries with it the risk of error, and it also requires some guesswork where internal details aren't documented in the photographic record. In instances where I haven't been able to view internal details, I've relied on standard furniture construction techniques to fill in the blanks. Furniture built using these drawings and the parts lists should honor the spirit of the originals even if they do not replicate them exactly.

TECHNIQUES

Entire books have been written on tools and techniques for building furniture—indeed, books have been written on single joints—so this chapter does not pretend to encyclopedic completeness. Rather the information presented here is intended to give the beginning woodworker a minimum of information required to build the furniture presented in later chapters. Note, too, that you can often accomplish the same end using very different methods depending on your tools, time and inclination. One woodworker might prefer to chop mortises by hand and another to rout or drill them. Most Arts and Crafts furniture can be built with only a few simple joints, and Limbert furniture is no exception (though slanted sides can present a challenge). Since joinery as ornamentation was a central tenet of the Arts and crafts movement, it makes sense to take care when cutting and fitting parts. If you have doubts about how to cut a joint, practice on scrap before sawing into your project wood.

TOOLS

Award-winning cabinetmaker and educator Gary Rogowski has observed that you could build anything with a bandsaw, router and chisel. This may be a slight exaggeration (keeping that chisel sharp, for one thing, is a skill unto itself and requires some equipment), but it emphasizes an important point. You don't need every tool or machine under the sun to build a piece of furniture. The Limbert and Stickley factories had rooms full of machinery, but many of their designs easily adapt to shops with much more limited tooling. Do your research before you buy, and use the techniques and tools you're comfortable with. You will need to be able to dimension stock, cut joinery, clamp pieces for assembly and prepare surfaces for finishing. Don't forget safety equipment either. Protect your eyes, your ears and your lungs.

Many of the pieces featured in the book can be built with surfaced lumber since they use only 3/4-inch stock. But other pieces require different thicknesses for slats and panels. Buying rough lumber gives you greater control over your material as well. Jack, jointer and smoothing planes allow you to true rough stock by hand, but most woodworkers save time by using powered jointers and planers. In the small shop, a combo machine will save space but at the cost of time spent changing between functions.

A table saw is at the center of many workshops since it allows for ripping and cross-cutting wood to size, and can be used to cut joinery, including dadoes, rabbets, grooves and tenons. While you can build without it, it does simplify many operations. A coping saw, bandsaw, or jigsaw allows you to cut curves, a common operation when building many Limbert pieces.

With the right bits, the router can cut tenons, dovetails, rabbets, dados and grooves. It can also profile edges. Guided by a template or bearing, it can also be used to duplicate parts using patterns, an extremely useful capability for reproducing the cutouts and curves that distinguish Limbert's best designs. See page 14 for more detail on pattern routing.

WOOD SELECTION

If your desire is to hew as closely to the originals when reproducing Limbert furniture, then white oak is an appropriate wood choice. The furniture in the 1903 catalog was, with few exceptions, available in ash or white oak. Oak predominated in later lines. The wood was readily available, durable, and machined and finished easily so it made a good furniture wood. But it isn't the only option available. Cherry or mahogany (the choice of the Greene brothers) suit the Craftsman-influenced pieces drawn here, and the more distinctly Limbert designs would look good in a variety of woods, or even painted.

Wood selection can make or break a project, so it pays to take your time at the lumberyard. Avoid twisted, cupped, bowed, or otherwise warped boards, then select to match for grain and color. Buy enough material to allow for mistakes and for choosing the right wood for a given part. Let stock acclimate in the shop before being used since solid wood will expand and contract with changes in humidity and temperature. Sheet goods are useful for panels and drawer bottoms, but care is required when cutting or sanding to avoid damage to the thin veneer faces.

When it comes time to cut parts, leave your options open: don't make a cut until you need to, and leave yourself slack when you can. When beginning a project, the impulse is often to cut all parts at once, but even the best cut list and most careful measurements may yield variation between the plan and the piece. Working with subassemblies simplifies work and minimizes risk. Try to cut similar parts at the same time so minor variations in tool setup don't lead to variations in the size of the parts. If a part's fit relies on how other parts come together — a drawer front in its opening, for example — grief can be avoided if you measure the actual distance between those parts instead of relying on the plan.

Since it is the most visible part of the completed project, use the best boards from your stack for the top. If you are finish planing, it can be useful to orient boards so the grain runs in the same direction, but otherwise place boards to yield the best looking top. Generally the goal is to produce a top that looks as much like a single board as possible. There is no need to alternate the direction of growth rings or to rip and re-glue wide boards to control movement. Often fewer boards used in a glue-up produce more attractive results, but boards of similar width will look better together than a wide board together with smaller boards.

Example of a through mortise and tenon.

MORTISE AND TENON

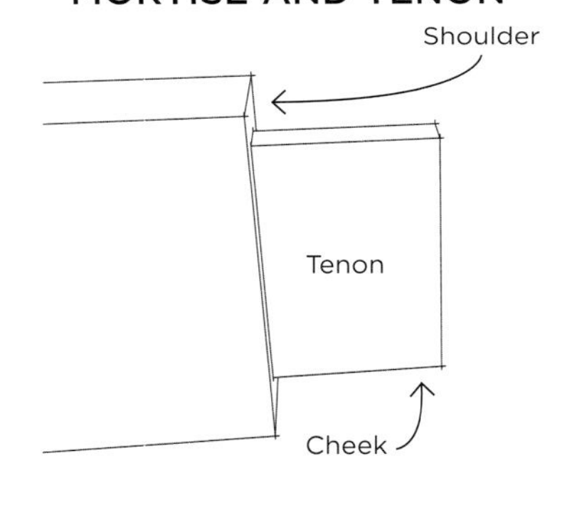

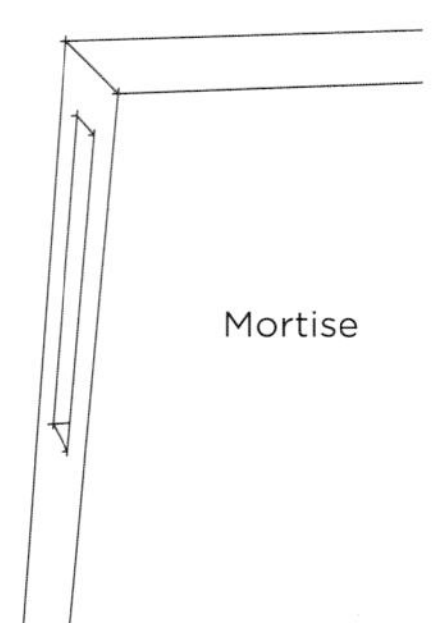

Rails and stiles look their best when grain runs along them. They'll also tend to stay straight over the passage of time. Avoid using stock with the arching lines of cathedral grain to make these parts. In the same way straight-grained wood can emphasize a straight piece, curved grain can complement a curved piece. And when building a row of drawers, try to cut the drawer fronts from a single piece of wood.

MORTISE AND TENON

The mortise-and-tenon joint featured prominently in Limbert furniture. It ties cases together, forms the frames for panels and doors, and connects table aprons and legs. In the through tenon, where the tenon passes all the way through the mortise and protrudes from the other side, the joint ceases to be merely functional and becomes decorative. The keyed tenon, a through tenon mortised to accommodate a wedge, adds a layer of complexity to the joint and allows furniture to be knocked down. The joint seems simple enough—remove wood at the end of a piece to form a tongue sized to fit in a hole cut in the mating piece—but care should be taken when cutting it, especially when it's a through or keyed mortise. The simplicity of Arts and Crafts furniture is part of its appeal, but that simplicity requires tight tolerances and is unforgiving of sloppy work.

It is easier to cut a tenon to fit a mortise than the reverse. Begin by marking out the location of the mortise. If cutting the mortise by hand, a marking knife or cutting gauge will help keep the edges of the joint neat. The depth of the mortise should account for the full length of the tenon and a little extra for excess glue. You can drill out most of the waste, then pare the edges of the mortise, but a dedicated mortising chisel makes quick work of them.

Chop down.

Pry the waste free.

The finished mortise.

MORTISE ROUTER JIG

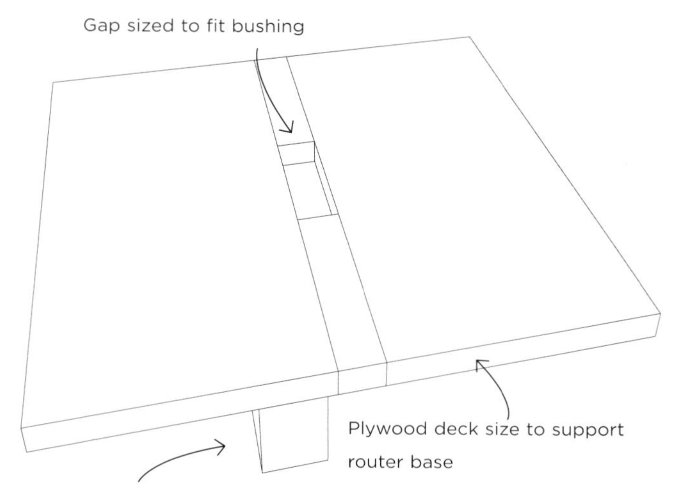

The router's template bushing rides in the jig to cut a mortise of a specific size.

The cutting gauge is set to the length of the tenon and passed around the work piece.

Define the shoulders.

With the shoulders defined, cut the cheeks.

There are a number of ways to cut a mortise using power tools. A hollow chisel mortiser drills a square hole, and by moving the work piece along the axis of the joint, a mortise of any length can be created. A router, guided by a template or a straight edge guide creates very clean walls, but the round ends it leaves will need to be squared or the tenon rounded to fit.

If cutting a tenon by hand, mark the joint, cut around the piece to establish the shoulder line, then cut the cheeks. A similar approach can be taken when cutting the tenon with power tools. Cut the shoulder line on the table saw using the miter gauge or sliding table, then cut the cheeks using a tenoning jig. If the piece being tenoned is too long for the table saw, a bandsaw can cut the cheeks. Passing the piece over a dado stack will also work, as will a straight bit in a router table.

However it's cut, the tenon should fit the mortise snugly without being forced. Shave a tight tenon with a rasp, block plane, or scraper, taking care to remove an even amount from either side of the tenon and to avoid tapering the thickness of tenon.

The through mortise and tenon is cut in much the same way, except the mortise passes completely through the piece. To maintain neat openings, cut the mortise from both sides, being sure to reference all cuts from

With the fence set to match the length of the tenon, the blade is set to the depth of the shoulder and the work piece passed over the blade to define the shoulders.

If the tenon is too long to safely use the table saw tenoning jig, the cheeks can be removed with a bandsaw.

the same side to ensure proper alignment. Take special care when cutting the show side of the joint since any mistakes will be on display. The tenon's end is left proud and chamfered or rounded over.

The keyed through tenon passes far enough past the mortise so that it can itself be pierced with a tapered mortise. A wooden key is then wedged in the mortise, locking the joint together. The tenon needs to be long enough so that the end won't blow out when the key is driven home. When the joint is assembled, the inside edge of the key mortise should fall just inside the mortise to ensure the key will pull the two pieces tightly together.

FRAME AND PANEL

Most of the case pieces featured in this book use frame and panel construction to join the parts of the case. The frame is joined with mortise and tenons and grooved to capture the panel. The tenons can be the same depth as the groove, which simplifies construction, or a deeper mortise can be cut in the groove for a longer tenon. When grooves need to be stopped, as they do when the stiles run long to form case legs, a straight or spiral bit of the appropriate width is probably the easiest approach to take. If the groove can run the whole length of the stile or rail, then it can be easily cut with a dado stack (or a standard blade in multiple passes) on the table saw or with a router using a straight or spiral bit, or a wing cutter.

TABLE SAW TENON JIG

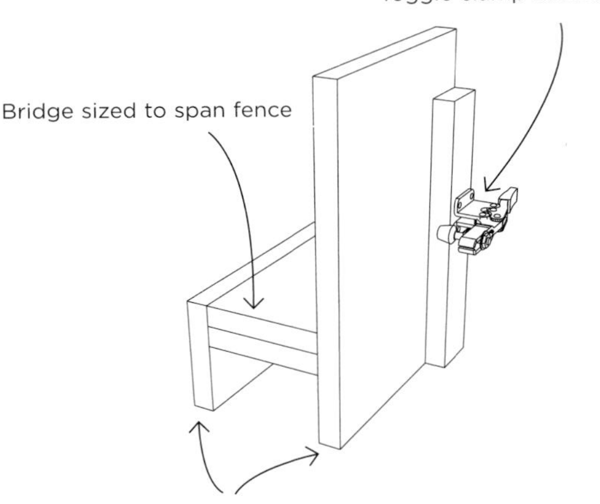

FRAME AND PANEL CONSTRUCTION

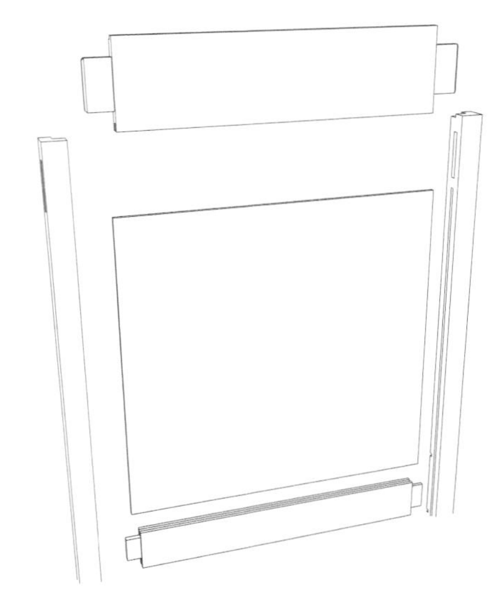

The panels can be cut from solid wood or veneered sheet goods. Since they can be easily cut to size and don't require glue ups, sheet goods require less effort. And since they are dimensionally stable, panels made from sheet goods can be glued to their grooves, making for stronger construction. Conversely, solid wood panels should be sized to leave an expansion gap left loose in their grooves so they can freely expand and contract with changes in temperature and humidity. Either veneered panels or solid wood panels can be made from quarter-inch stock to match the thickness of the groove, but a half-inch panel, rabbeted around the edges to fit the groove, makes a piece feel more solid.

PATTERN ROUTING

Many Limbert pieces make use of multiple copies of identical pieces, oftentimes featuring cutouts. These can be cut individually, but for more than one or two pieces, it is more effi-

A pattern doesn't have to be full size. This pattern captures the key details—feet, square cutout, and rounded corner—of the No. 367's side while omitting the length. To reproduce the full-size part, reposition the pattern as needed.

The pattern is traced on the blank and roughed out on the bandsaw.

Guided by a bearing, the flush cut bit follows the contours of the pattern.

cient to prepare a pattern and use it to guide a router fit with a pattern-routing bit. Wood, plywood, mdf, or hardboard of appropriate size can be used to create the pattern. Any flaws in the pattern will be replicated in the final parts, so take pains to make a perfect pattern. Consider, too, completing a test run with the pattern before using project lumber.

Use the completed pattern to trace the part on the wood, then rough out the part. Once all blanks are rough cut, affix the pattern to the wood. If the design of the part allows it, the template can be built with toggle clamps. Otherwise, double-sided tape can be used, or if part of the piece won't show in the finished project, a couple of screws will hold the pattern in place. The bit's bearing will follow the contours of the pattern, trimming the rough blank to finished size.

ASSEMBLY

Dry-fitting, where the pieces of the project are assembled without glue and clamped to verify the final fit of all parts, goes a long way to ensuring piece of mind when assembling a project. Gather all parts and a sufficient number of clamps and cauls to protect the wood from being marred by clamps. Decide on a sequence for assembly and then put the piece together. Smaller pieces will come together easily, but larger projects are better managed in subassemblies. For example, you might assemble the ends of the table, wait for them to dry, then connect the ends with the front and back aprons. If anything comes together with difficulty, refine the joints until they fit.

Having rehearsed final assembly, it will go more smoothly. Original pieces were assembled with hot hide glue, and that's still an option today, as is liquid hide glue. Hide glue has the benefit of being reversible when treated with heat and moisture, a convenient feature should the piece ever need to be repaired. PVA, or yellow wood glue is more commonly used today. Apply a thin layer to both surfaces of the joints, fit them together, then tighten your clamps.

Before the glue has a chance to set, measure case goods (and drawers) for square by measuring the diagonals. If the diagonals are the same length, the piece is square. If they don't match, a clamp across the longer diagonal or a few blows with a wood mallet should bring things into square.

The square cutouts on a pattern can be roughed out with a jigsaw and refined with a rasp and sandpaper, but it is easier to prepare a quick template to shape them. To produce the square here, a four-inch strip was ripped from the center of the board, then crosscut. With those pieces spaced four inches apart, the pattern is glued together, producing a four-inch square.

It is tempting to wipe any glue squeeze out with a damp rag, but unless you're thorough, you run the risk of smearing a thin layer of glue along the joint. It is easier to allow the glue to dry to a gel state, then scrape with a chisel. Leave the clamps on long enough to allow the glue to cure (anywhere from a few hours to overnight, depending on the glue). If you've prefinished the piece, you can remove your painter's

TYPICAL DRAWER CONSTRUCTION

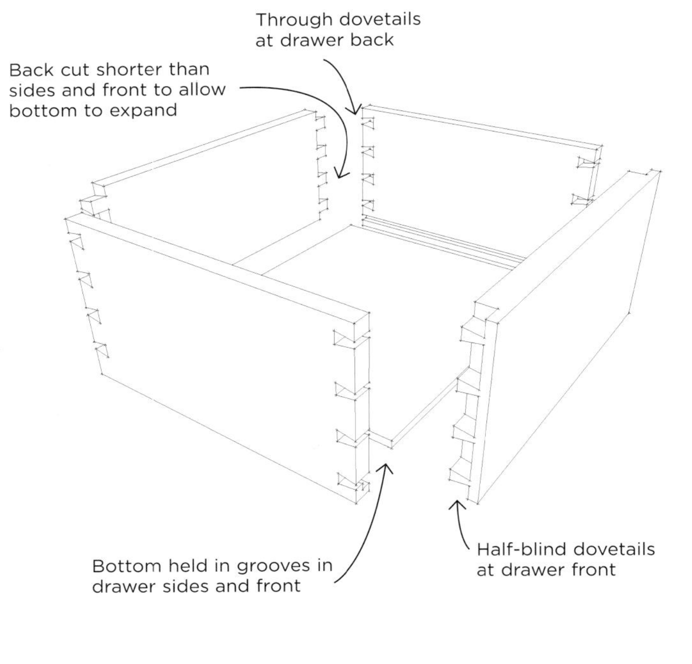

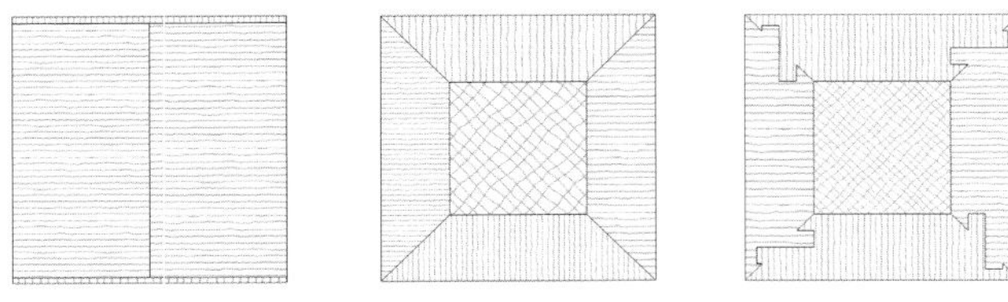

To produce quartersawn figure on all faces of a leg, Gustav Stickley veneered the plain faces (left). His brothers Leopold and John George mitered four pieces around a solid core (center). A locking miter bit refines the technique (right).

tape and put your completed project in its new home. If you are assembling before applying finish coats, double check to make sure you've cleaned up any squeeze out since it will show under a finish. Wiping the piece with mineral spirits should show any problems.

DRAWER CONSTRUCTION

The drawers in Limbert pieces used half-blind dovetails at the front and through dovetails at the back to join the drawer box together, with the drawer bottom held in place by a groove. This is a common drawer construction, and it makes for a strong drawer since the dovetails provide mechanical resistance to forces acting on the drawer. If the thought of cutting dovetails doesn't appeal, there are other ways to join a drawer. Pinned or locking rabbets will also work in place of dovetails, and with an applied front, the box can also be assembled using box joints. Plywood drawer bottoms can be glued in grooves in the sides, front, and back of the drawer, but a solid-wood bottom should be captured in the sides and front of the drawer and left to expand towards the back of the drawer, which should be cut so that it ends flush with the top of the drawer bottom.

THE QUADRILINEAR LEG

Since quartersawn figure will only show on two sides of a piece of wood, legs present a challenge when building Arts and Crafts furniture. Different makers tackled the problem with different approaches. Gustav Stickley veneered the plain faces of his legs. His brothers mitered four pieces and glued them around a core to create a solid leg with four faces of quartersawn figure. The modern take on this solution is to use a lock miter bit on the router table to create the joints, mechanically locking the edges together as well as creating ample gluing surface.

THE TAPERED COLUMN BASE

The tapered column base occurs regularly in Limbert furniture, especially the occasional tables (see the No. 164 Pagoda Table and No. 251 Tabouret). The slight taper (usually 3-5 degrees) yields a miter angle of just under 45 degrees. Miter the edges of the piece using the table saw or a chamfer bit in a router, then join the piece with its mate using packing tape along the outside edges. Fold the pieces along this tape hinge and then run a folded-over piece of sand paper along both edges of the joint to fine-tune the fit.

Packing tape can also be used to clamp the pieces during final assembly. When all four miters fit, place the four pieces together with their outsides facing up. Run packing tape along the joints, flip over, spread glue along the mitered edges, and roll up the base. Captured shelves require a different strategy: glue up two sub-assemblies of two side each, place the shelf between the two sub-assemblies, and glue them together.

FINISHING

A good finish begins with good surface preparation. If sanding, begin with a low enough grit to easily remove milling marks, then work up through the grits, stopping at 180 or 220, then vacuum the work or blow it off with compressed air to remove all dust. You can also plane and scrape your parts smooth using a smoothing plane and card scraper. Surfaced stock can be sharp where two edges meet, so break all edges with 220 grit sand paper or a light pass with a block plane.

I like to pre-finish my parts when I can, since it helps minimize drips and runs and eases surface preparation. Using blue painter's tape, I tape joints and then apply my finish. During glue up, I then tape surfaces at risk of glue squeeze out. If you choose to assemble your work then apply your finish, pay particular attention to where glue has squeezed out during assembly since any residual glue will show under a finish coat.

Much effort has been given trying to replicate the traditional fumed finish of Arts and Crafts furniture without actually fuming in order to avoid the risks of working with ammonia. These alternatives range in complexity, some requiring multiple stages of stains, dyes, and glazes. The results can be satisfactory, but fuming with ammonia is not difficult, and the safety risks can be minimized with care. Begin by acquiring ammonia of proper strength. Fuming requires a greater concentration of ammonia than the weak solution used in household cleaning. A 26% solution is available at blueprint supply stores, and a gallon jug should see you through many projects. When working with the ammonia, take appropriate precautions. Work outside or an extremely well ventilated area, wear safety goggles, a respirator with appropriate chemical cartridges, long sleeves and gloves.

The piece is placed in an airtight container and exposed to the ammonia fumes, which react with the tannins present in white oak. Smaller items can be placed in a plastic container, but larger items will need to be tented. A suitable tent can be made from 1 x 2 stock and plastic sheeting. Build a frame large enough to house your work and staple sheeting to the frame. Place the piece under the tent and pour ammonia into a glass or plastic dish (glass pie pans work well). Expose the furniture until the desired darkness is reached. 12 to 48 hours should be sufficient. To gauge progress, place offcuts in the tent along with the project. You can then pull an offcut and check and see if the wood has reached the desired color. Be warned: fumed oak doesn't take its final color until a finish coat is applied, so give the sample offcut a quick wipe with boiled linseed oil to gauge color.

Spent ammonia can be diluted in a large bucket of water and spread on the lawn. Let the piece air out, then proceed with your topcoat. I like to wet sand my fumed projects with 320 grit and boiled linseed oil, then apply a couple of coats of de-waxed garnet or orange shellac and a coat of dark paste wax. If the piece will see heavy use or exposure to moisture, I'll add a final coat of satin polyurethane and skip the wax.

If ammonia fuming seems intimidating, you can try one of the many less-noxious alternatives. One easy one is to use stain, oil and shellac. Begin by sanding to 150 grit, then raise the grain by dampening it with water (a spray bottle works well here). Let dry overnight, then sand with 220 grit and remove sanding dust from the project by blowing with compressed air or vacuuming.

A base coat of oil-based stain in a walnut tone provides the first layer of color. Apply the stain following the manufacturer's instructions and let dry overnight. Watco Danish Oil (again in a walnut tone) finishes the color base coat. Apply per directions and let dry. Then apply a coat or two of thinned amber or garnet shellac. If the piece will see heavy use or moisture, topcoat it with your preferred varnish or lacquer.

These are just two ways to finish quarter-sawn white oak Arts and Crafts furniture. Other methods will yield attractive results or apply to different woods, but however it is finished, the furniture looks best with a satin or matte finish.

HARDWARE

Sourcing Arts and Crafts hardware is easier today than ever before thanks to the rise of online commerce. A web search will yield a staggering variety of sources. The list below contains those I've used and recommend.

Craftsman Hardware
www.craftsmanhardware.com
509.766.4322

Horton Brasses
www.horton-brasses.com
1.800.754.9127

Lee Valley
www.leevalley.com
1.800.871.8158

Rockler
www.rockler.com
1.800.279.4441

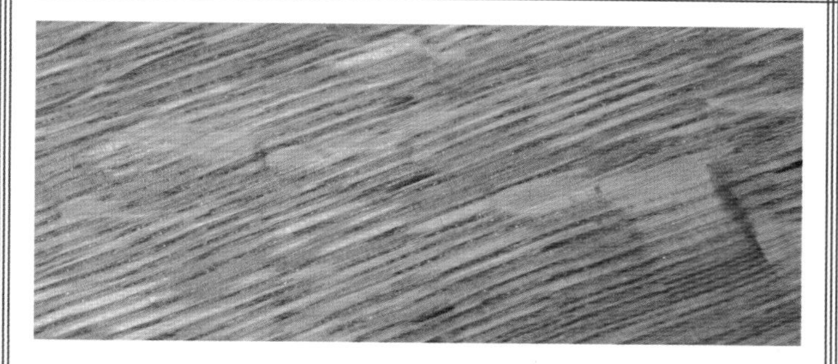

A coat of boiled linseed oil highlights the ray flakes of fumed quartersawn white oak.

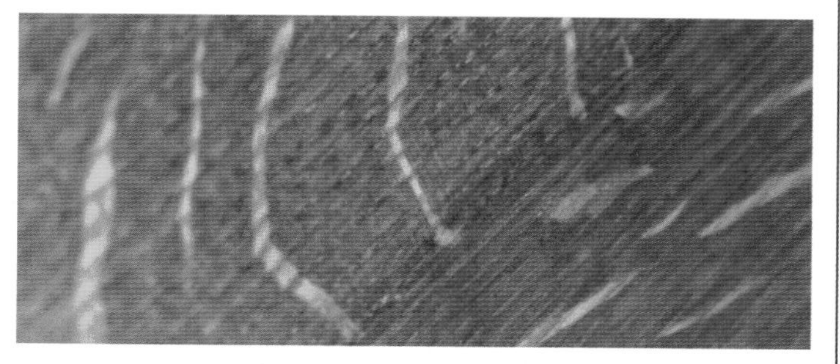

Garnet shellac warms oiled and fumed quartersawn white oak.

UPHOLSTERY

Couch cushions and spring seats are probably better left to a professional, especially if made from leather, but the slip seat cushion featured in the No. 676 Rocker, No. 911 Dining Chair, and No. 500 Café Chair is one of the easiest upholstery projects to tackle. A plywood or hardwood frame forms the foundation of the seat. Size the frame to allow some room for layers of fabric along all edges. Jute webbing is then woven across the frame opening, stretched tight, and stapled or tacked in place. For a single seat, the webbing can be stretched with a large pair of pliers, but a webbing stretcher is a worthwhile investment for more than a couple of chairs. The webbing supports a polyurethane foam cushion, which is wrapped in batting. A muslin cover is then stapled over the cushion to shape it and to hold it in place. With the cushion shaped and the muslin in place, apply the show fabric and attach it to the chair.

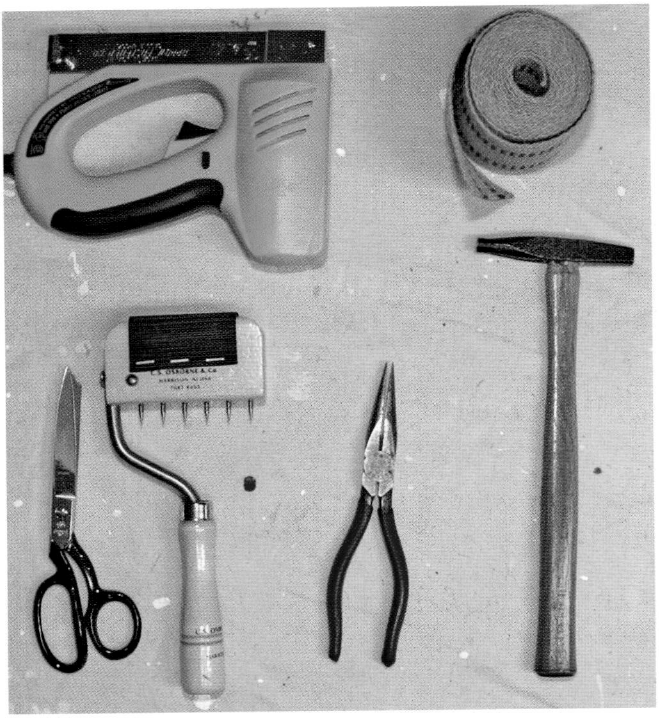

Clockwise from upper left: staple gun, jute webbing, tack hammer, pliers, gooseneck webbing stretcher, fabric shears.

Jute webbing is woven across the seat frame.

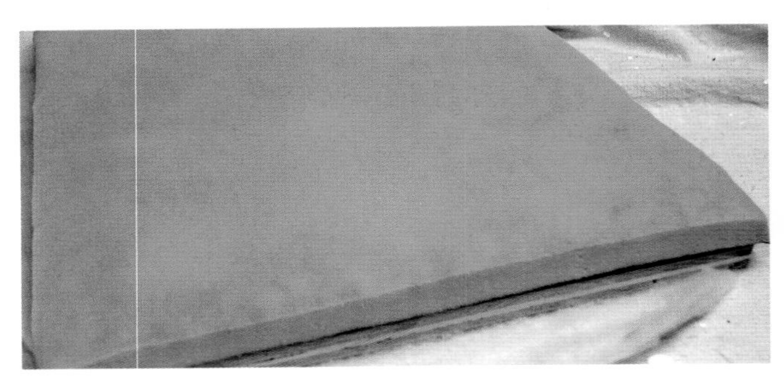

Polyurethane foam is cut to size to form the cushion.

Batting is stretched over the foam.

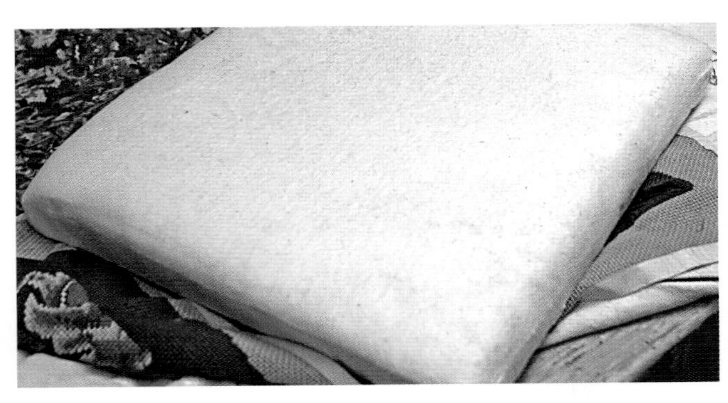

Muslin is wrapped over the foam and stapled to the bottom of the frame.

Show fabric is wrapped over the cushion and stapled to the frame.

No. 21

MIRROR

23 1/4" high x 37 1/2" wide

Limbert produced numerous variations of the arched-rail mirror, modifying the length of the rails and stiles to change scale. The No. 21 features the arch on the bottom, but other versions had it on top. The varying thickness of the frame members creates shadowlines, providing more visual interest than if they were all the same thickness. The original featured coat hooks on the stiles and across the bottom rail. It was meant to be hung on a chain mounted to eyelets mortised into the tops of the stiles, but heavy-duty picture mounting hardware would serve as well.

EXPLODED VIEW

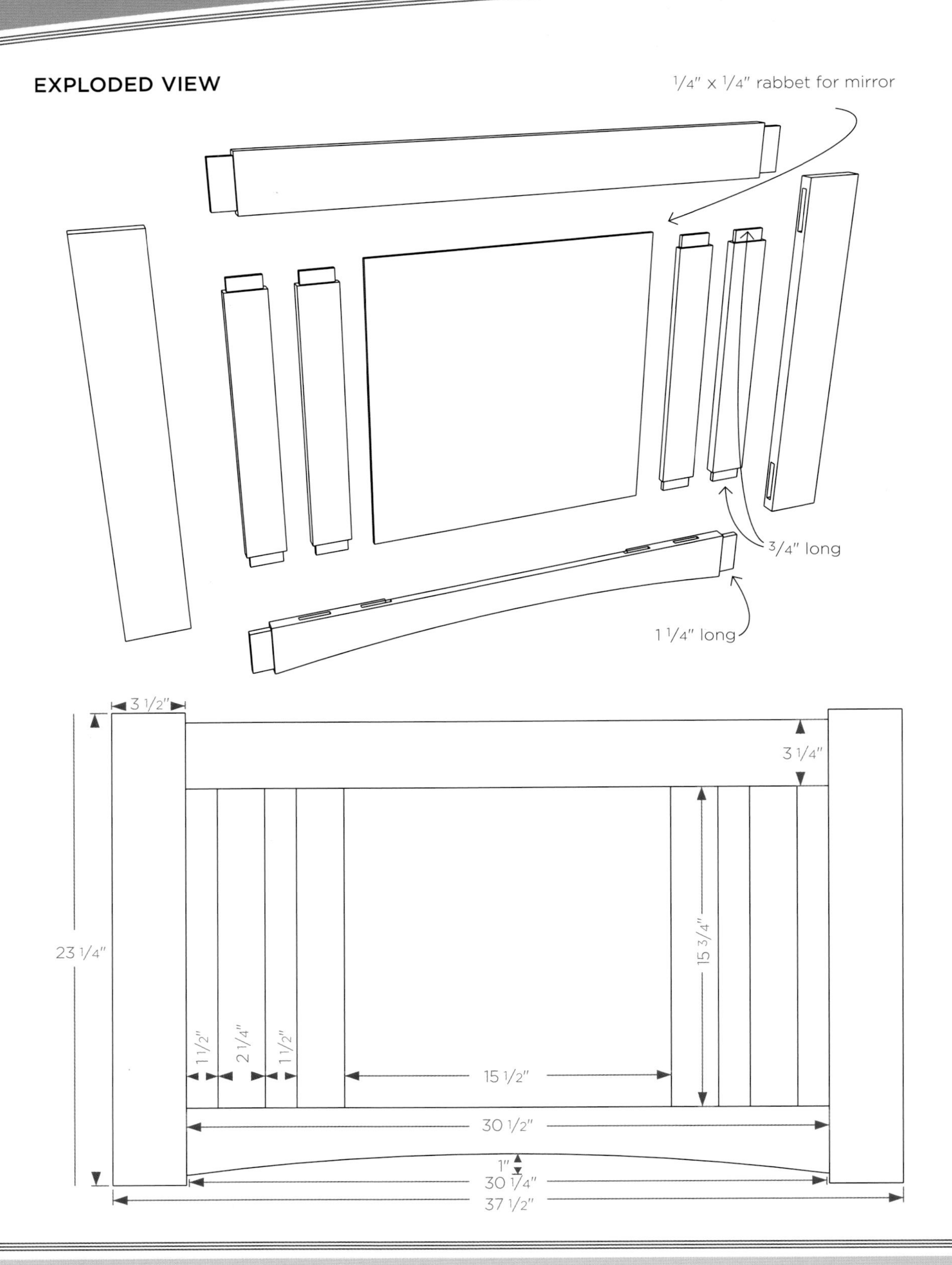

PART LIST

Qty	Description	Length	Width	Thickness
1	bottom rail	33"	3 1/4"	3/4"
4	slat	17 1/4"	2 1/4"	5/8"
2	stile	23 1/4"	3 1/2"	7/8"
1	top rail	33"	3 1/4"	3/4"
1	back	17 3/4"	17 1/2"	1/4"

No. 81

HALL CHAIR

45″ high x 14″ wide x 16″ deep

The stark lines, asymmetric cutouts, and splayed sides of the No. 81 hall chair make this one of Limbert's most distinctive forms. They also complicate construction. If the thought of cutting angled mortise and tenons seems daunting, note that the original likely featured dowelled joinery.

The sides slant inward 5 degrees from vertical, and the back reclines the same amount. The back is screwed into the edge of the seat and stretcher.

EXPLODED VIEW

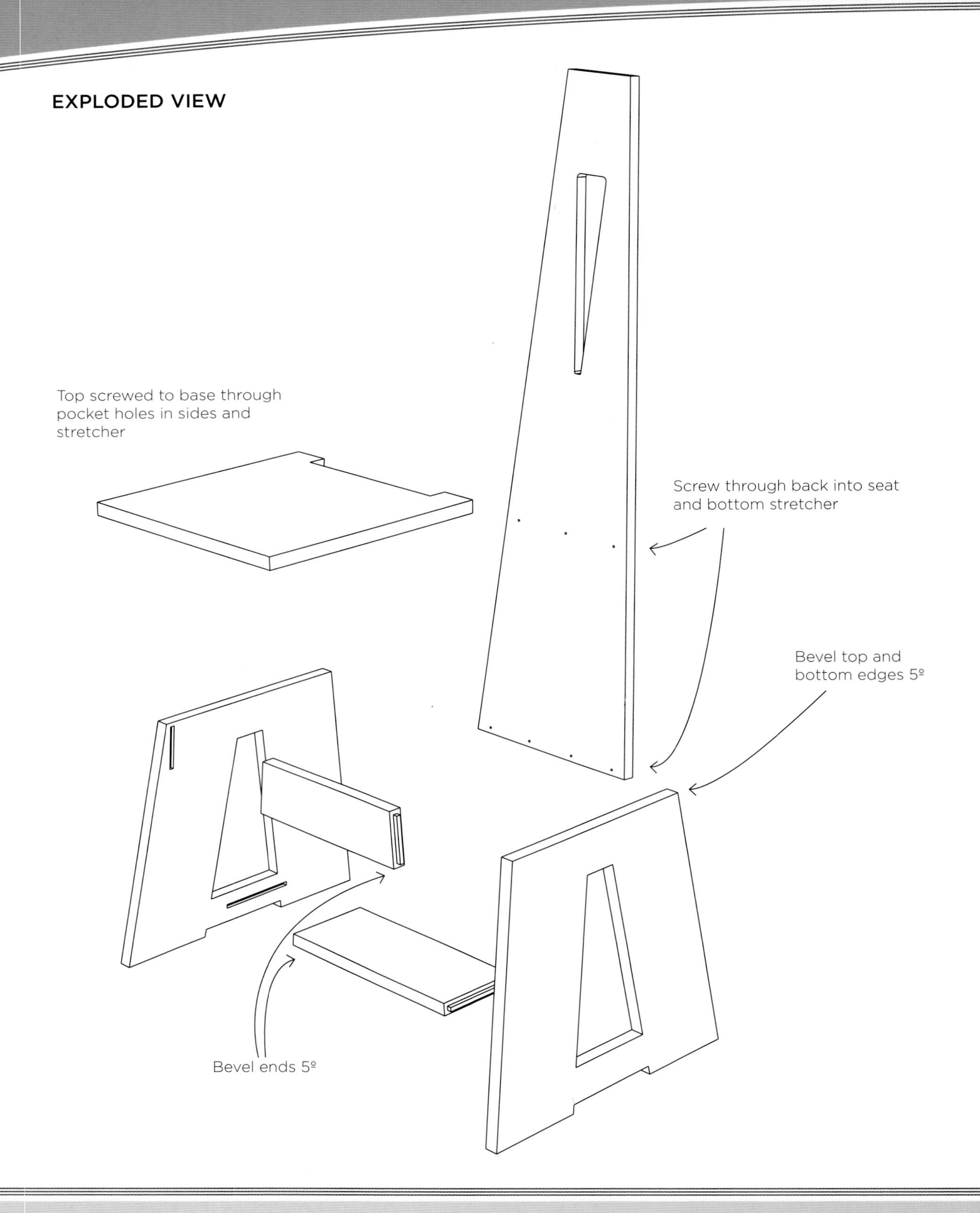

PART LIST

Qty	Description	Length	Width	Thickness
1	back	42 1/2"	12 5/16"	4 7/16"
1	bottom stretcher	12 3/4"	5 1/8"	3/4"
1	front stretcher	1 13/16"	3 1/4"	3/4"
1	seat	14 3/8"	14"	3/4"
2	side	17"	15 3/16"	2 1/16"

FRONT VIEW

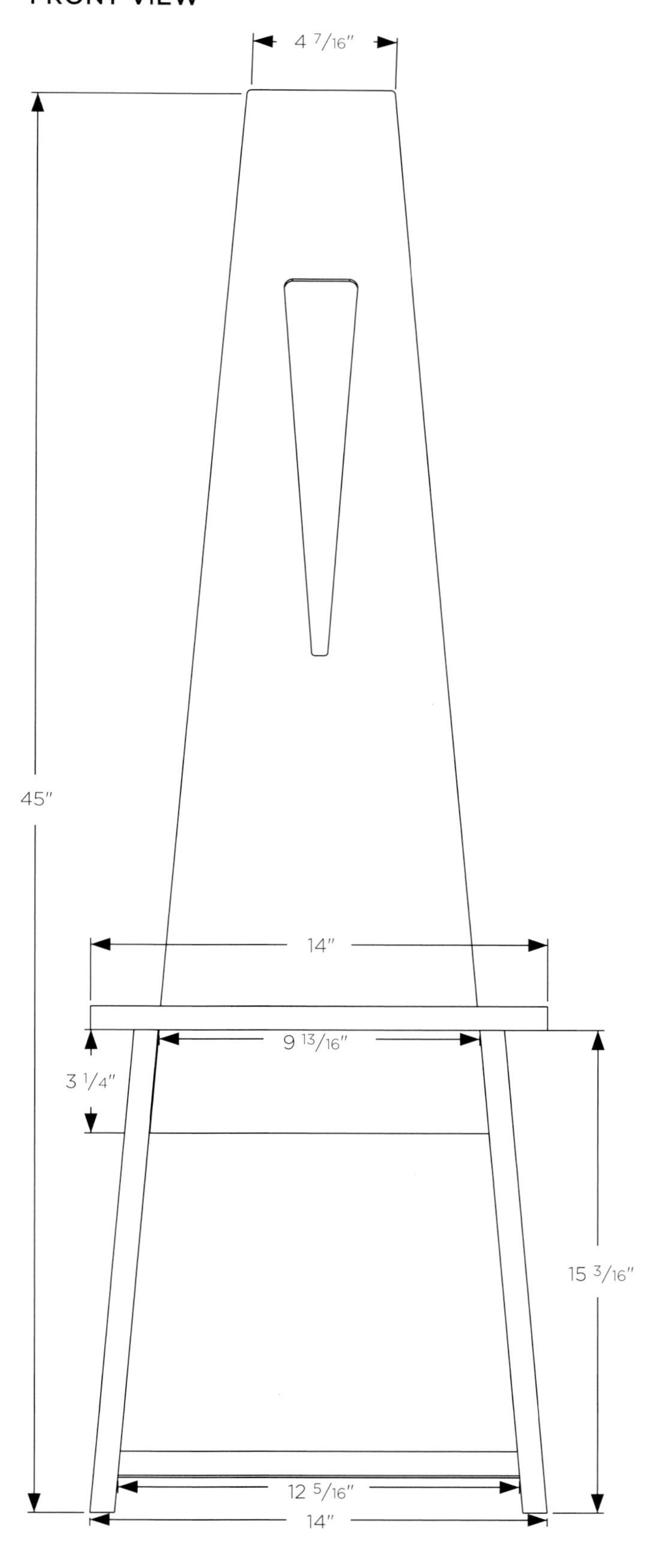
4 7/16″
45″
14″
9 13/16″
3 1/4″
15 3/16″
12 5/16″
14″

FRONT STRETCHER FRONT VIEW

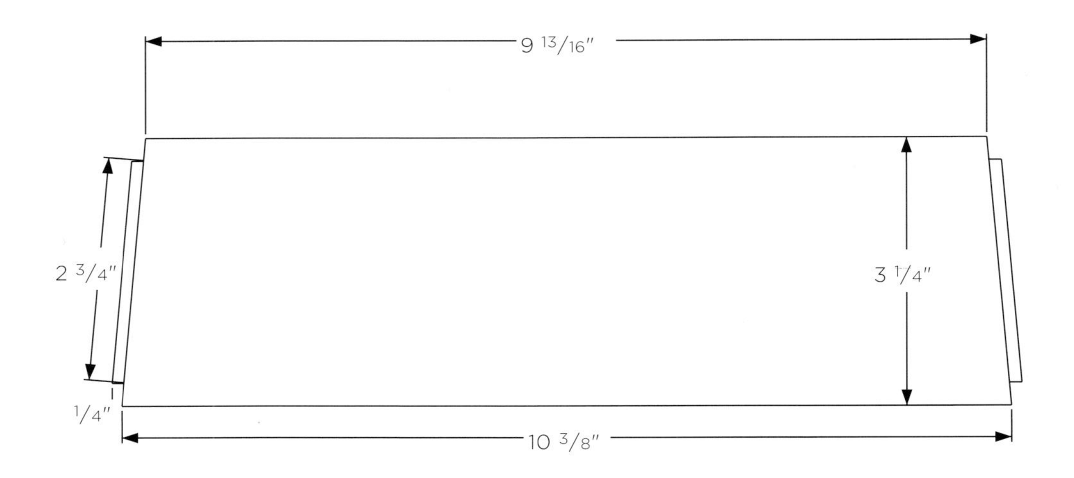

BOTTOM STRETCHER TOP VIEW

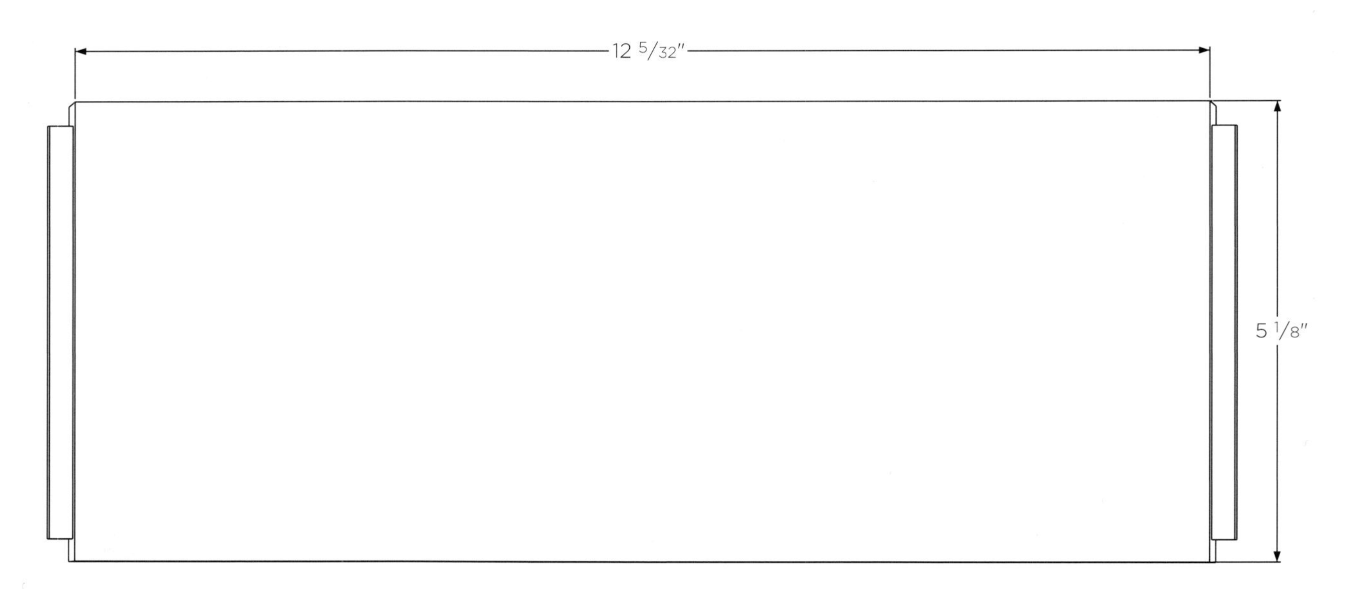

BOTTOM STRETCHER FRONT VIEW

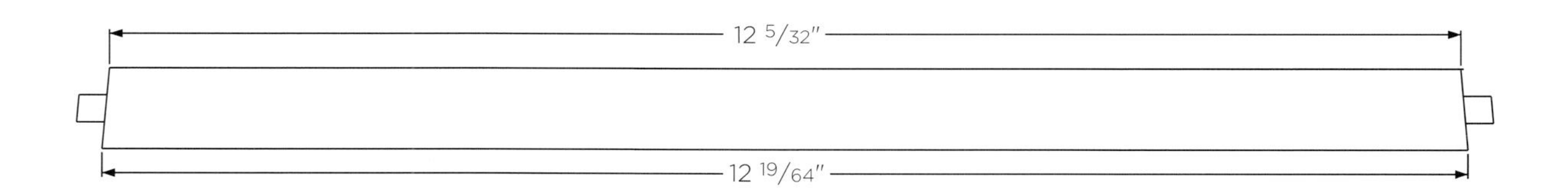

CHAIR BACK FRONT VIEW

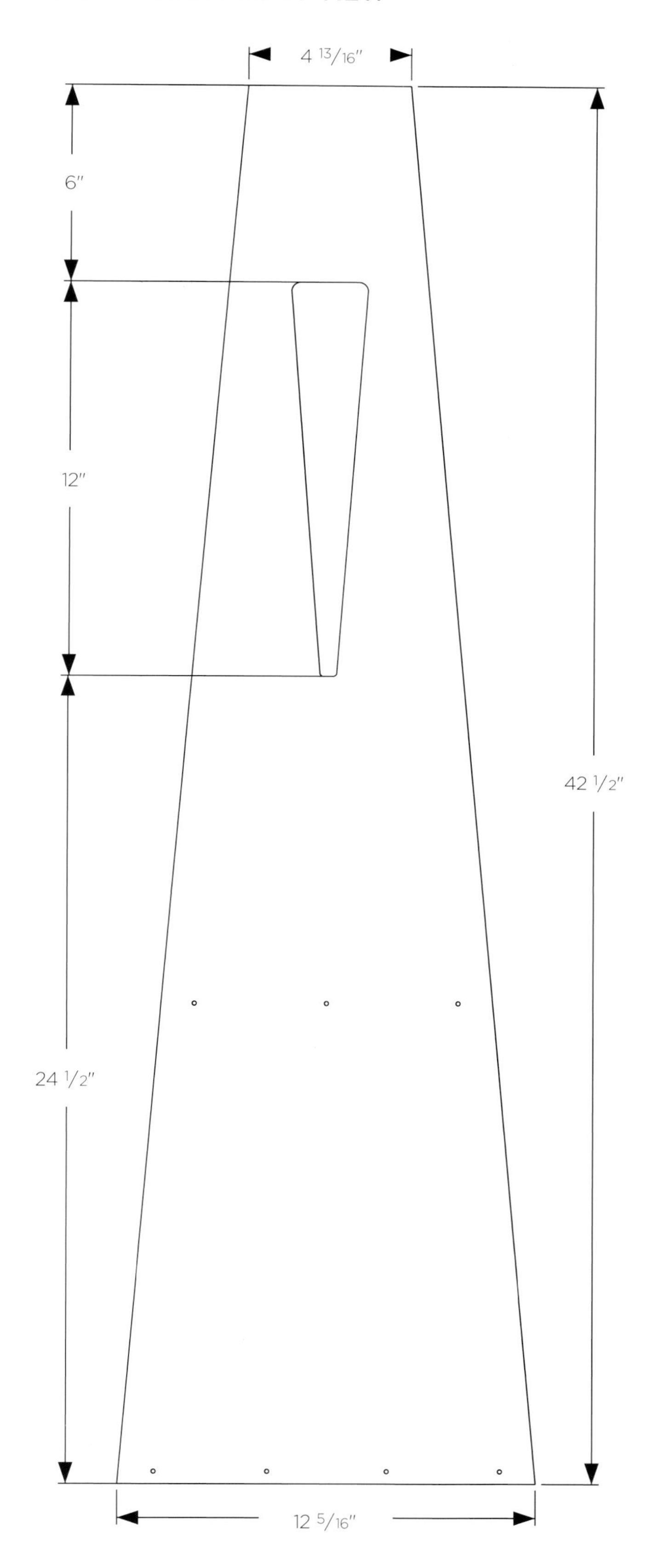

BACK CUTOUT

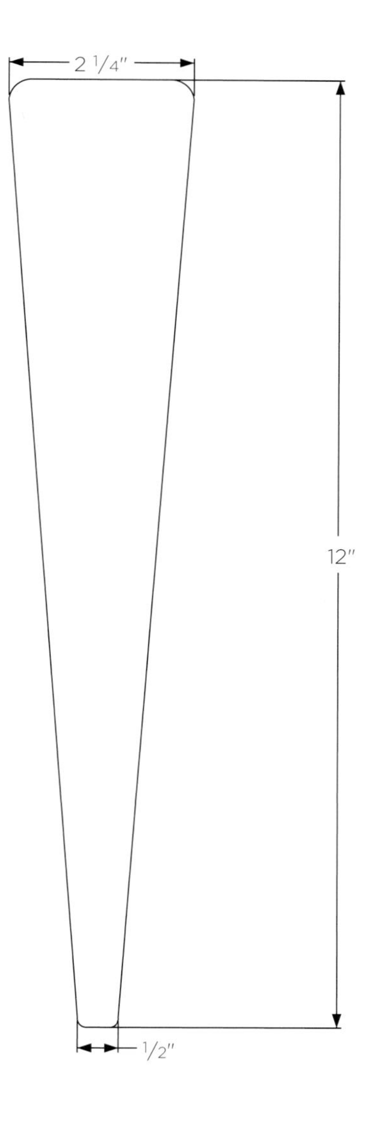

SIDE DETAIL

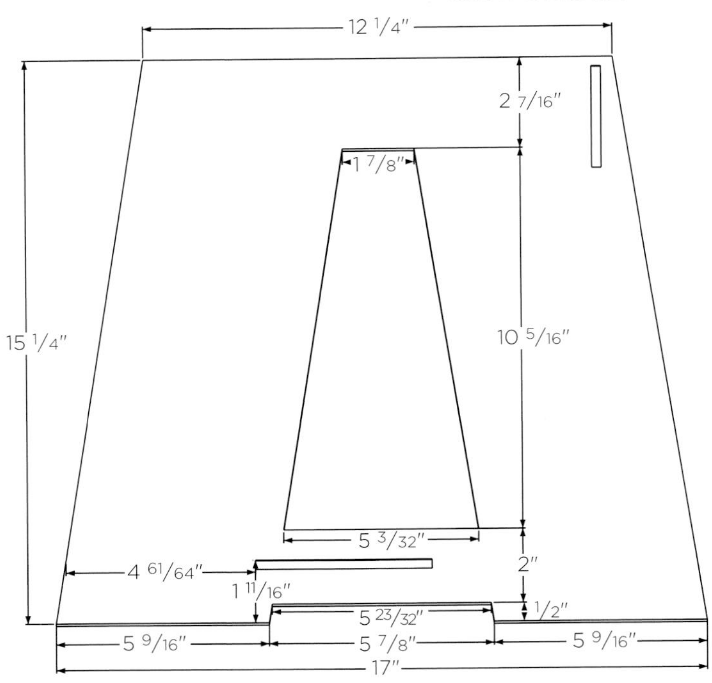

SEAT TOP VIEW

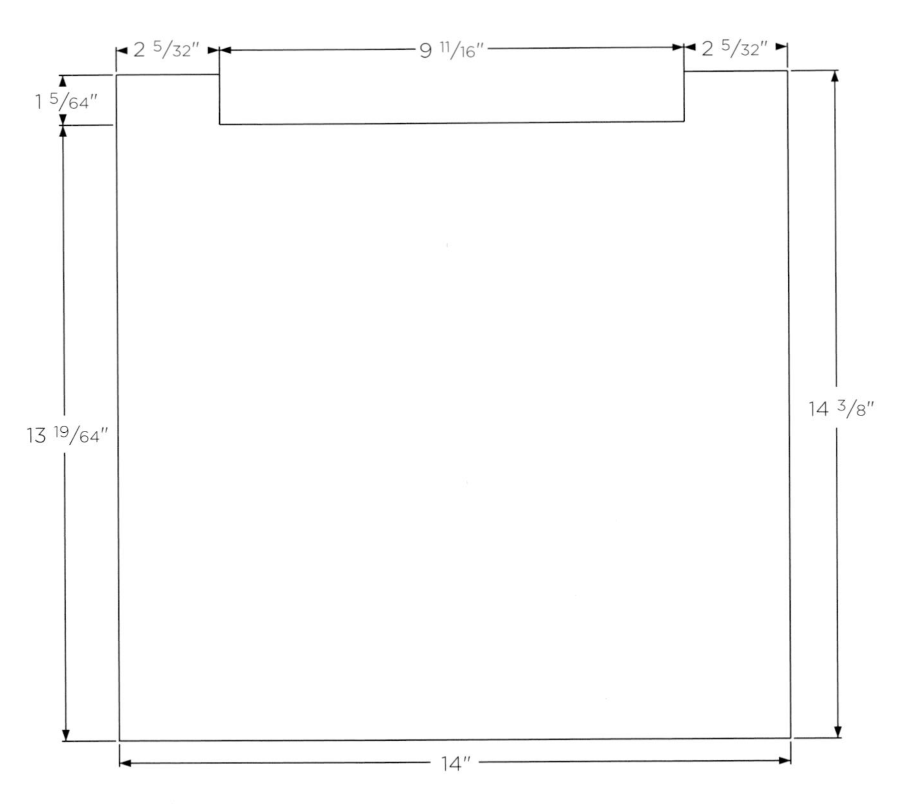

SEAT BACK VIEW

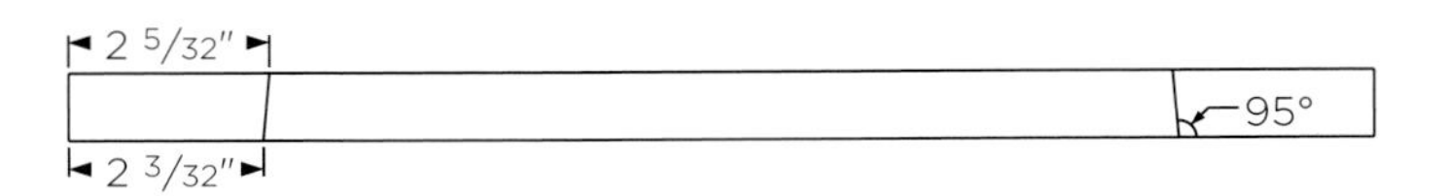

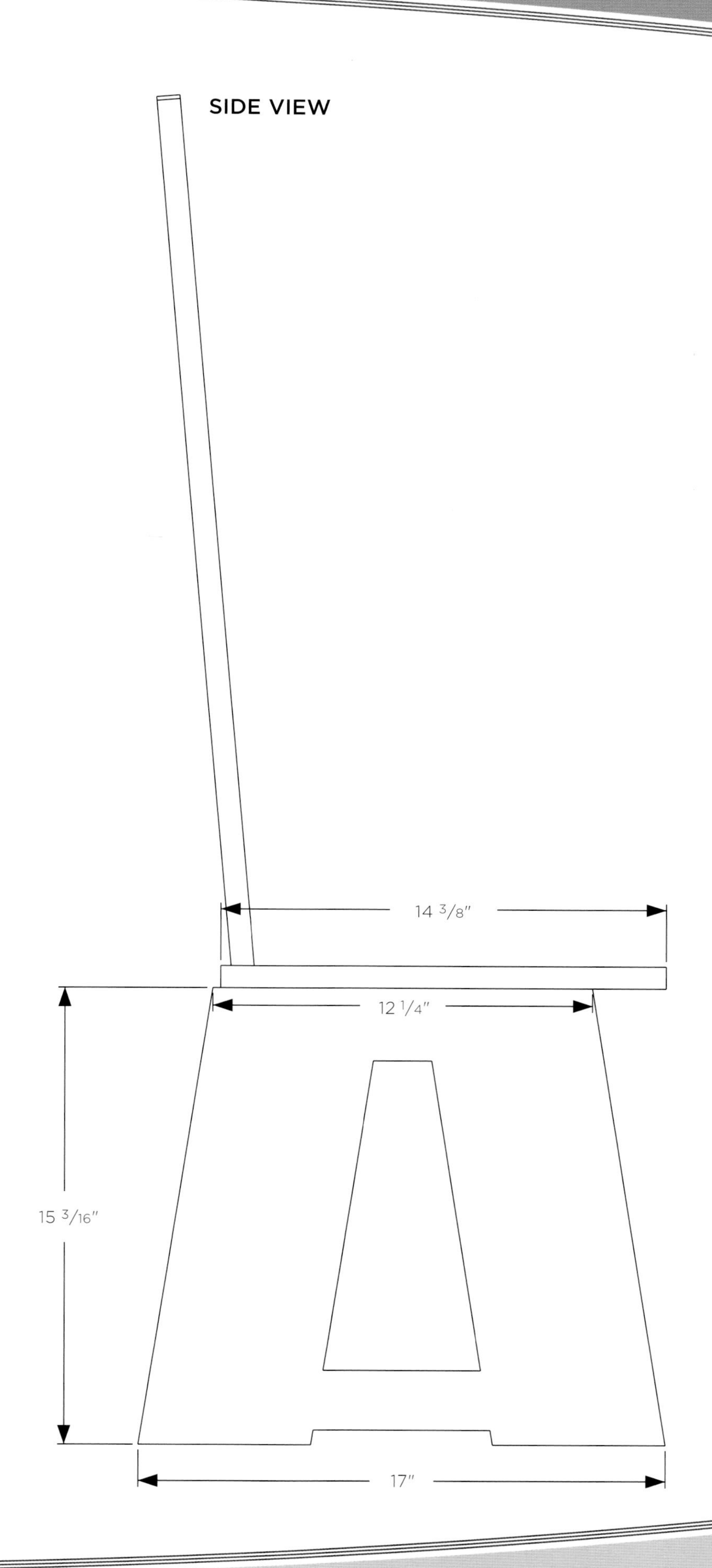
SIDE VIEW
14 3/8″
12 1/4″
15 3/16″
17″

No. 126

HALL TABLE

34″ high x 36″ wide x 16″ deep

This table shares the inset "cushion" top and rounded top edges of many other Limbert pieces (see No. 499 Somnoe and No. 1162 Library Table). These touches soften the hard lines of similar work by other makers.

As with most Limbert pieces, the No. 126 features copper hardware, though pyramid pulls in wood would also suit.

EXPLODED VIEW

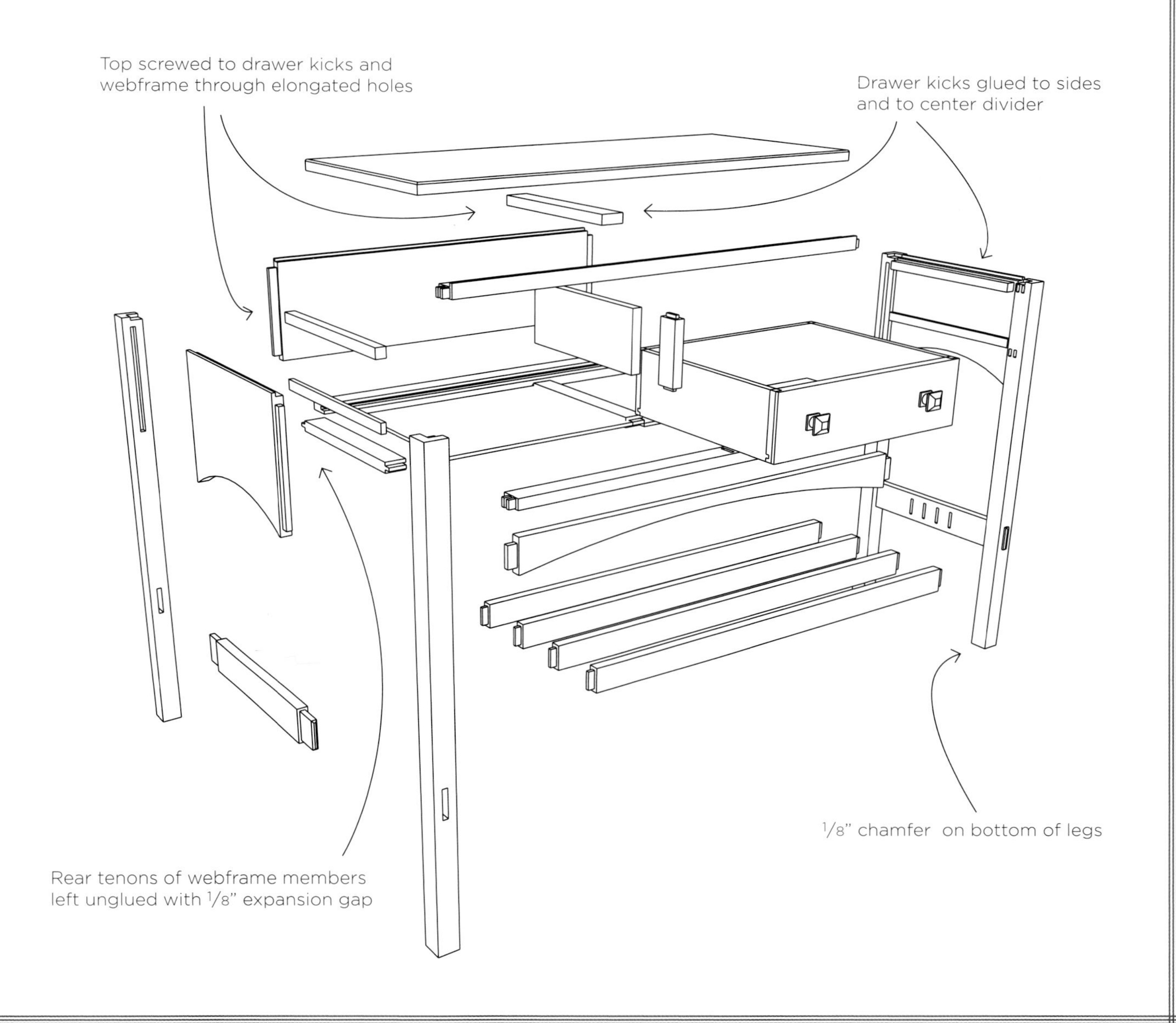

PART LIST

Qty	Description	Length	Width	Thickness
1	back	34 1/2"	9 1/4"	3/4"
1	bottom arch	34 1/2"	2 3/4"	3/4"
1	bottom drawer rail	34"	1 1/2"	3/4"
1	divider	5 1/4"	1 1/2"	3/4"
2	drawer back	16 1/8"	4 3/4"	1/2"
2	drawer bottom	15 5/8"	13 1/2"	1/4"
2	drawer front	16 1/8"	4 3/4"	3/4"
2	drawer guide	13"	3/4"	23/64"
1	drawer kick	11 11/16"	1 3/4"	3/4"
4	drawer side	13 3/4"	4 3/4"	1/2"
2	dust panel	14 3/4"	11 61/64"	1/4"

Qty	Description	Length	Width	Thickness
4	knob	1 1/4"	1 1/4"	1 1/8"
4	leg	33 1/2"	1 1/2"	1 1/2"
4	shelf stretcher	34 3/4"	2"	3/4"
2	side	14"	9 1/4"	3/4"
2	side top cleat	12 5/8"	3/4"	3/4"
2	stretcher	16 1/2"	2 1/2"	3/4"
1	top	34 3/4"	14 3/4"	3/4"
1	top drawer rail	34"	1 1/2"	1"
1	web frame back	33"	1 37/64"	3/4"
1	web frame divider	11 45/64"	4 3/4"	3/4"
3	web frame side	12 5/16"	1 1/2"	3/4"

TOP VIEW

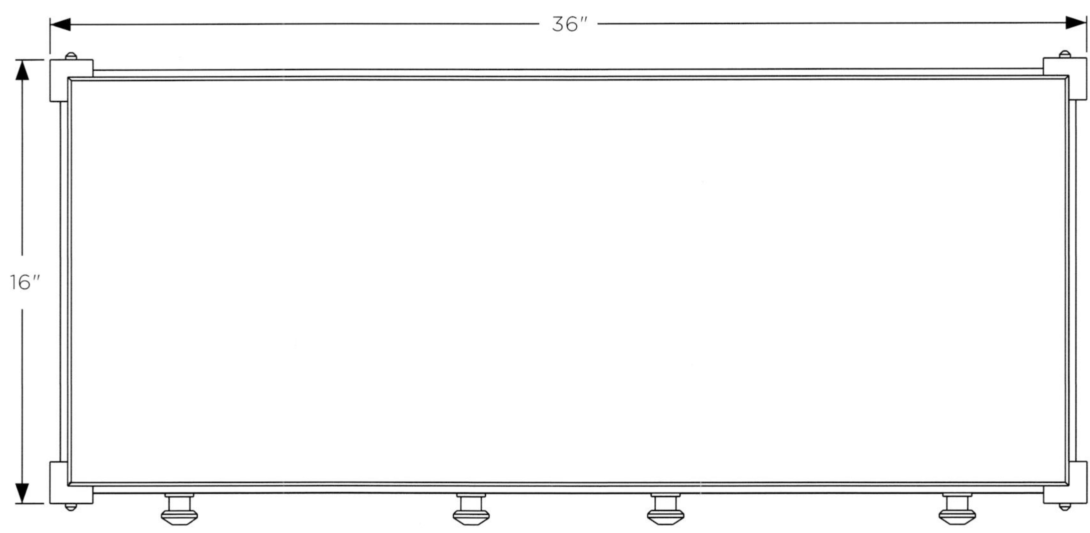

FRONT VIEW

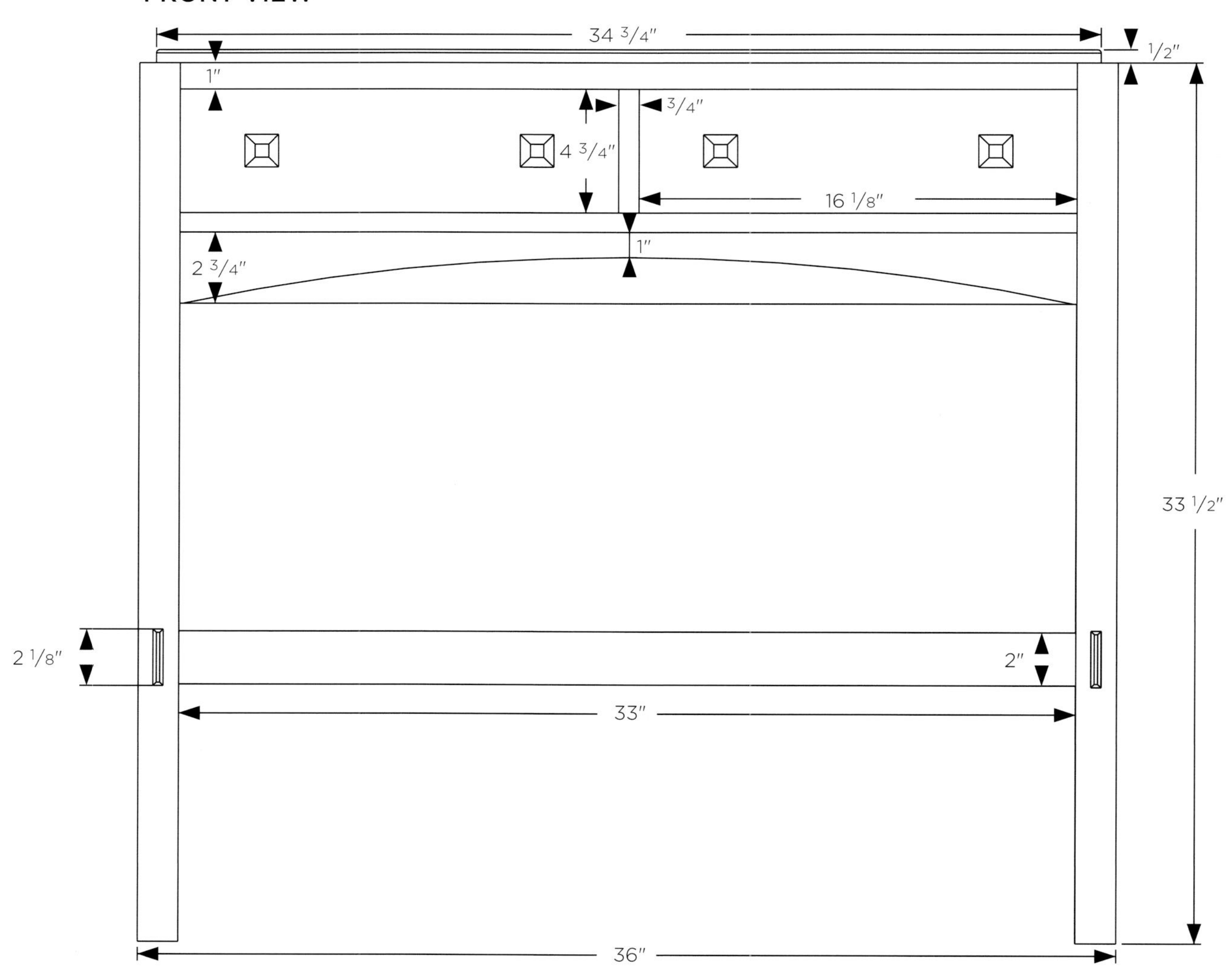

SIDE SECTION VIEW

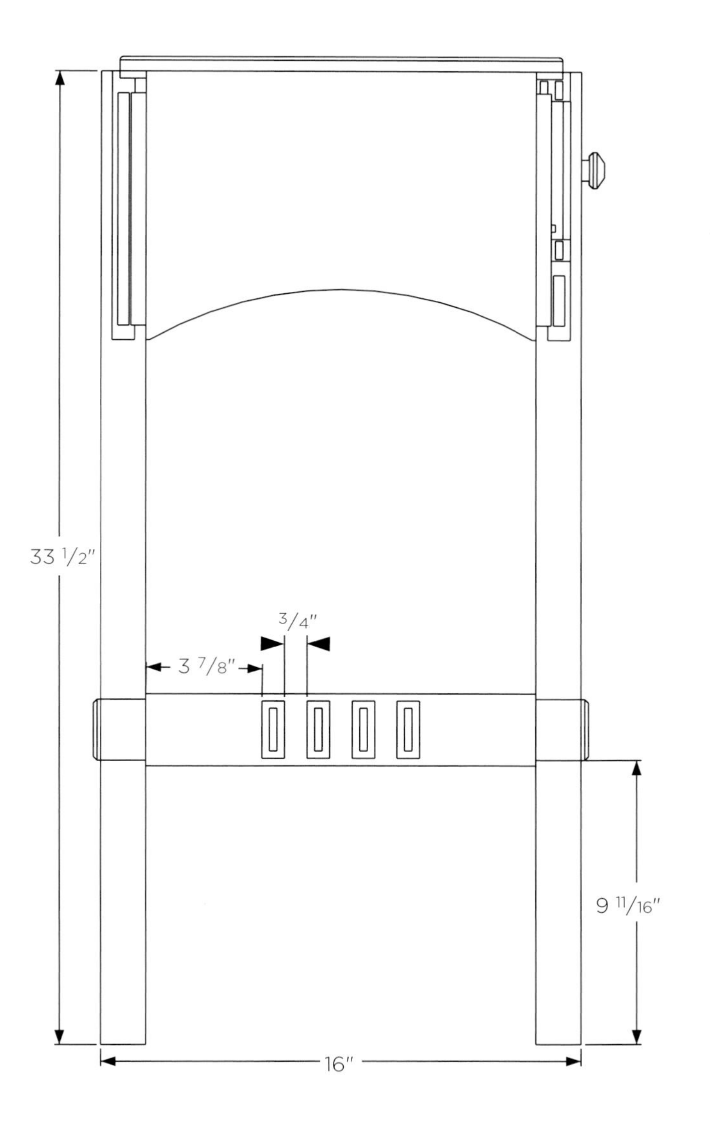

SIDE VIEW

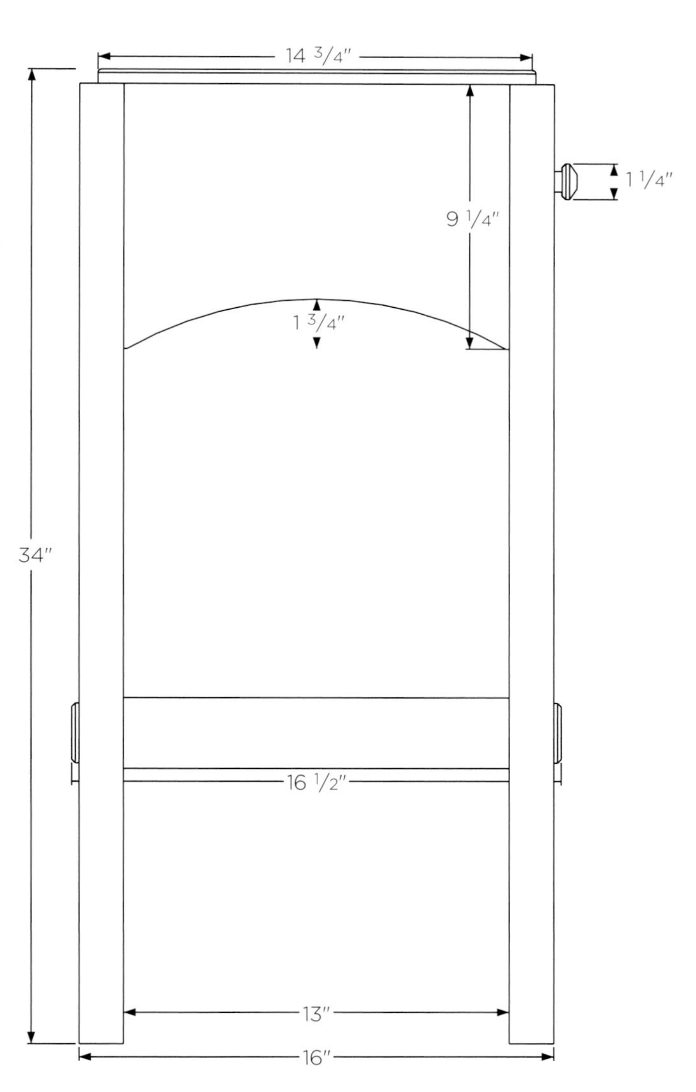

No. 254

UMBRELLA STAND

27″ high x 12″ wide x 12″ deep

With its trapezoidal column (a common Limbert element), this umbrella stand coordinates nicely with the No. 81 chair. A copper drip pan lines the base.

The sides are joined with a miter just under 45 degrees (44.78º). Cut them to 45 degrees and then fine tune the joint by running a piece of doubled-over sandpaper along both edges until they fit. The bevel on top and bottom edge is 5 degrees.

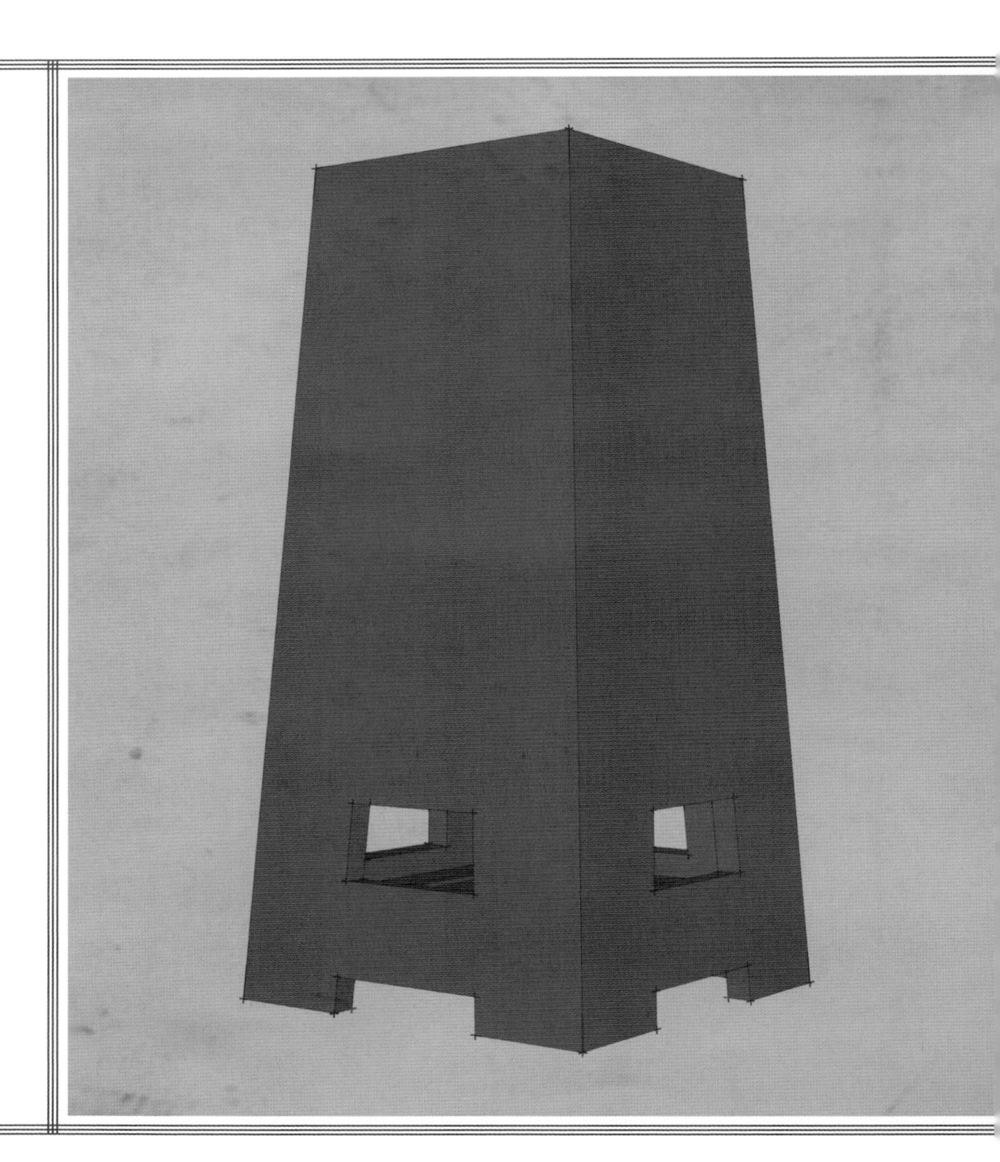

EXPLODED VIEW

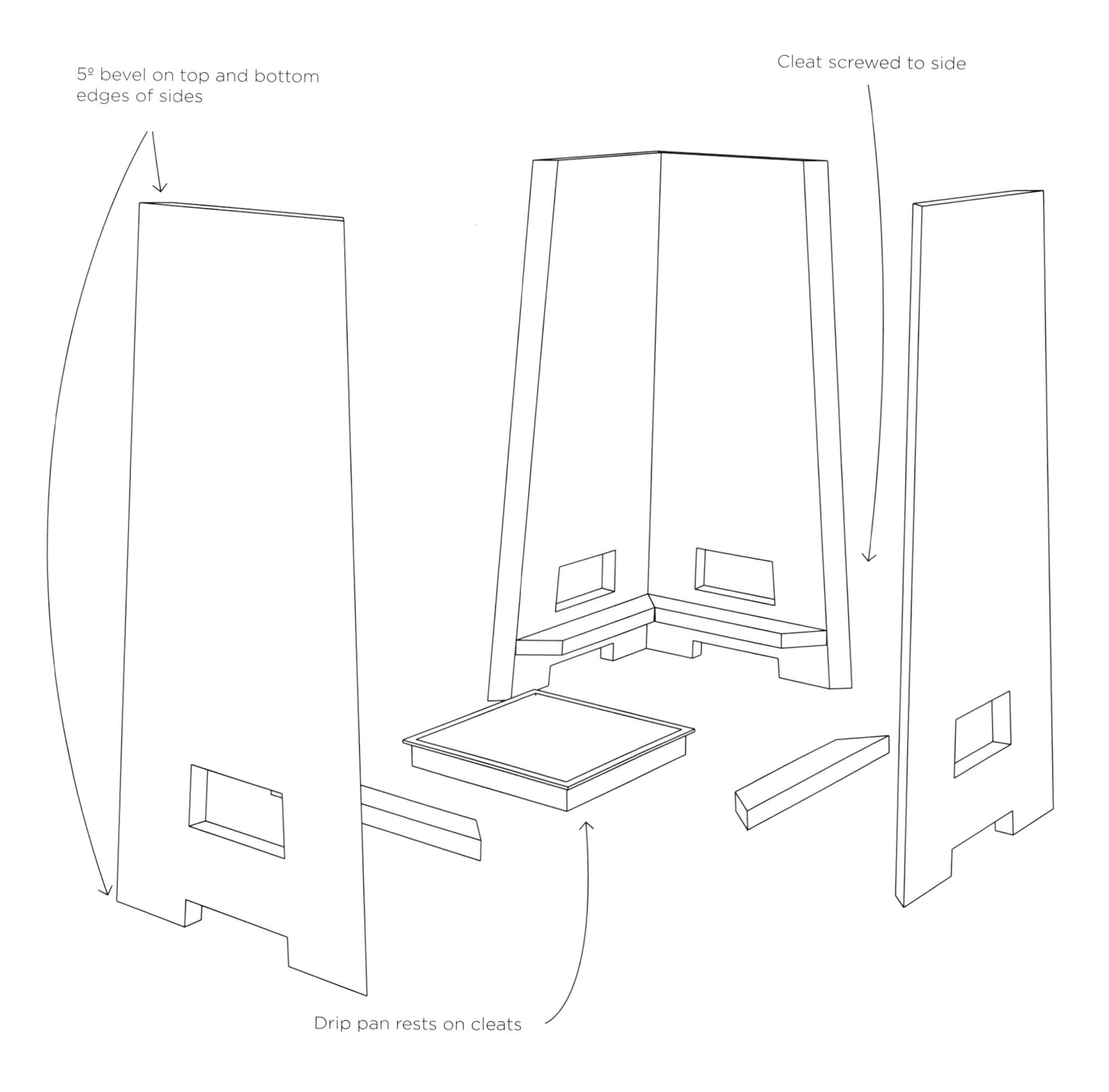

PART LIST

Qty	Description	Length	Width	Thickness
1	drip pan	8 1/8"	8 1/8"	1 1/8"
4	side	25"	12"	3/4"
4	slat	10 3/16"	1 9/16"	3/4"

SIDE VIEW

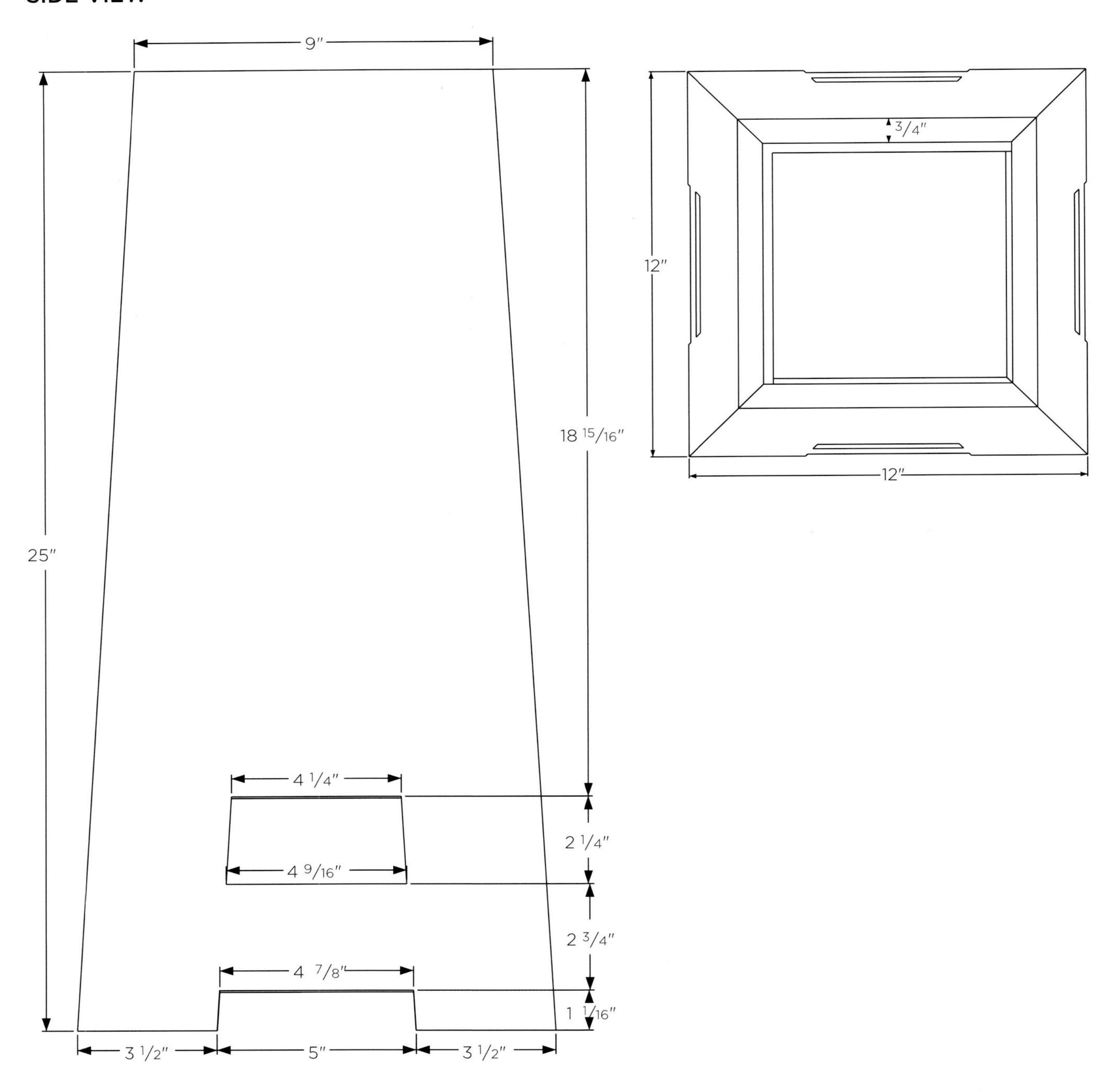
9″
25″
18 15/16″
4 1/4″
2 1/4″
4 9/16″
2 3/4″
4 7/8″
1 1/16″
3 1/2″
5″
3 1/2″
3/4″
12″
12″

No. 39-7

PORCH SWING

24″ high x 81″ wide x 25″ deep

Limbert produced a wide range of outdoor furniture, including a number of swings in ash or oak, as well as rockers, chairs and occasional tables. Here the cutouts in the slats distinguish the 39-7 from the other offerings. Catalog photos show the swing with large cushions at the arms and seat (customers could order them in green denim for an additional charge). At 81 inches long, the 39-7 is sized for larger porches. Eliminate a back slat or two to tailor the size to a smaller space.

The drawings substitute a slatted seat for the cane seat in the original. The slats can be screwed through the top into the supporting frame, but pocket holes or hidden deck fasteners create a more finished appearance. A solid plank would also serve for a seat but drains less easily than slats.

EXPLODED VIEW

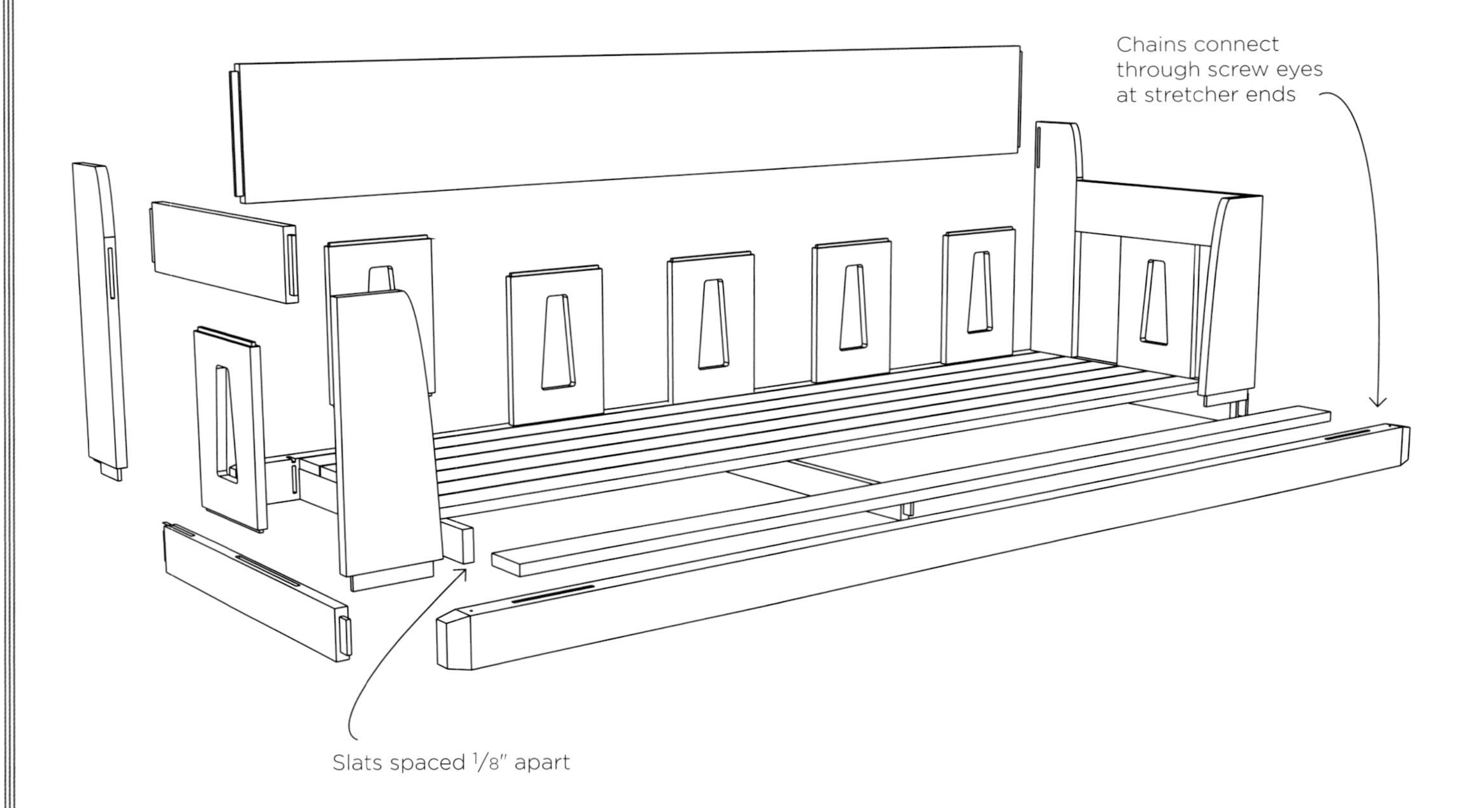

PART LIST

Qty	Description	Length	Width	Thickness
2	back arm stile	22"	5"	3/4"
2	front arm stile	17"	6	3/4"
2	arm rail	20"	4 1/2"	3/4"
1	back top rail	73"	9 1/2"	3/4"
2	base side rail	23 5/8"	3"	3/4"

Qty	Description	Length	Width	Thickness
1	center support	23 1/2"	2 1/4"	3/4"
2	end seat cleat	22"	2 1/4"	3/4"
2	base long rail	81"	3"	1 1/2"
7	seat slats	72"	3"	3/4"
7	slats	12"	8"	5/8"

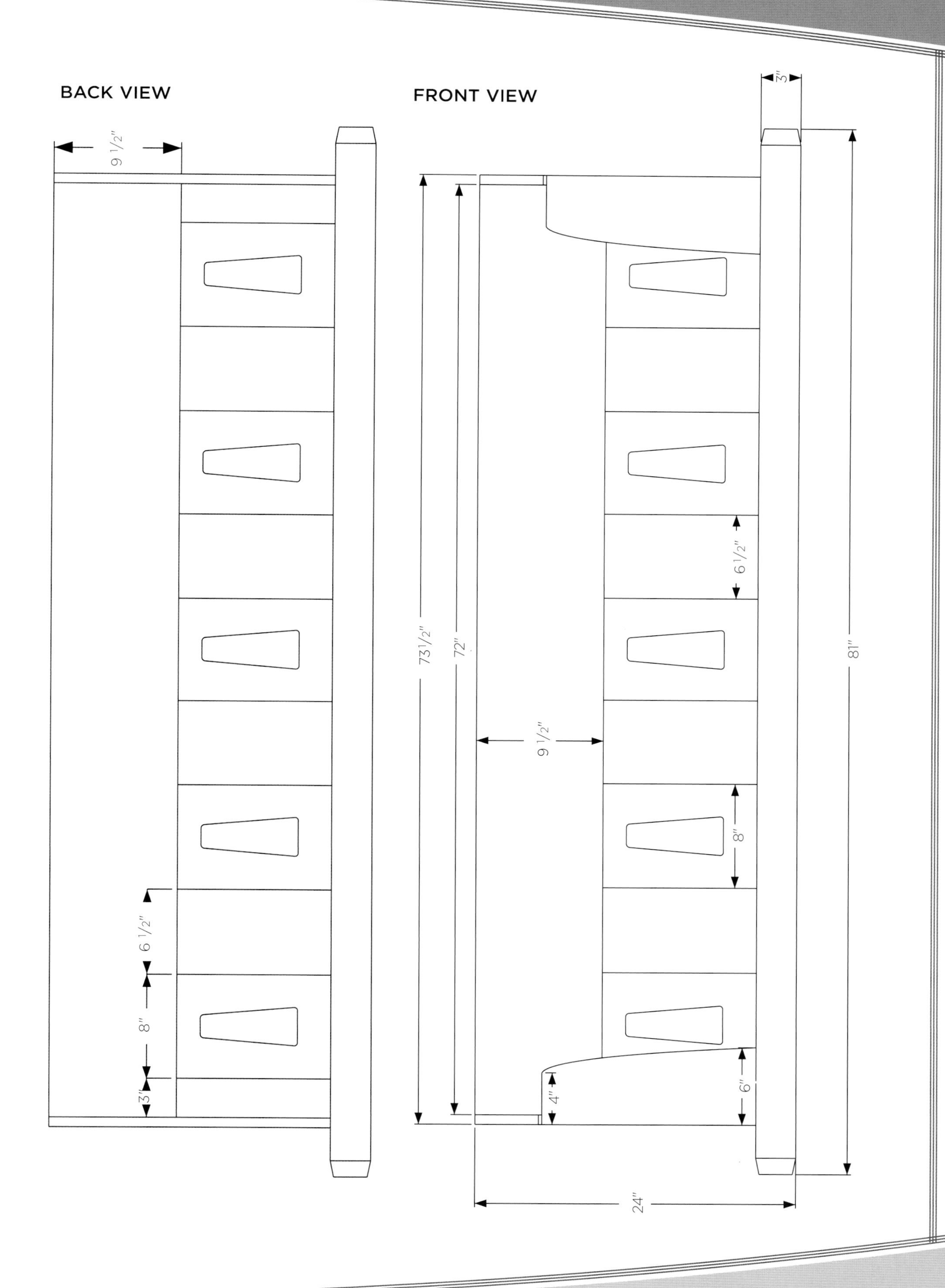
BACK VIEW
FRONT VIEW
9 1/2"
6 1/2"
8"
3"
3"
73 1/2"
72"
81"
6 1/2"
9 1/2"
8"
4"
6"
24"

SIDE VIEW

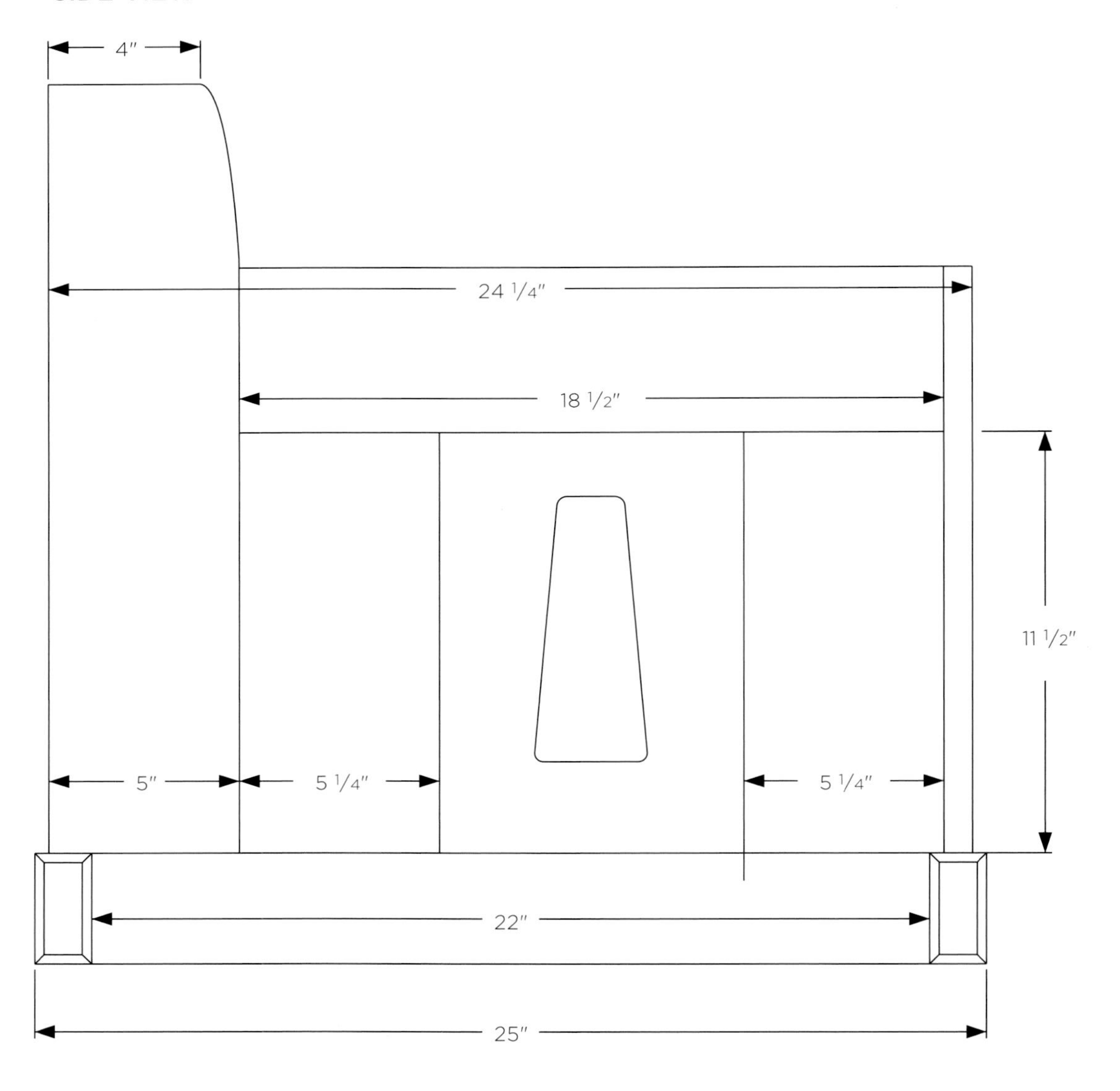

TOP VIEW

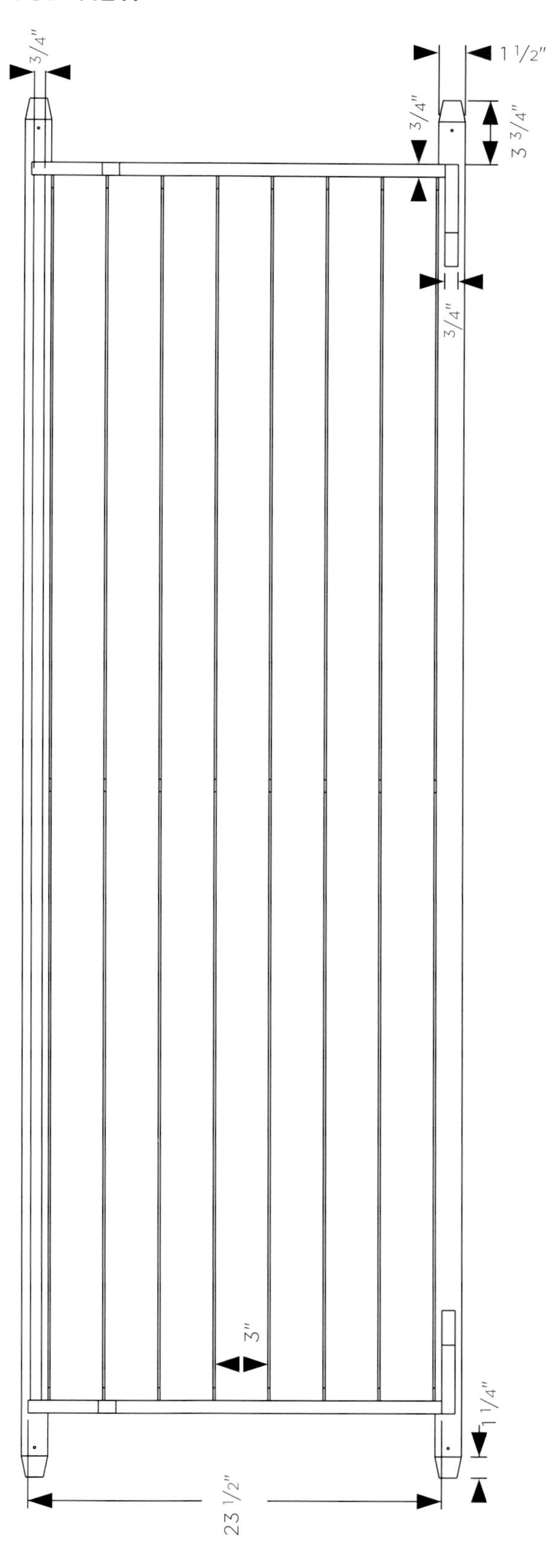
3/4"
1 1/2"
3/4"
3 3/4"
3/4"
3"
1 1/4"
23 1/2"

No. 50

SCREEN

24″ high x 81″ wide x 25″ deep

Many Craftsman homes featured an open-plan living space, with the living room only partly separated from the dining room by a knee wall or sometimes not at all. The design creates a sense of expansiveness, but sometimes it's desirable to divide up that open space. A screen offers an easy way to do that. The No. 50's Mission-inspired lines put it at home in a bungalow, and substituting different fabric for the original's linen canvas lower panels provides an easy way to customize the screen.

EXPLODED VIEW

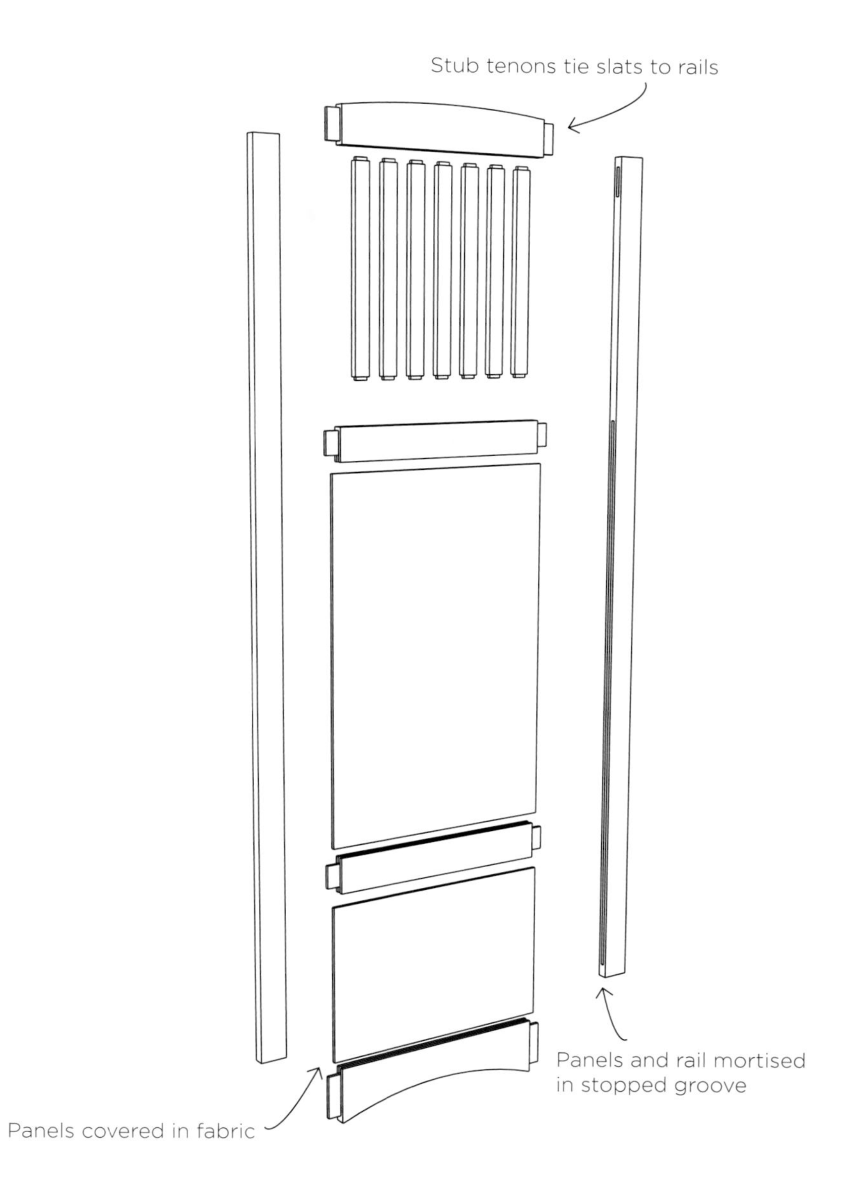

FRONT VIEW

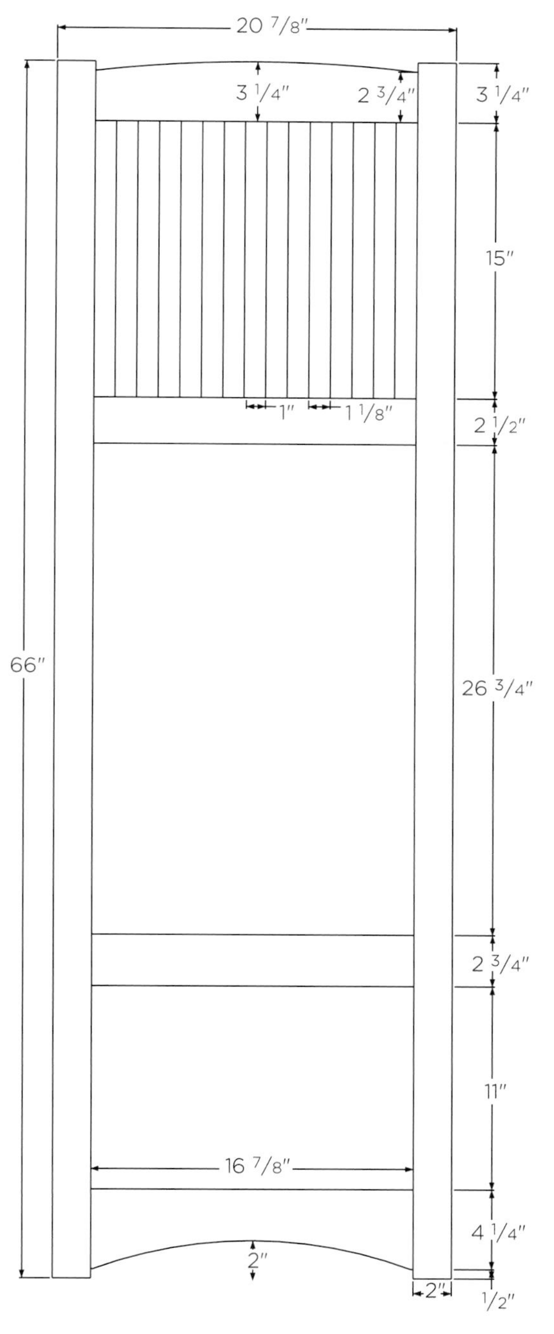

PART LIST

Qty	Description	Length	Width	Thickness
3	bottom rail	18 7/8"	4 1/4"	3/4"
3	lower middle rail	18 7/8"	2 3/4"	3/4"
3	lower panel	17 7/8"	12"	1/4"
21	slat	15 1/2"	1 1/8"	1/2"
6	stile	66"	2"	3/4"
3	top rail	18 7/8"	3 1/4"	3/4"
3	upper middle rail	18 7/8"	2 1/2"	3/4"
3	upper panel	27 3/4"	17 7/8"	1/4"

No. 140

SIDE TABLE

38″ high x 32″ wide x 39 1/2″ deep

This is a substantial side table and would work best in larger rooms. The use of cutouts adds a layer of interest by balancing negative and positive space.

The sides lend themselves to pattern routing, and once the pattern is prepared it is relatively easy to produce another for a matched set.

EXPLODED VIEW

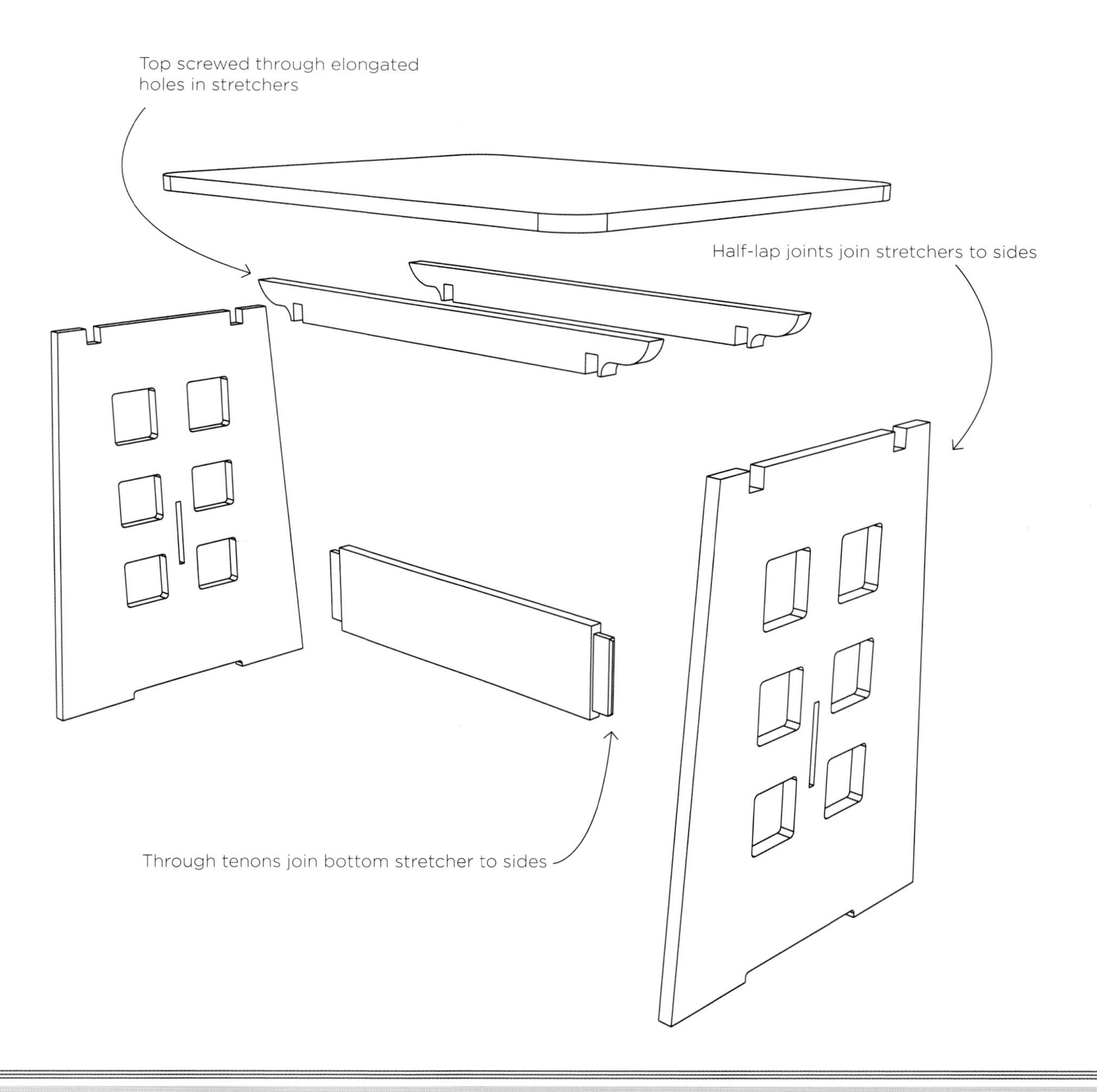

PART LIST

Qty	Description	Length	Width	Thickness
1	bottom stretcher	23"	5 1/2"	3/4"
2	side	26 1/4"	20"	3/4"

Qty	Description	Length	Width	Thickness
1	top	3	24"	3/4"
2	top stretcher	28	2"	1"

FRONT VIEW

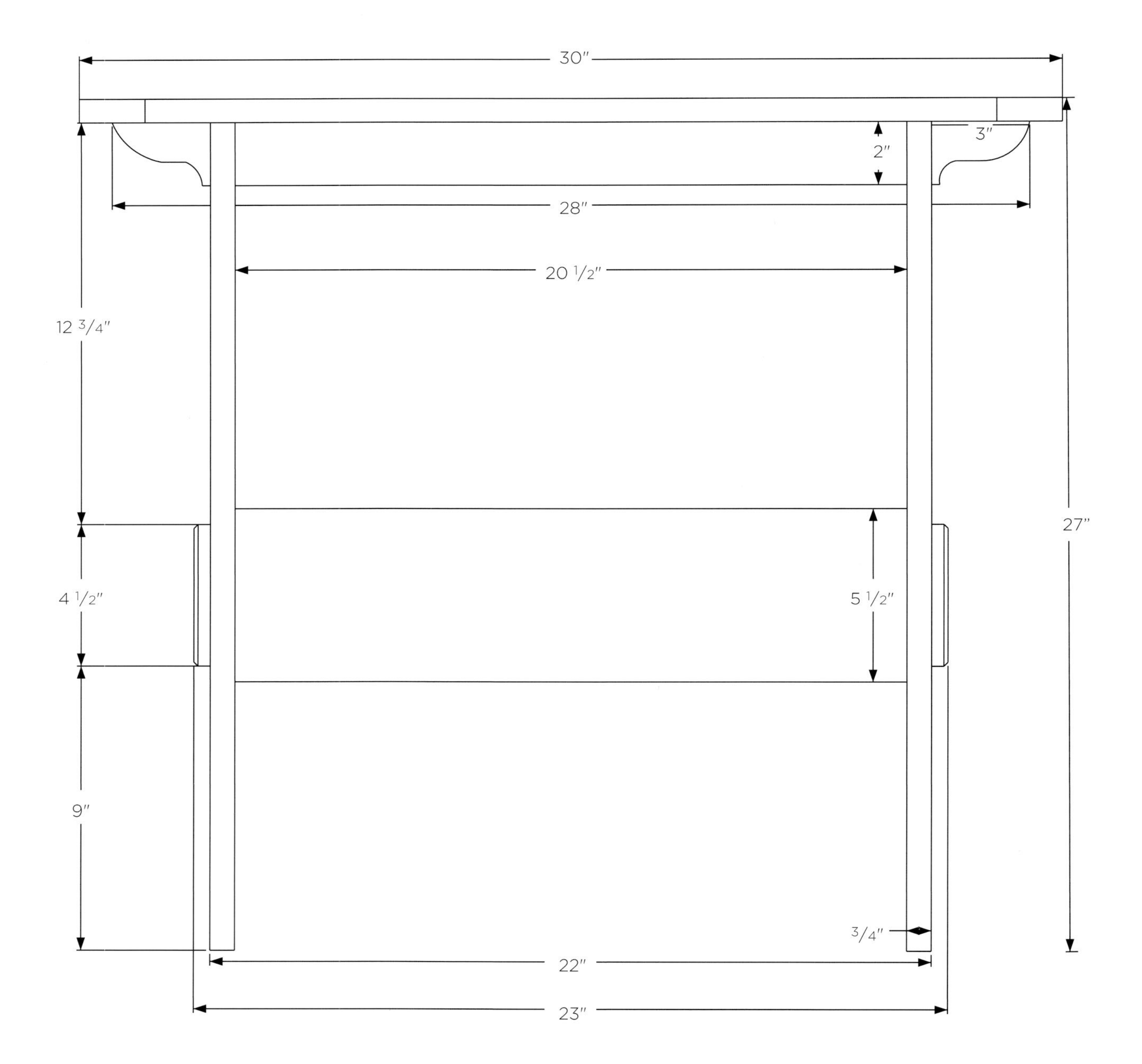

SIDE VIEW

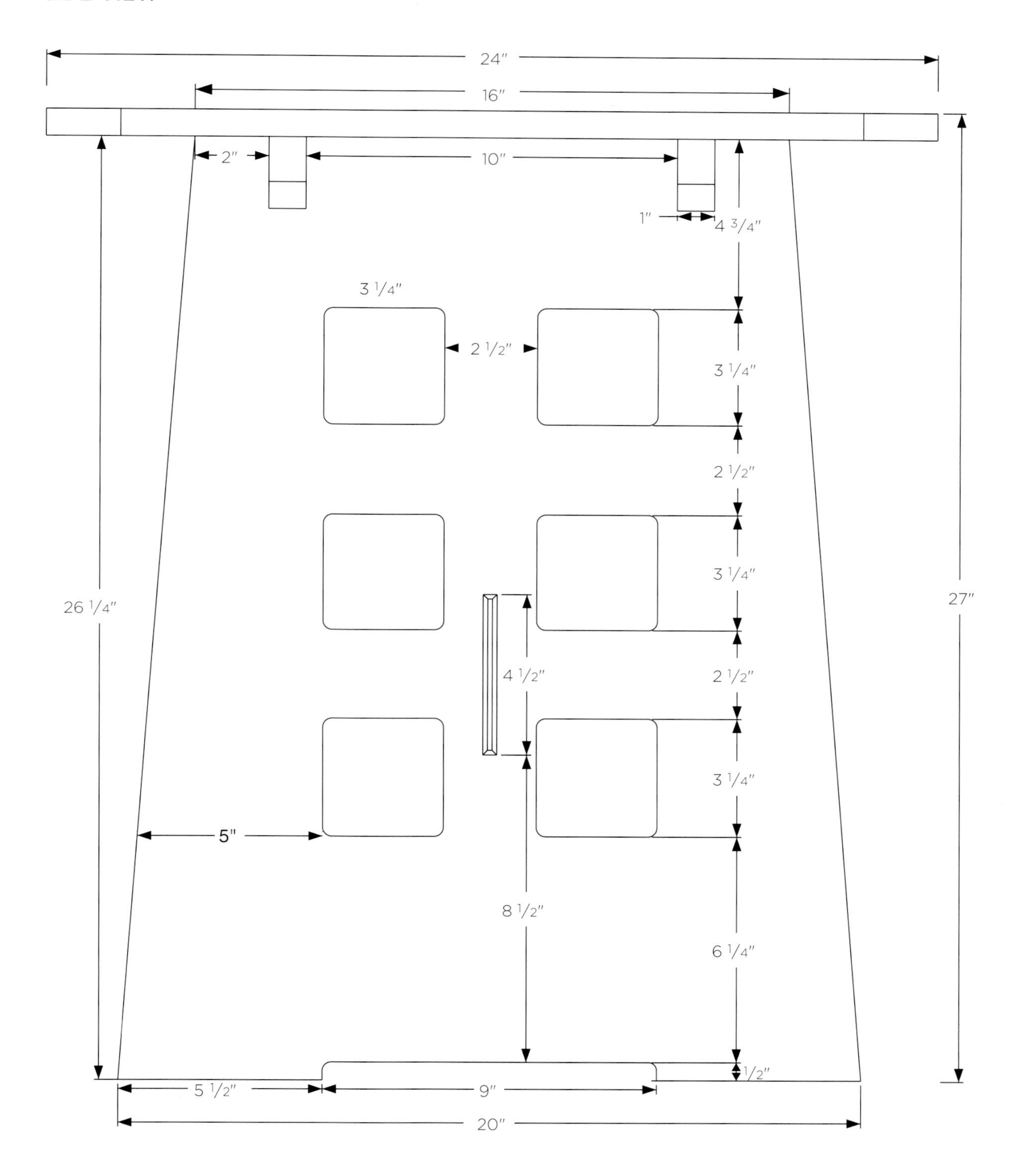

24″
16″
2″
10″
1″
4 3/4″
3 1/4″
2 1/2″
3 1/4″
2 1/2″
3 1/4″
26 1/4″
27″
4 1/2″
2 1/2″
3 1/4″
5"
8 1/2″
6 1/4″
1/2″
5 1/2″
9″
20″

TOP SECTION VIEW

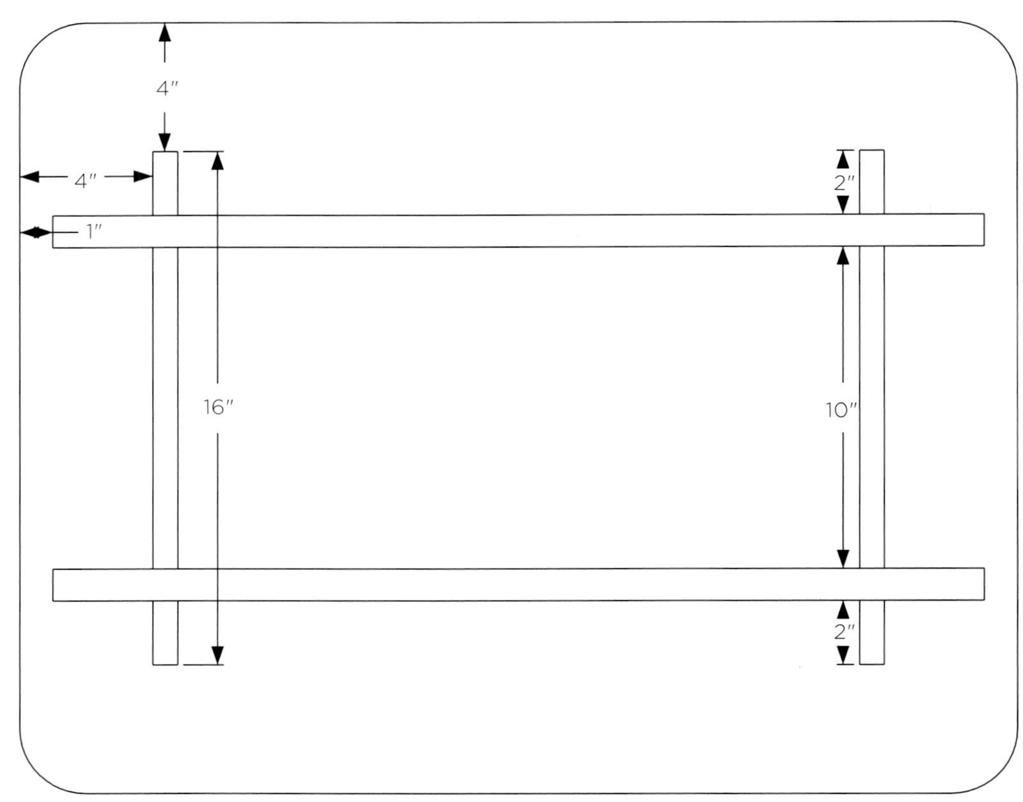

TOP VIEW

No. 251

TABOURETTE

24″ high x 17″ wide x 17″ deep

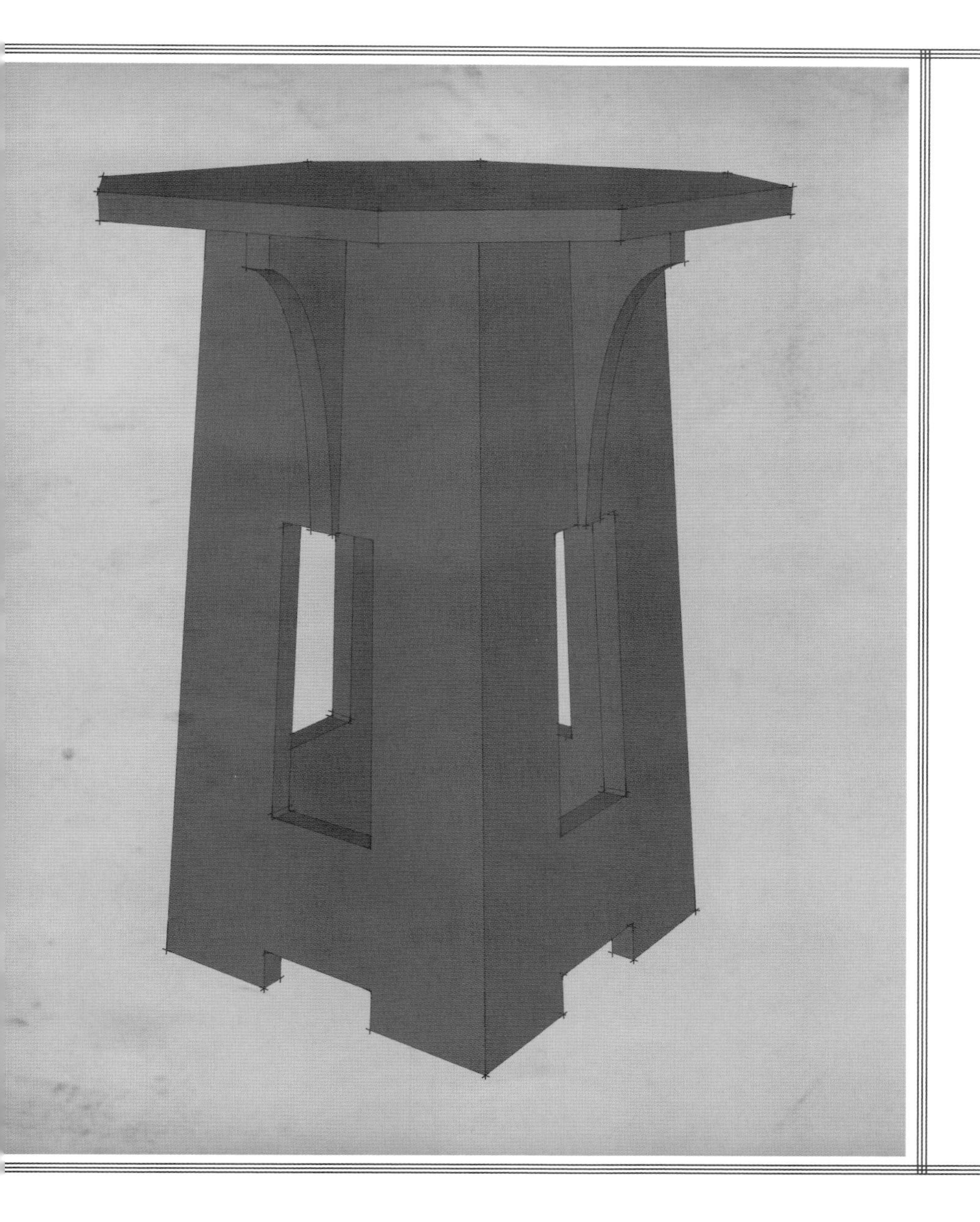

Here is another version of the tapered column form. The Limbert company produced the No. 251 and the taller No. 239 with an additional cutout. The octagonal top calls to mind several different tables from the 1903 catalog, but this table featured in the later line.

EXPLODED VIEW

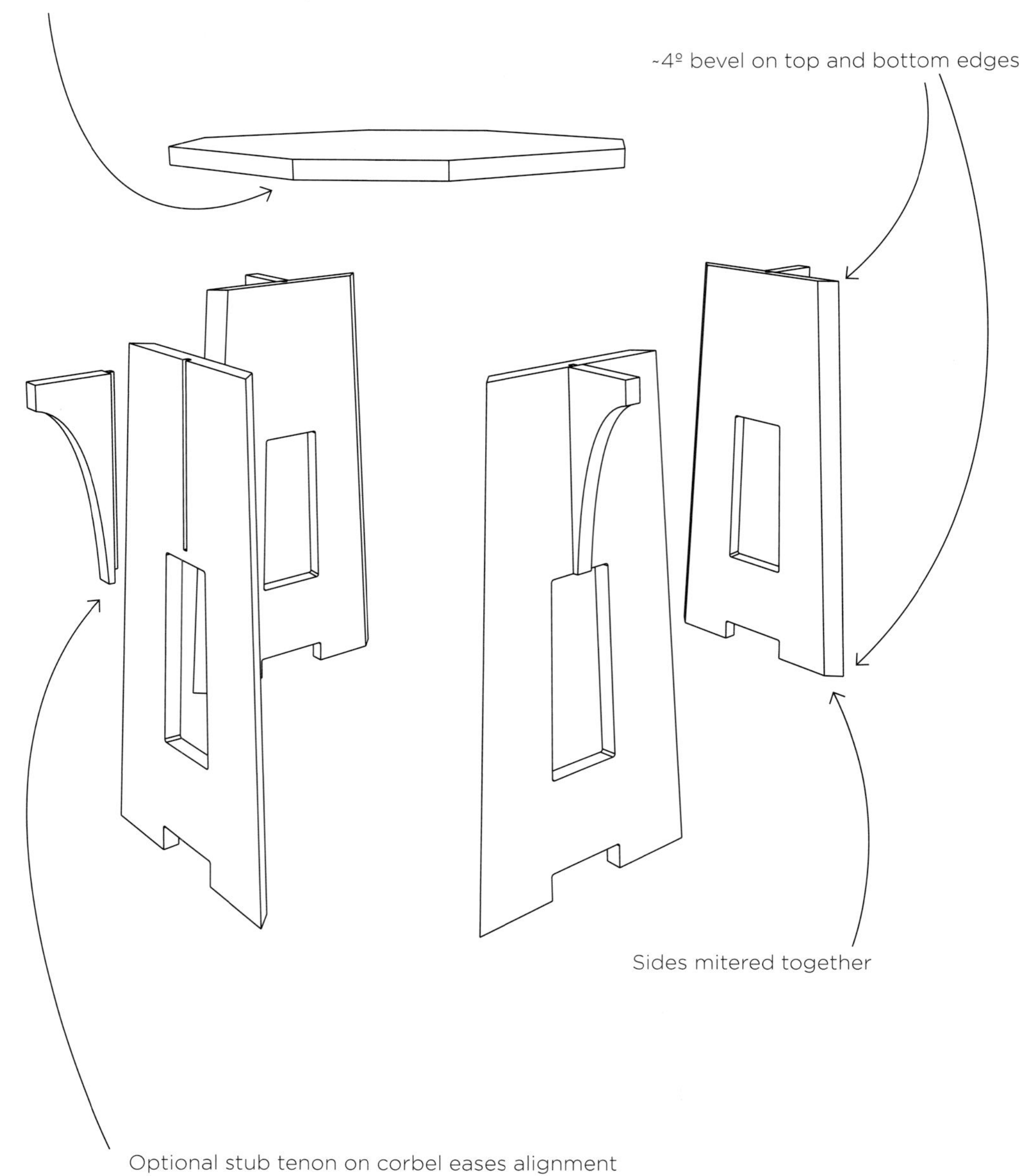

Top attached to sides with fasteners or pocket holes
~4º bevel on top and bottom edges
Sides mitered together
Optional stub tenon on corbel eases alignment

PART LIST

Qty	Description	Length	Width	Thickness
4	corbel	8 9/16"	3 21/64"	3/4"
4	side	23 13/64"	12"	3/4"

Qty	Description	Length	Width	Thickness
1	top	17"	17"	3/4"

SIDE VIEW

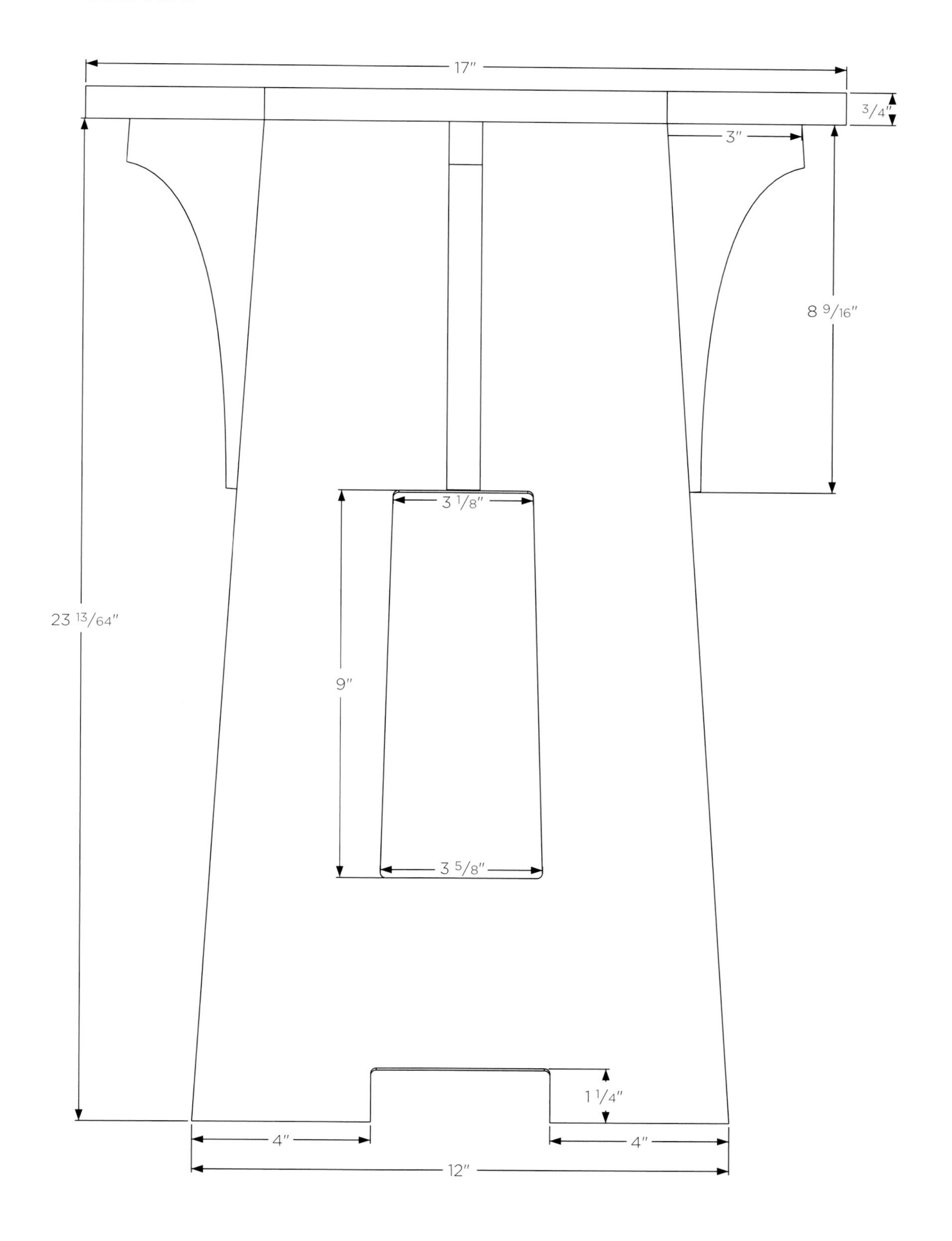

SIDE PANEL

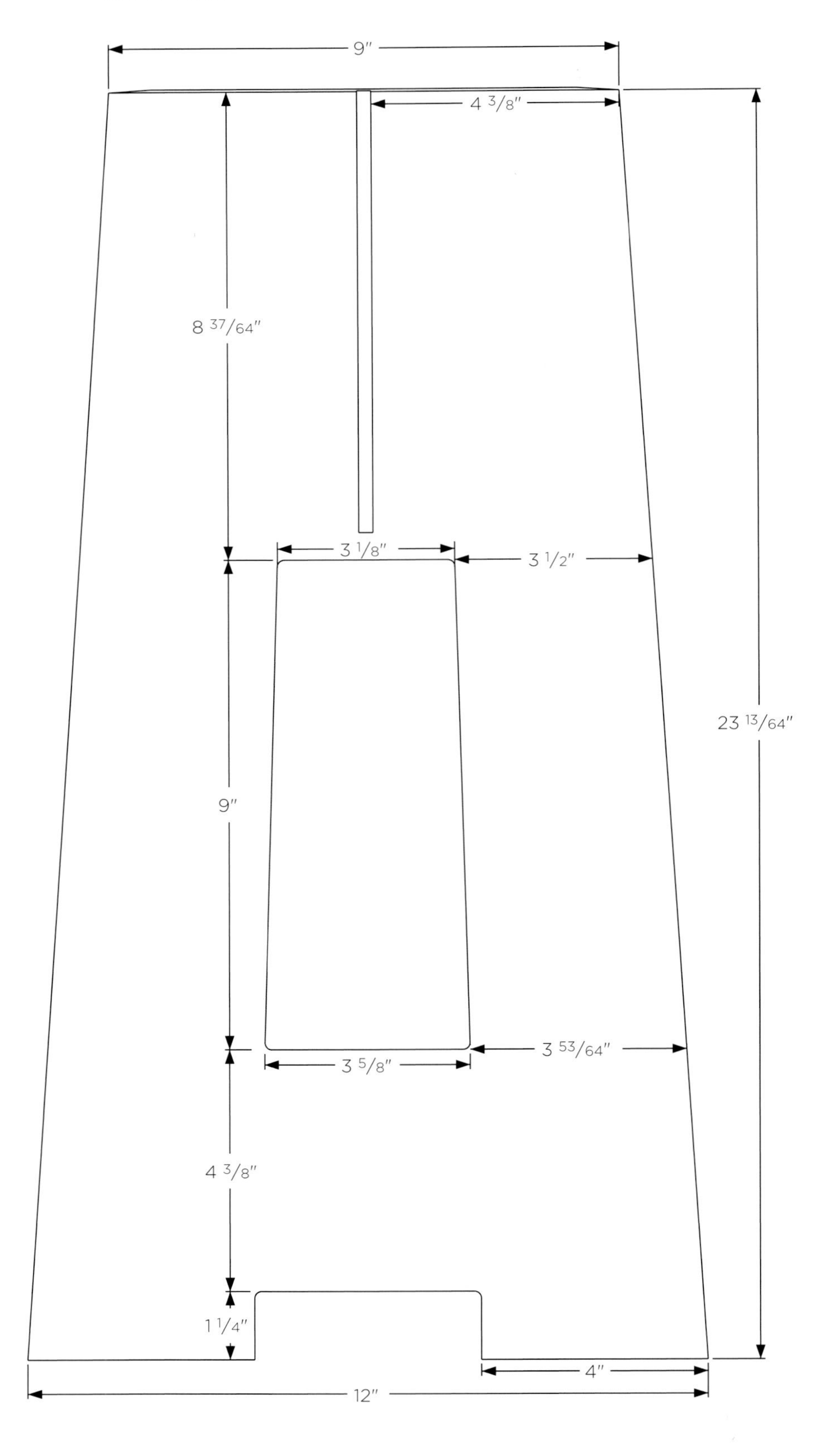

TOP SECTION VIEW

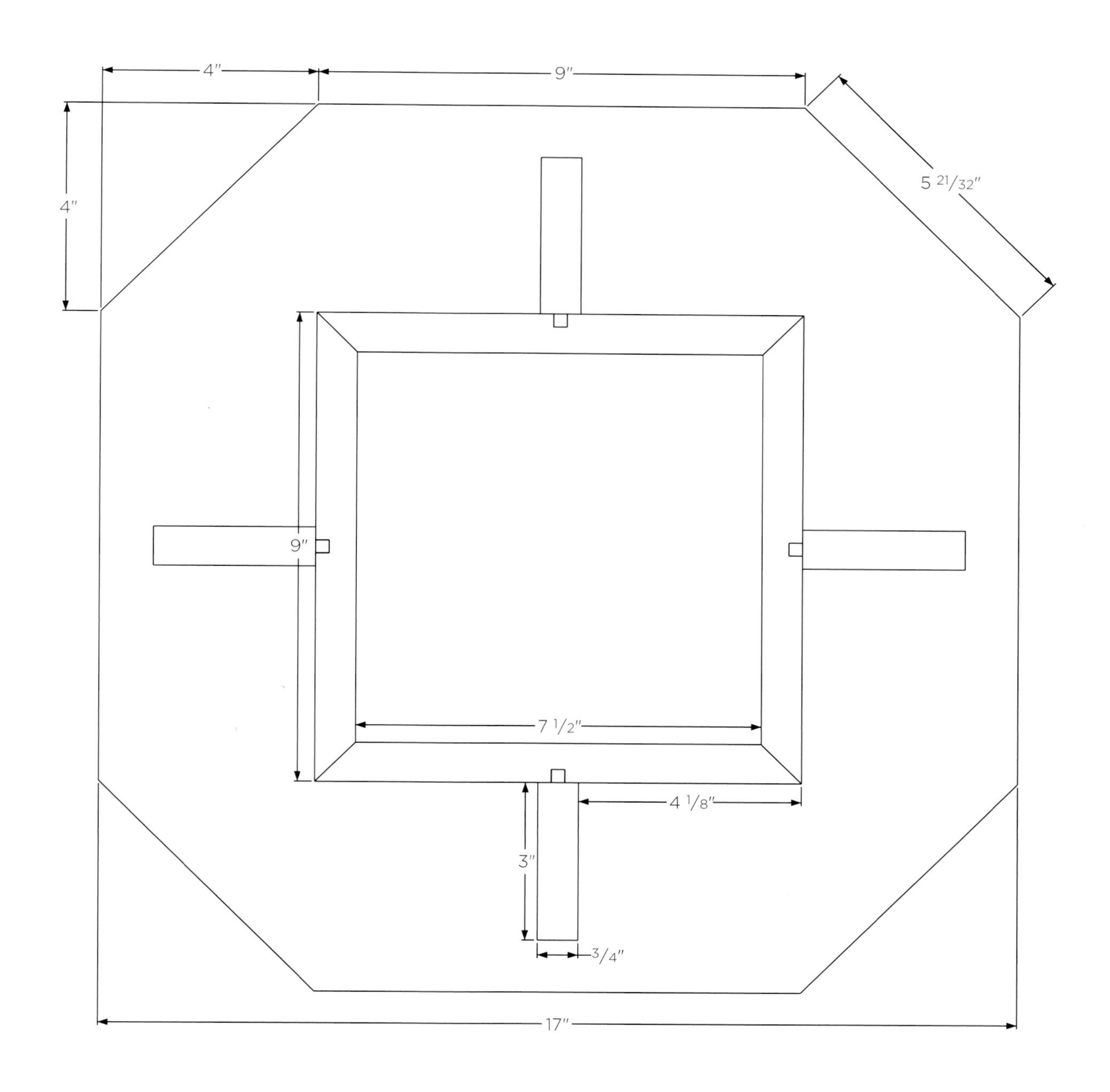

No. 234

SIDE TABLE

18″ high x 16″ wide x 16″ deep — $6.00 (1905)

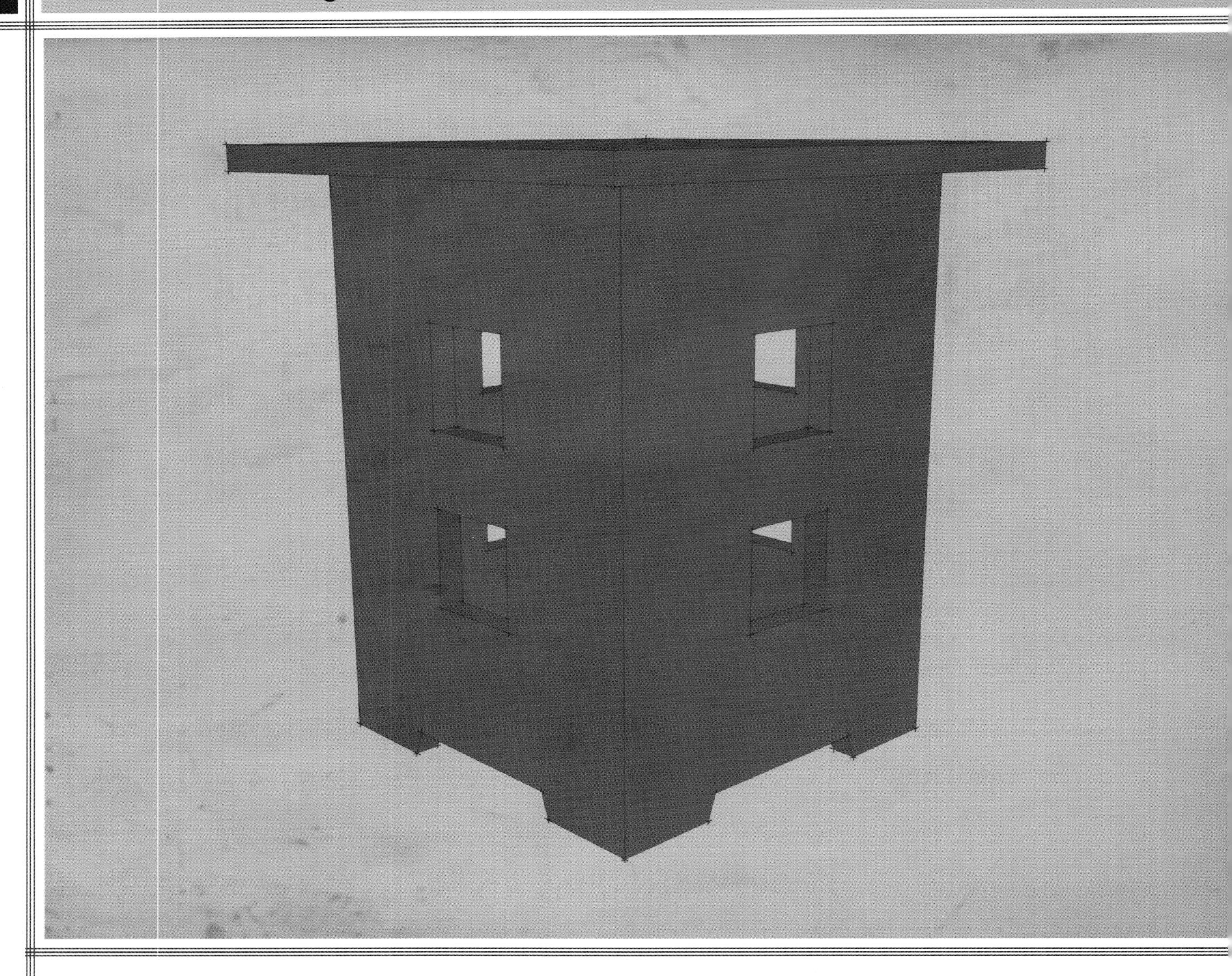

This table's diminutive stature makes it a flexible piece, useful at the side of a couch or bed. In a smaller living room, two in a row would serve instead of a coffee table. The mitered base and cutouts provide a good introduction to working with two features common to Limbert furniture.

EXPLODED VIEW

Top attached with fasteners or through pocket holes in sides
Sides joined with a simple miter, splined miter, or locking miter

PART LIST

Qty	Description	Length	Width	Thickness	Qty	Description	Length	Width	Thickness
4	side	17 1/4"	12"	3/4"	1	top	16"	16"	3/4"

FRONT VIEW

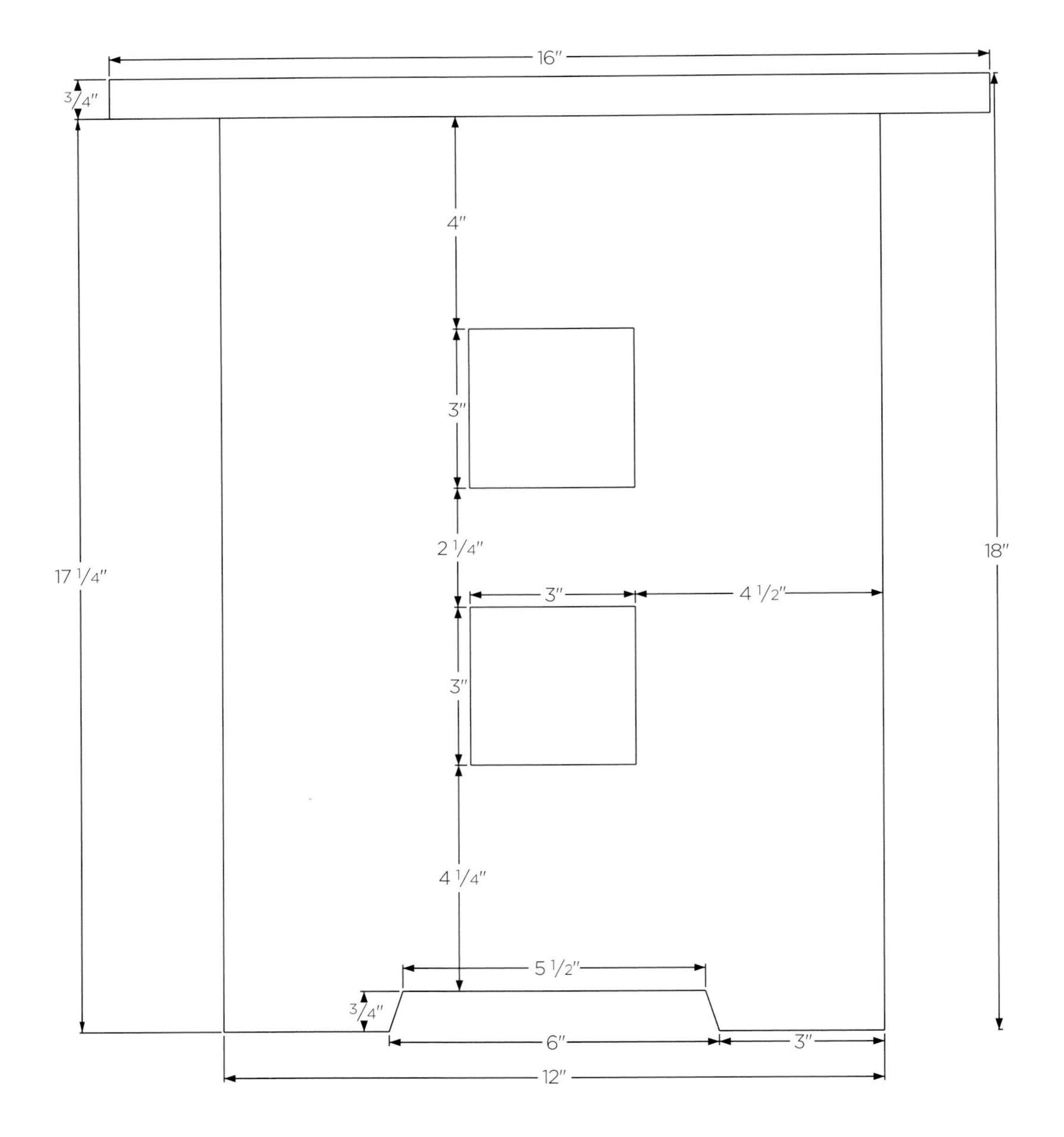

TOP SECTION VIEW

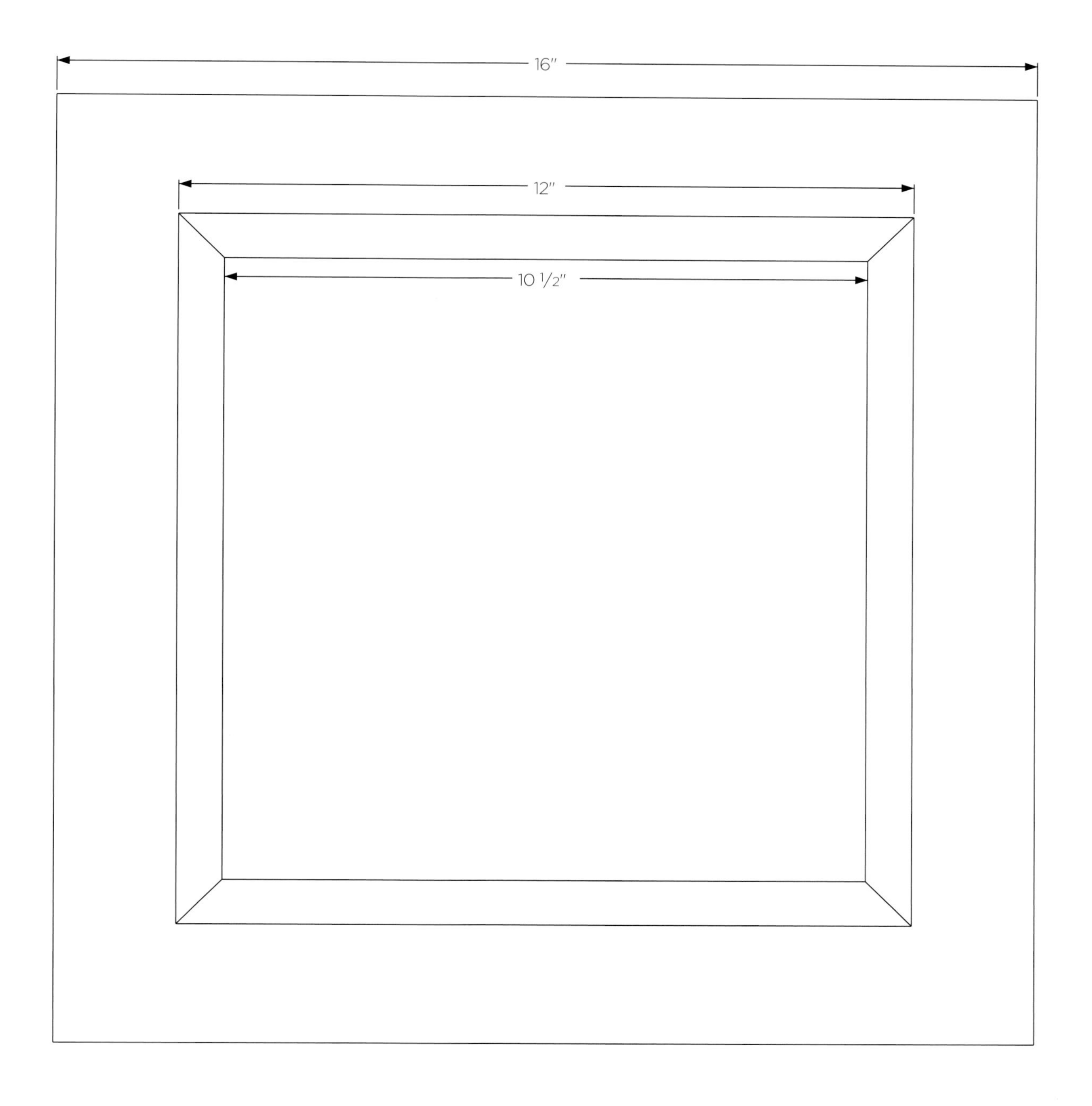

No. 500

CAFE CHAIR

34″ high x 26″ wide x 22″ deep — $15.00 (1905)

Limbert's debt to Mackintosh is most obvious in the No. 500 café chair. Mackintosh's version was built for Glasgow's Rose Team Room, and Limbert hews closely to the original. Critics may dismiss it as a mere copy, but Limbert made several changes that improve upon Mackintosh's design. The No. 500 eliminates the arched front apron and substitutes a single wide stretcher for two narrow slats at the base. These changes give the chair greater horizontal visual weight and help ground the design. The altered cutout in the back ties the chair to other Limbert pieces, and the wider arms of the No. 500 make for a more comfortable seat. The corbels add a nice Mission detail as well as supporting the wider arms.

The original features an upholstered seat. The drop-seat cushion is one of the easiest upholstery jobs to tackle, but a wood seat can be substituted for the upholstered. The different cutouts in the Mackintosh and Limbert versions, too, suggest an opportunity for individual expression. You could use the half-moon shape of the Mackintosh version or adopt a different cutout entirely: one contemporary maker substitutes a series of small square cutouts for the organic shape. This alludes to Mackintosh while associating the chair with other Limbert furniture that uses the square cutout.

EXPLODED VIEW

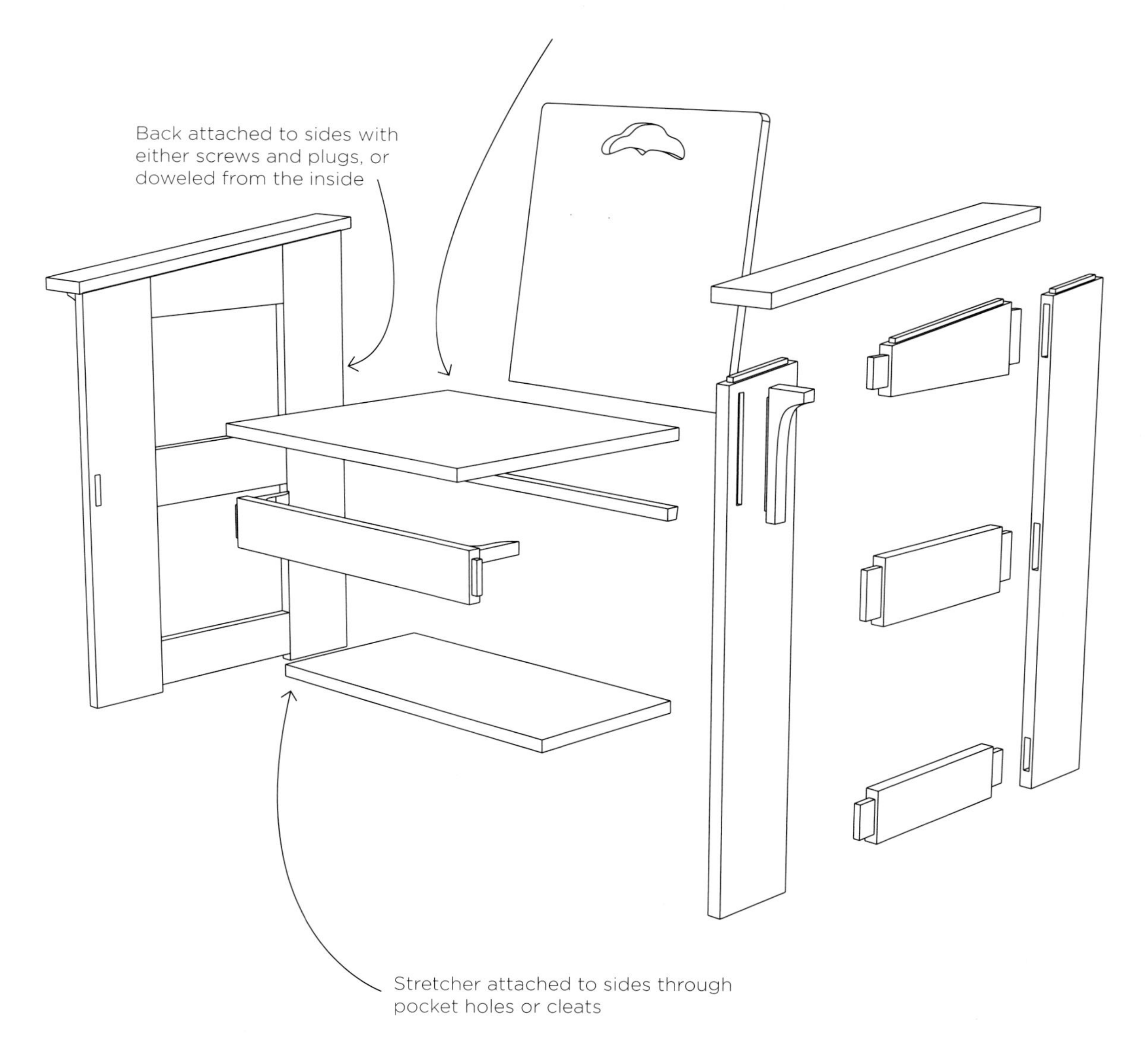

Seat attached to corner blocks and cleats
Back attached to sides with either screws and plugs, or doweled from the inside
Stretcher attached to sides through pocket holes or cleats

PART LIST

Qty	Description	Length	Width	Thickness
2	back side stile	29 3/4"	5"	3/4"
1	back	19 13/64"	19"	3/4"
2	corbel	6 19/32"	2 15/64"	3/4"
2	corner brace	3 1/2"	3 1/2"	3/4"
2	front side stile	27 49/64"	5"	3/4"
1	front stretcher	19 3/4"	3"	3/4"
2	arm	21 37/64"	3 1/2"	3/4"
2	lower side rail	13"	3"	3/4"
2	middle side rail	13"	3 3/4"	3/4"
1	rear seat cleat	19"	7/8"	3/4"
1	seat	19"	17 23/64"	3/4"
1	stretcher	21 1/2"	1 1/2"	3/4"
2	upper side rail	13"	4 11/64"	3/4"

FRONT VIEW

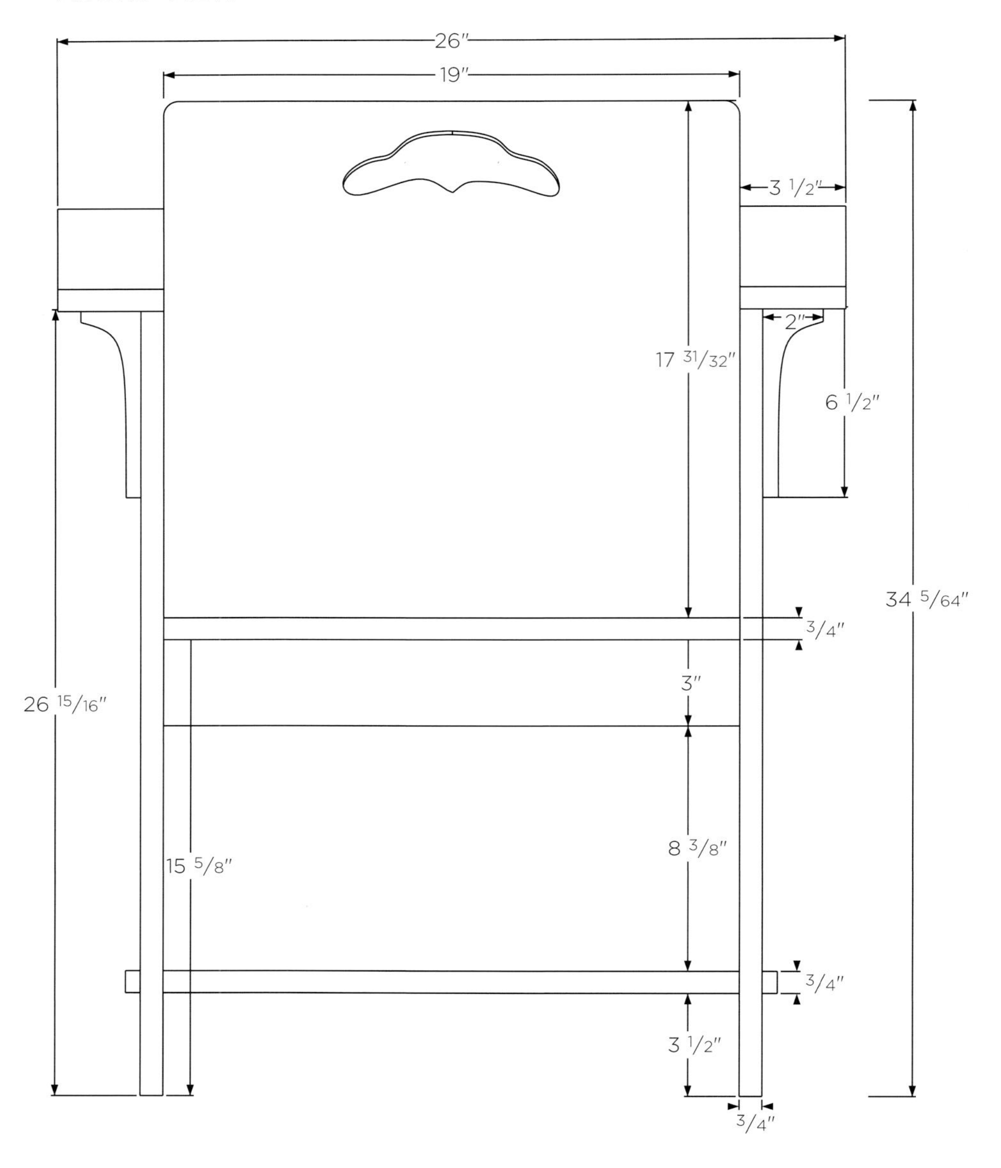

26″
19″
3 1/2″
2″
17 31/32″
6 1/2″
34 5/64″
3/4″
3″
26 15/16″
8 3/8″
15 5/8″
3/4″
3 1/2″
3/4″

BACK CUTOUT FULLSIZE PATTERN

1 square = 1″

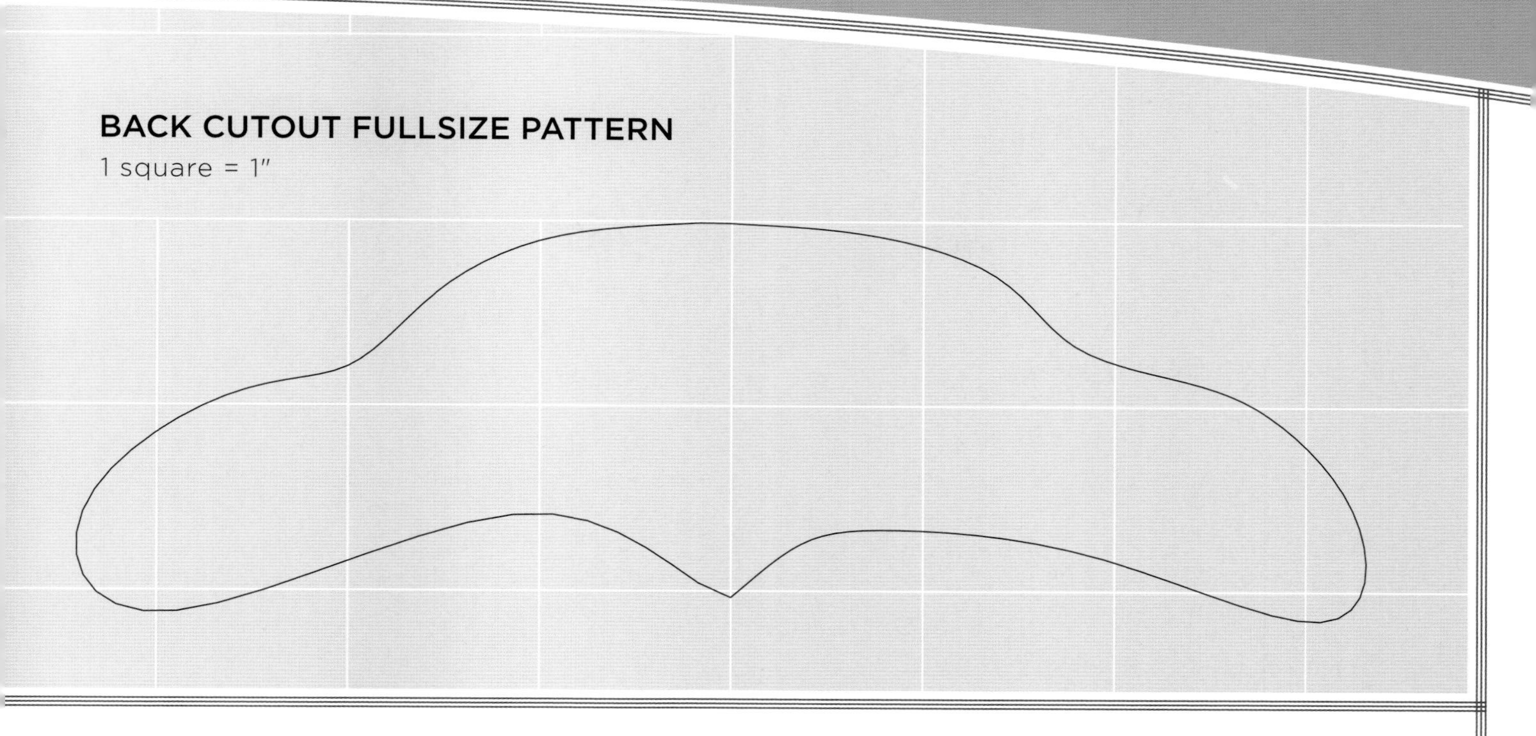

TOP VIEW

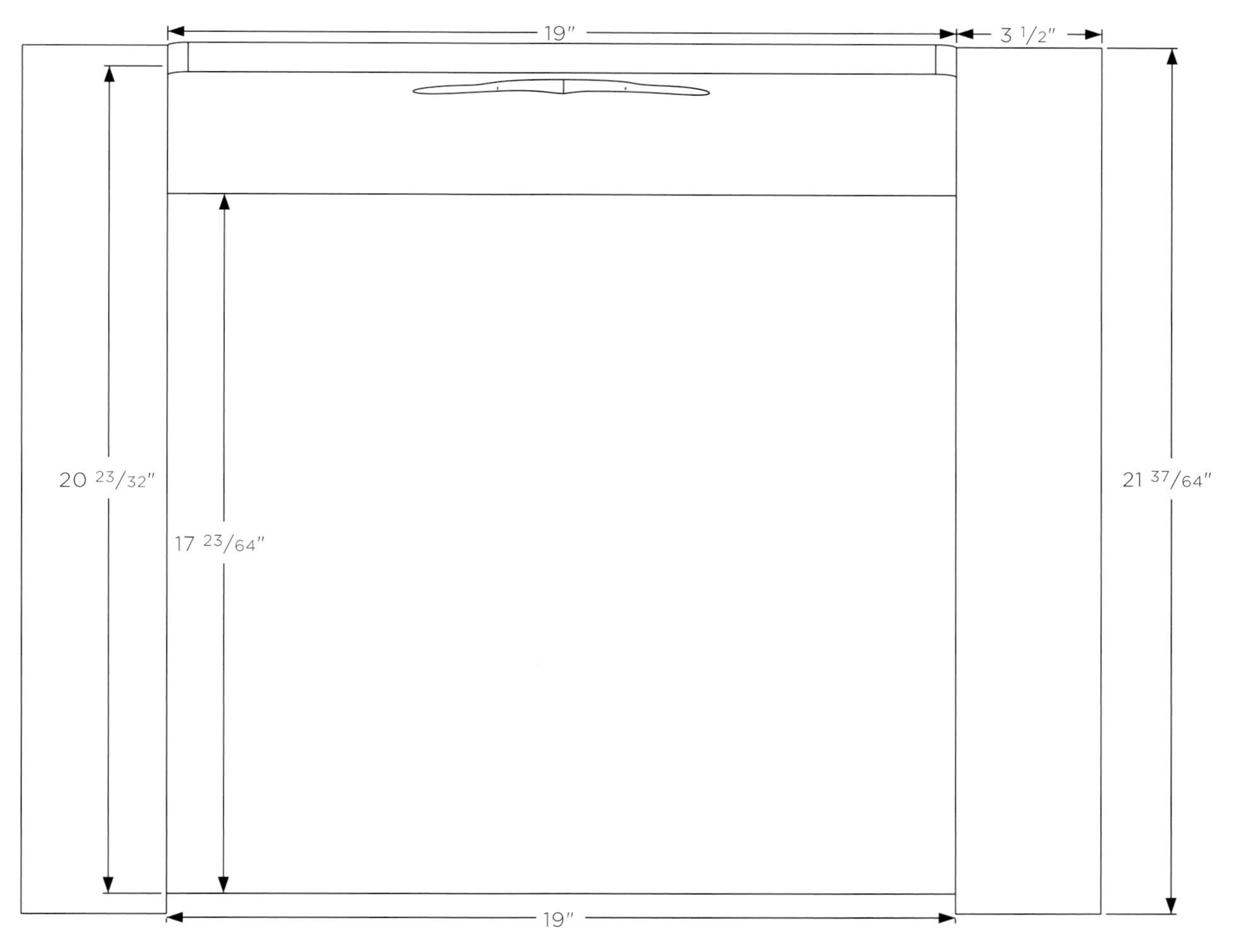

SIDE SECTION VIEW

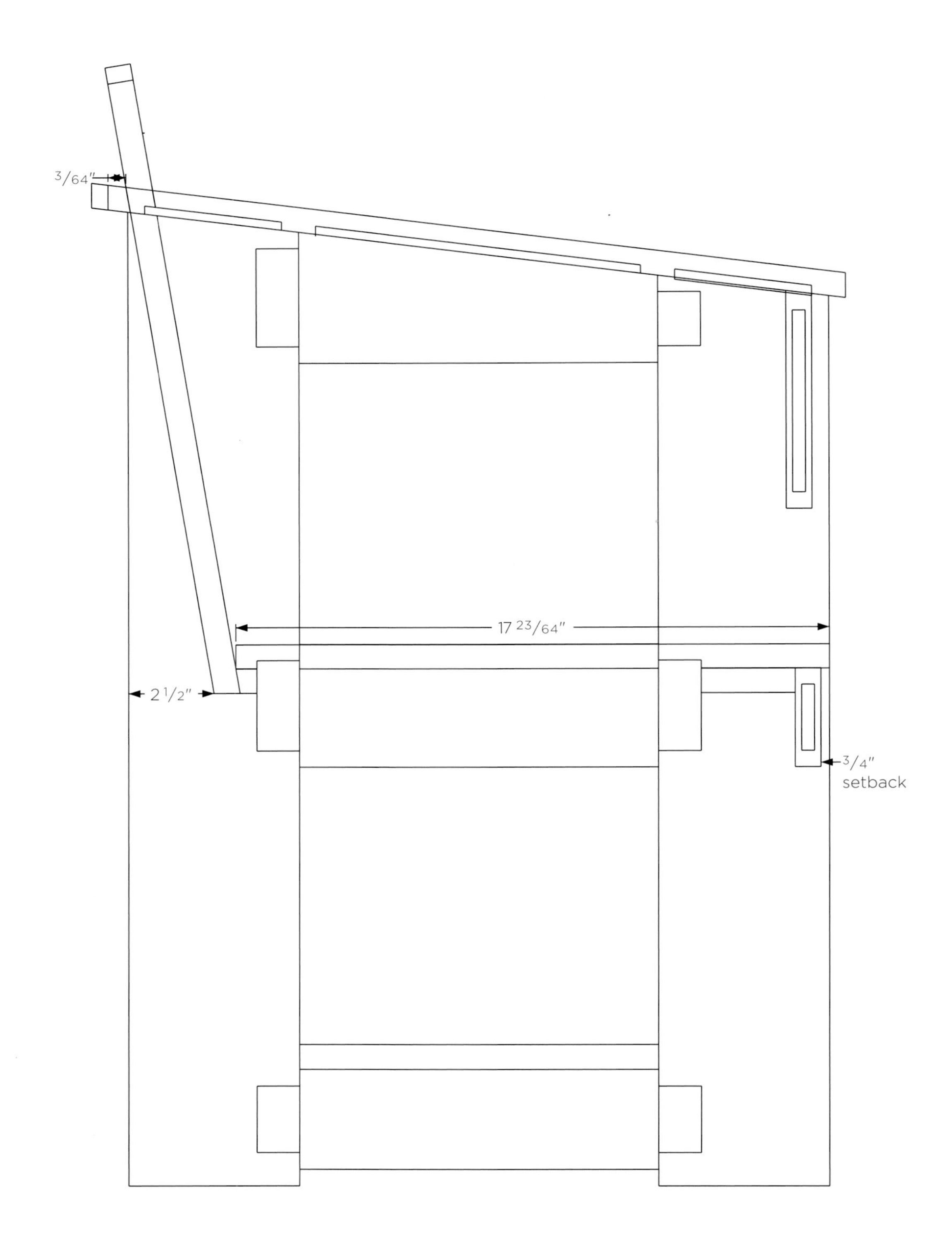

SIDE VIEW

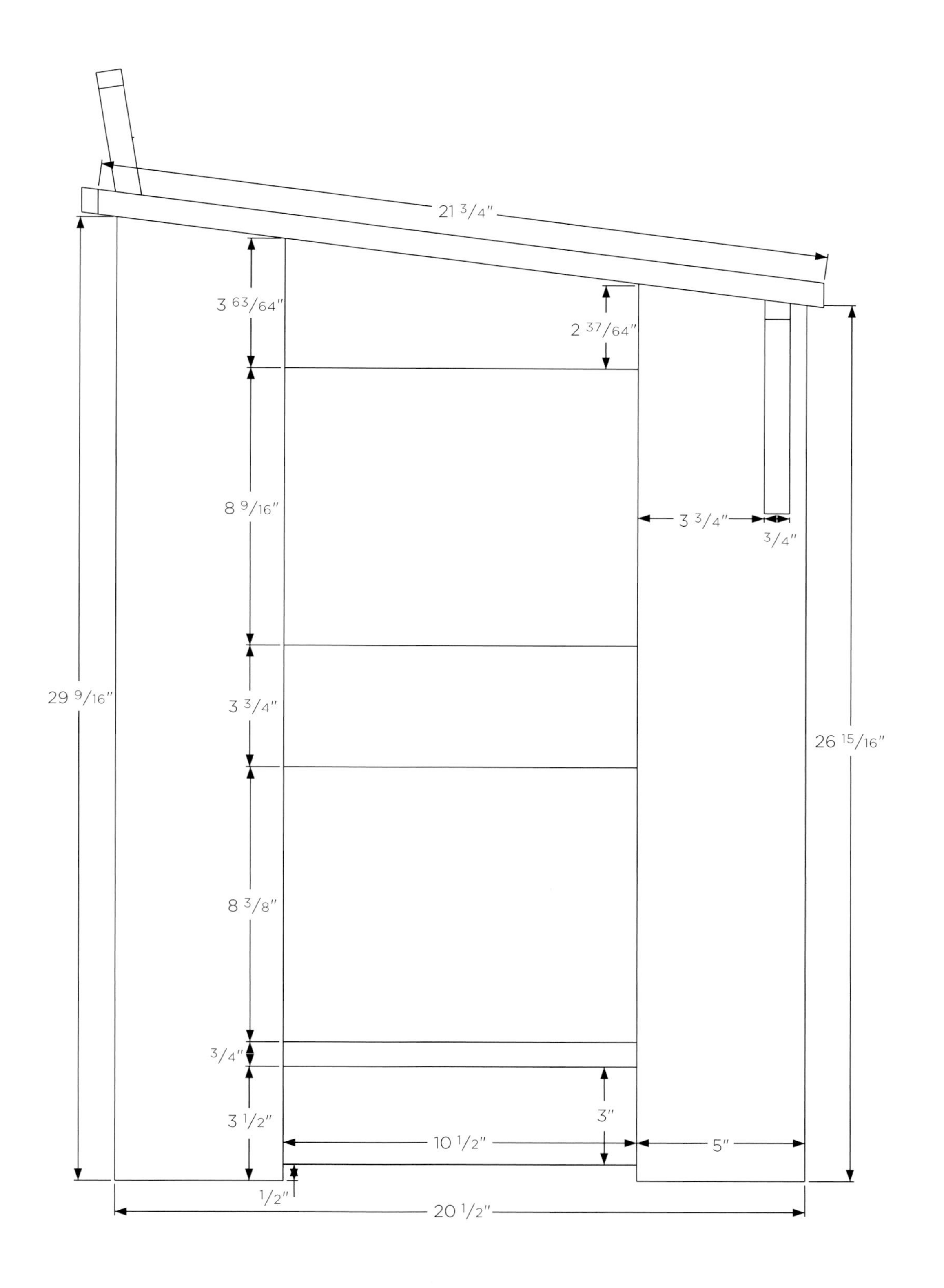

21 3/4"
3 63/64"
2 37/64"
8 9/16"
3 3/4"
3/4"
29 9/16"
3 3/4"
26 15/16"
8 3/8"
3/4"
3 1/2"
3"
10 1/2"
5"
1/2"
20 1/2"

No. 710

MAGAZINE SHELF

66" high x 24 3/4" wide x 14" deep

Striking in its close resemblance to a large magazine shelf produced by Roycroft, the 710 is also noteworthy for its absence from the publishing record Limbert left behind in catalogs, booklets, and advertisements. It features in one 1906 ad, but doesn't appear in any of the facsimile editions of catalogs and booklets available today. Nor do examples show in any readily-available auction catalogs. Since information on the No. 710 is so scarce, these drawings are based on the measurements of the Roycroft magazine shelf. The No. 71 varies from the Roycroft version with its dropfront desktop (hinged to the fourth shelf from the bottom) and lack of through tenons.

EXPLODED VIEW

PART LIST

Qty	Description	Length	Width	Thickness
1	back panel	60 3/8"	23 5/8"	3/4"
1	back rail	17 19/64"	4 3/8"	3/4"
1	door batten	20 1/4"	1 1/32"	3/4"
1	door panel	20 7/64"	15 3/64"	3/4"
1	shelf 1	17 5/16"	9 3/16"	3/4"
1	shelf 2	18 3/16"	9 5/8"	3/4"
1	shelf 3	19 13/64"	10 1/8"	3/4"
1	shelf 4	20 7/32"	10 21/32"	3/4"
1	shelf 5	21 1/4"	11 11/64"	3/4"
1	shelf 6	22 3/8"	11 49/64"	3/4"
1	shelf 7	23 39/64"	12 41/64"	3/4"
2	side	66"	14"	3/4"
1	toe kick	23 1/4"	1 1/4"	3/4"

DOOR DETAIL FRONT VIEW

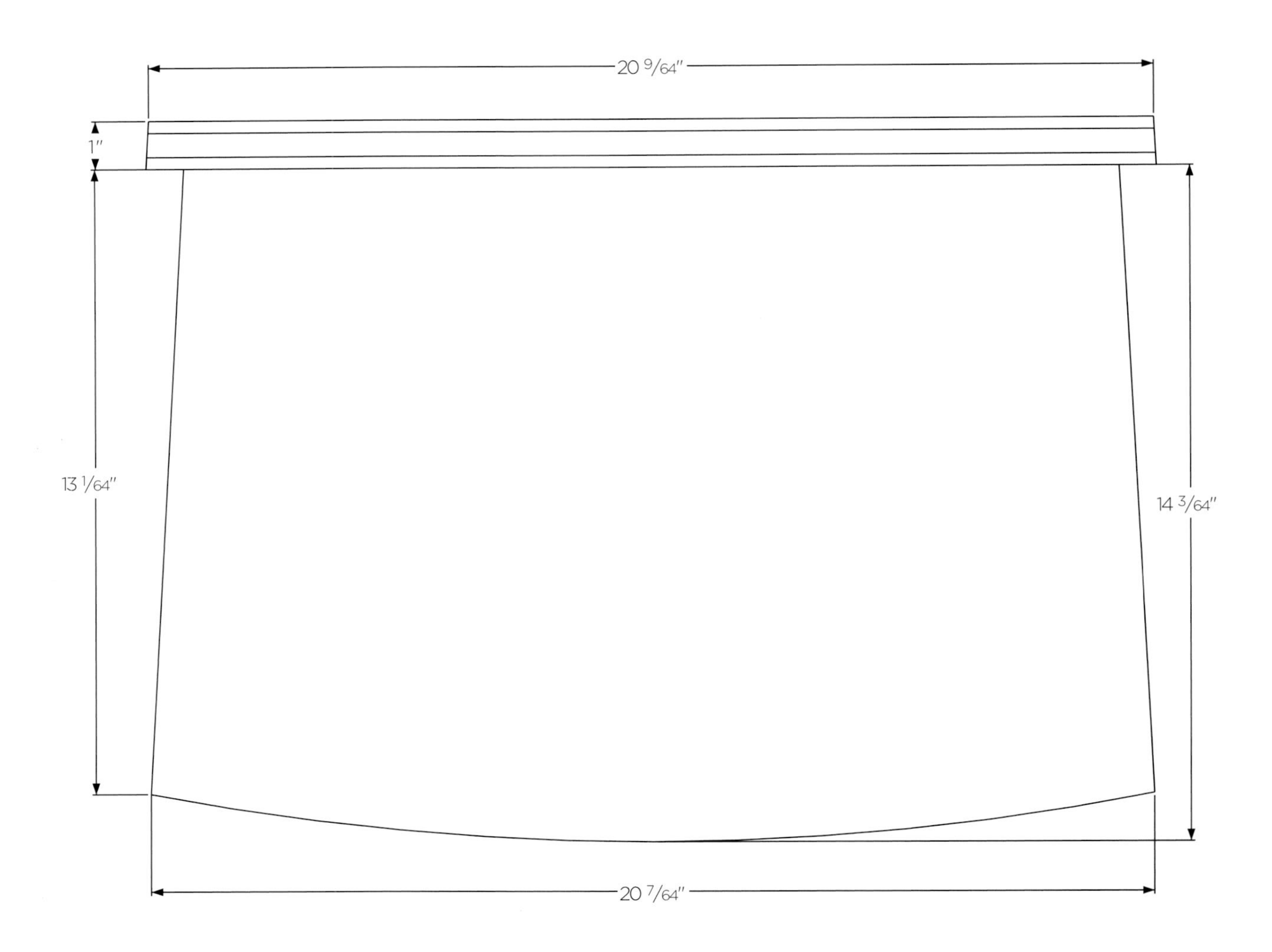

FRONT VIEW

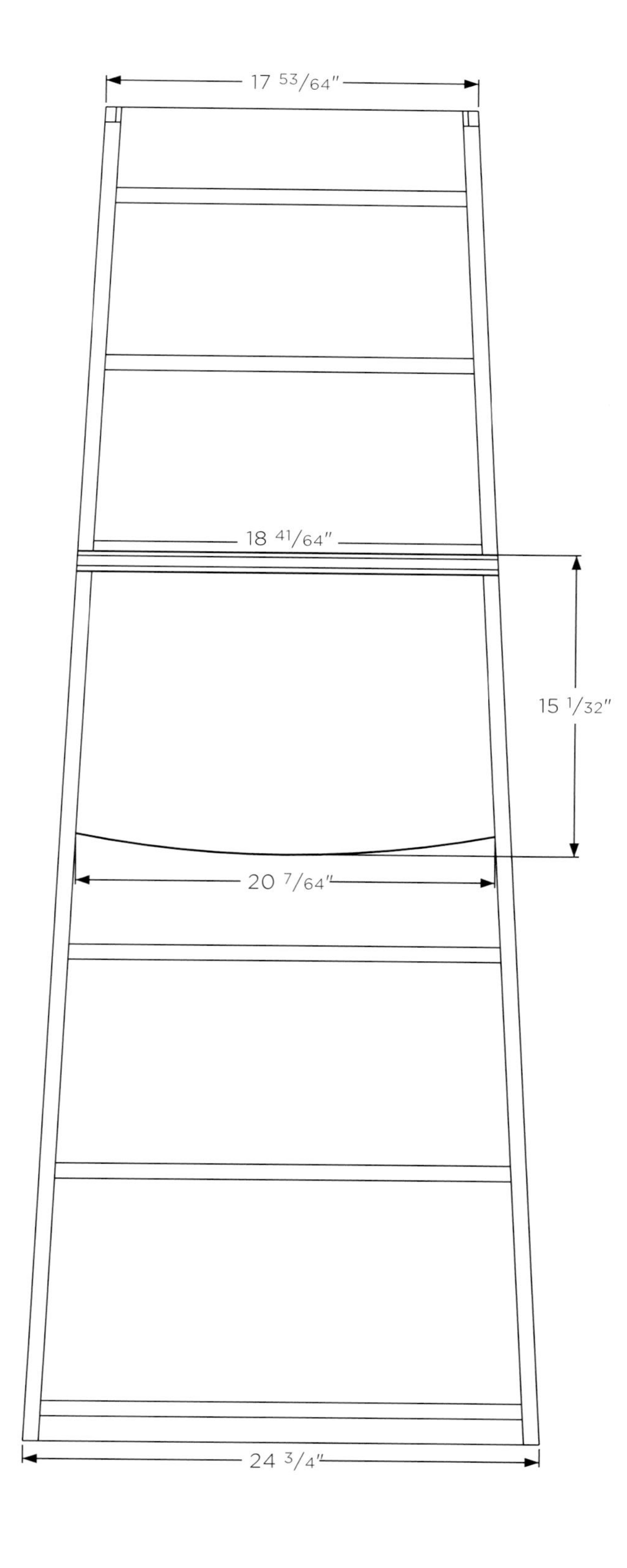

FRONT VIEW WITHOUT DOOR

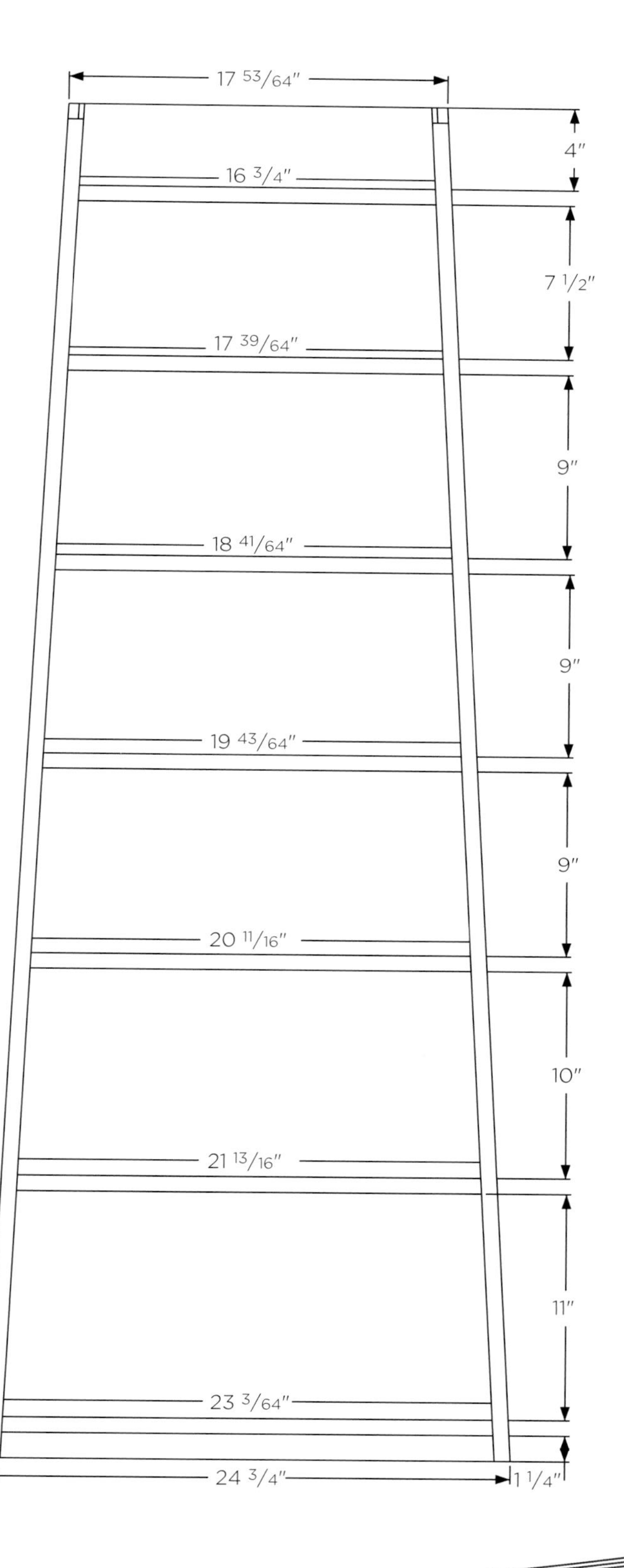

SIDE SECTION VIEW

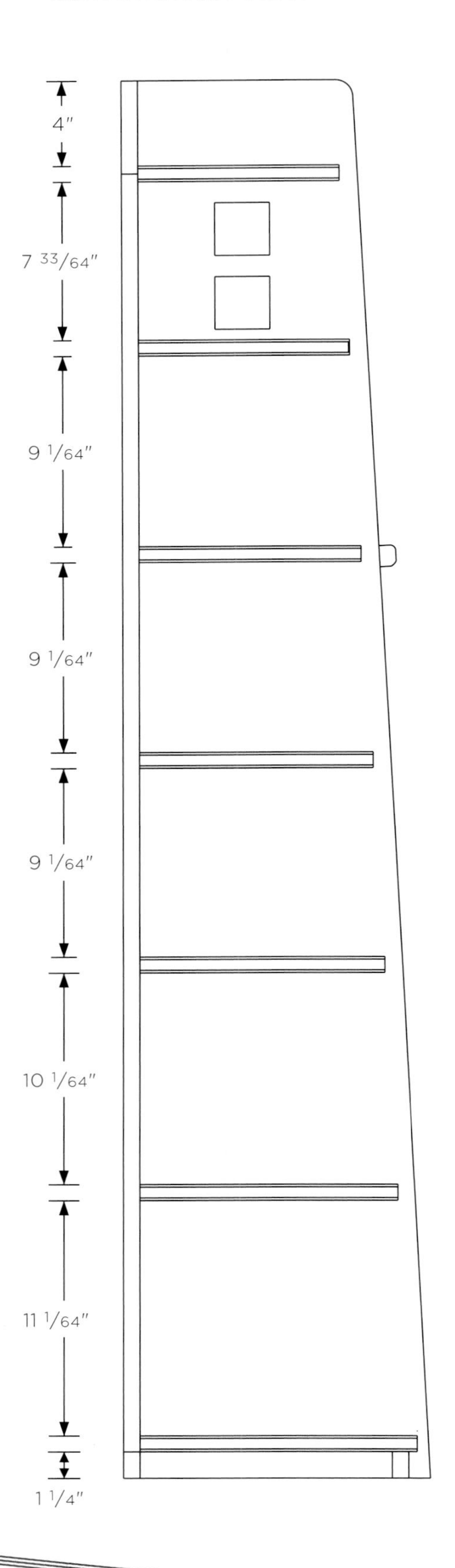

SIDE VIEW

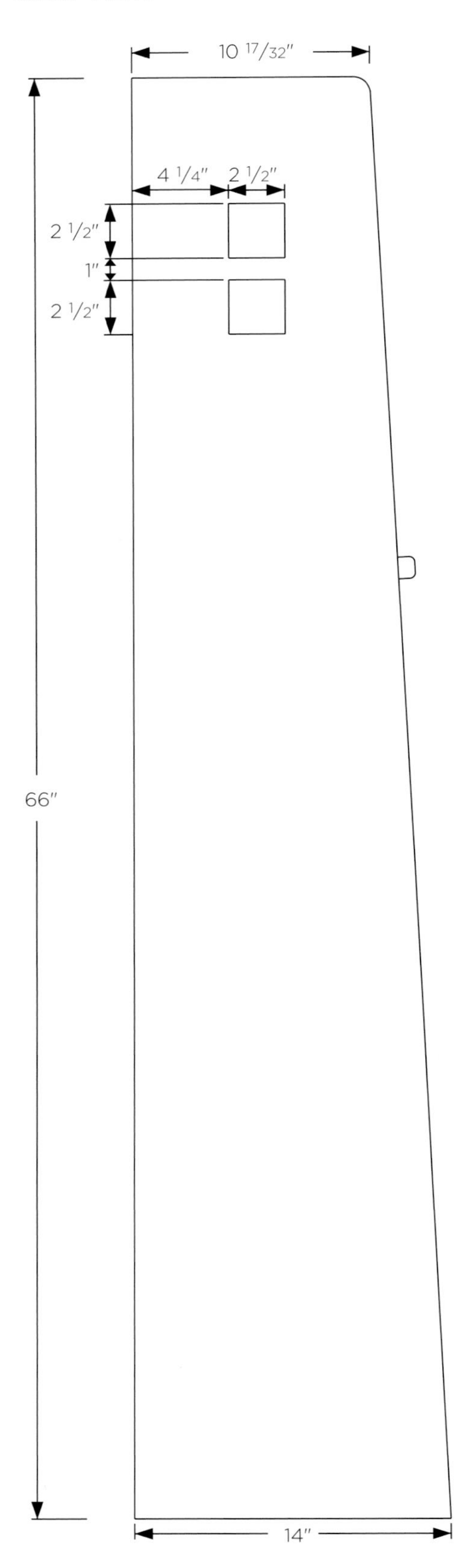

No. 565-1/2

SETTLE

34 1/2" high x 61" wide x 28" deep

The No. 565 1/2 is an even-arm form in the Craftsman style. The length could be varied by adding or removing a slat or two and extending or shortening the front and back rails as needed. If through tenons were subsituted for the blind tenons in the side rails, it would liven the face of the settle and make it resemble the No. 567 1/2.

EXPLODED VIEW

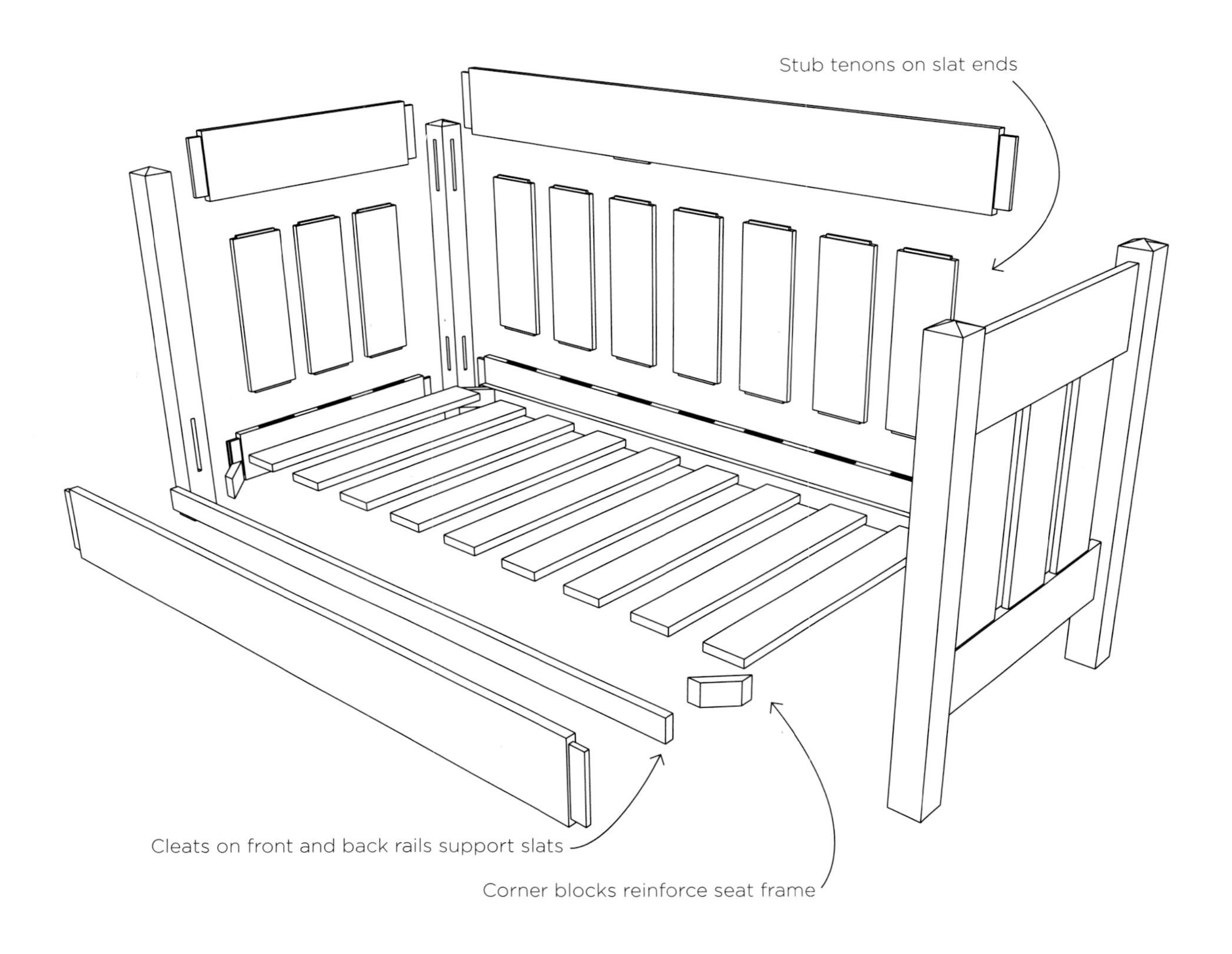

PART LIST

Qty	Description	Length	Width	Thickness
1	back bottom rail	58 1/2"	5"	3/4"
1	back upper rail	58 1/2"	6 1/2"	3/4"
4	corner block	4 1/4"	2"	3/4"
1	front rail	58 1/2"	6 1/2"	3/4"
4	leg	34 1/2"	2 1/2"	2 1/2"
9	seat slat	24 3/4"	3 1/2"	3/4"
2	side bottom rail	25 1/2"	5"	3/4"
13	slat	16"	5 1/8"	1/2"
2	slat support	56"	2"	3/4"
2	upper side rail	25 1/2"	6 1/2"	3/4"

SIDE VIEW

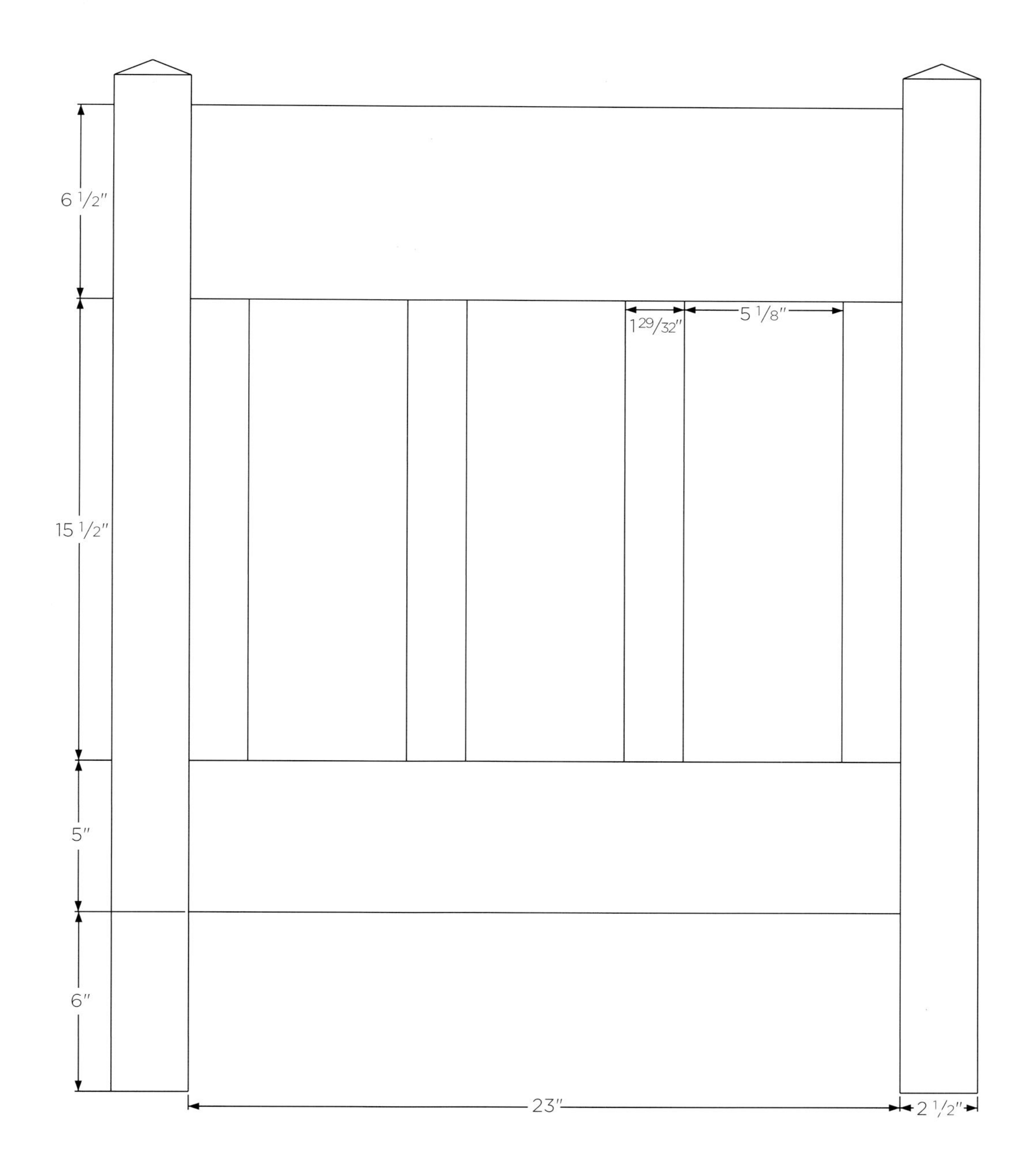

6 1/2"
15 1/2"
5"
6"
1 29/32"
5 1/8"
23"
2 1/2"

FRONT VIEW

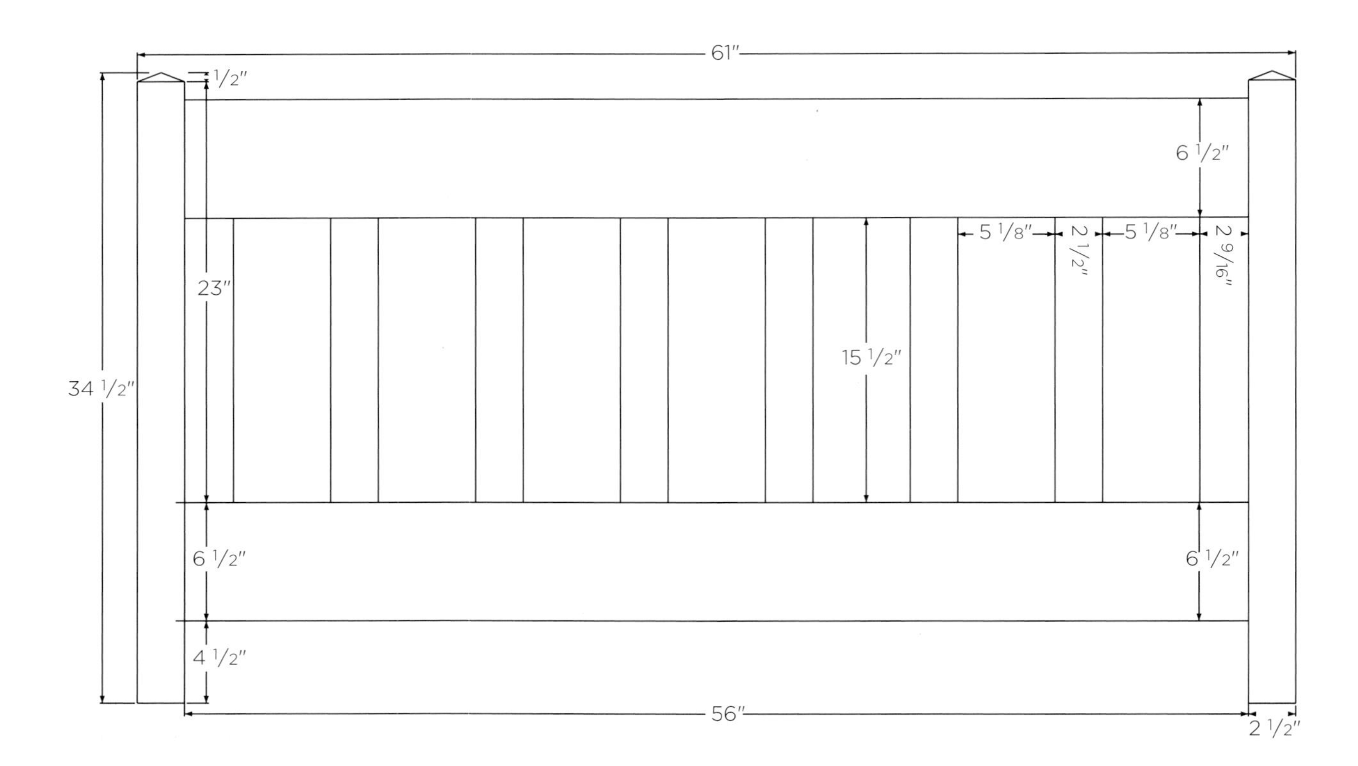

TOP VIEW

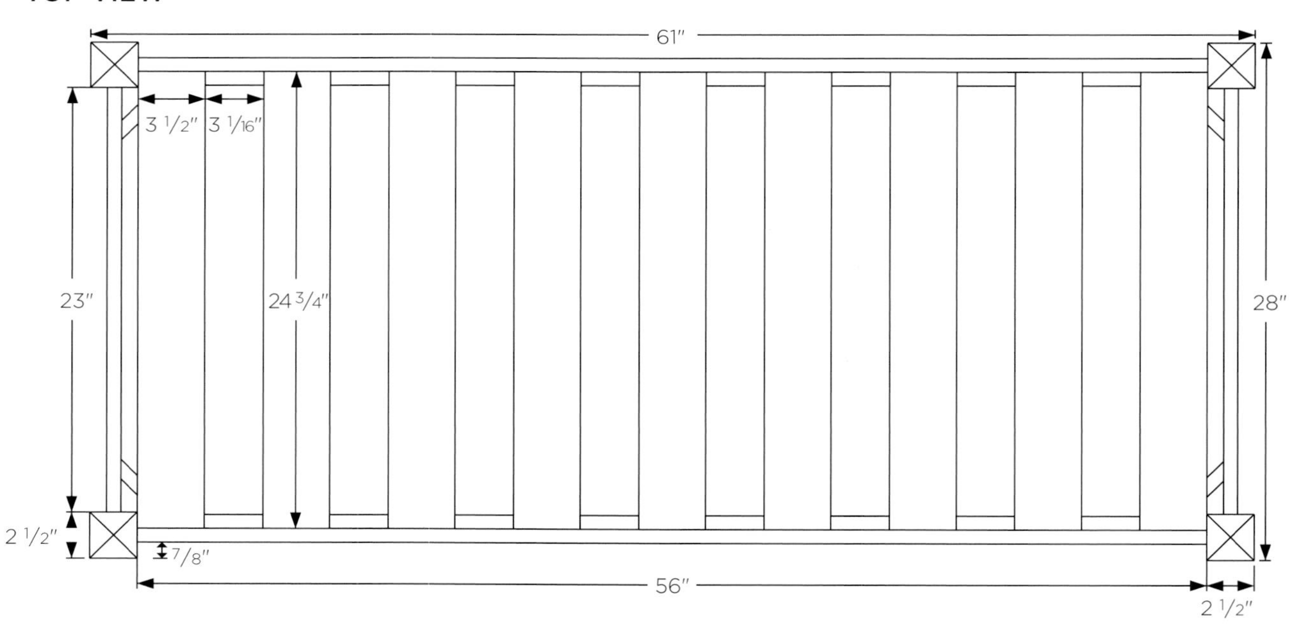

No. 148

CAFE TABLE

30″ high x 30″ wide x 30″ deep

The Limbert Furniture Company produced the round table with slanted legs and cutout bottom stretchers in a number of sizes. With a thirty inch top, the No. 148 makes a cozy table for two in a smaller eat-in kitchen. It would also complement the No. 500 café chair.

EXPLODED VIEW

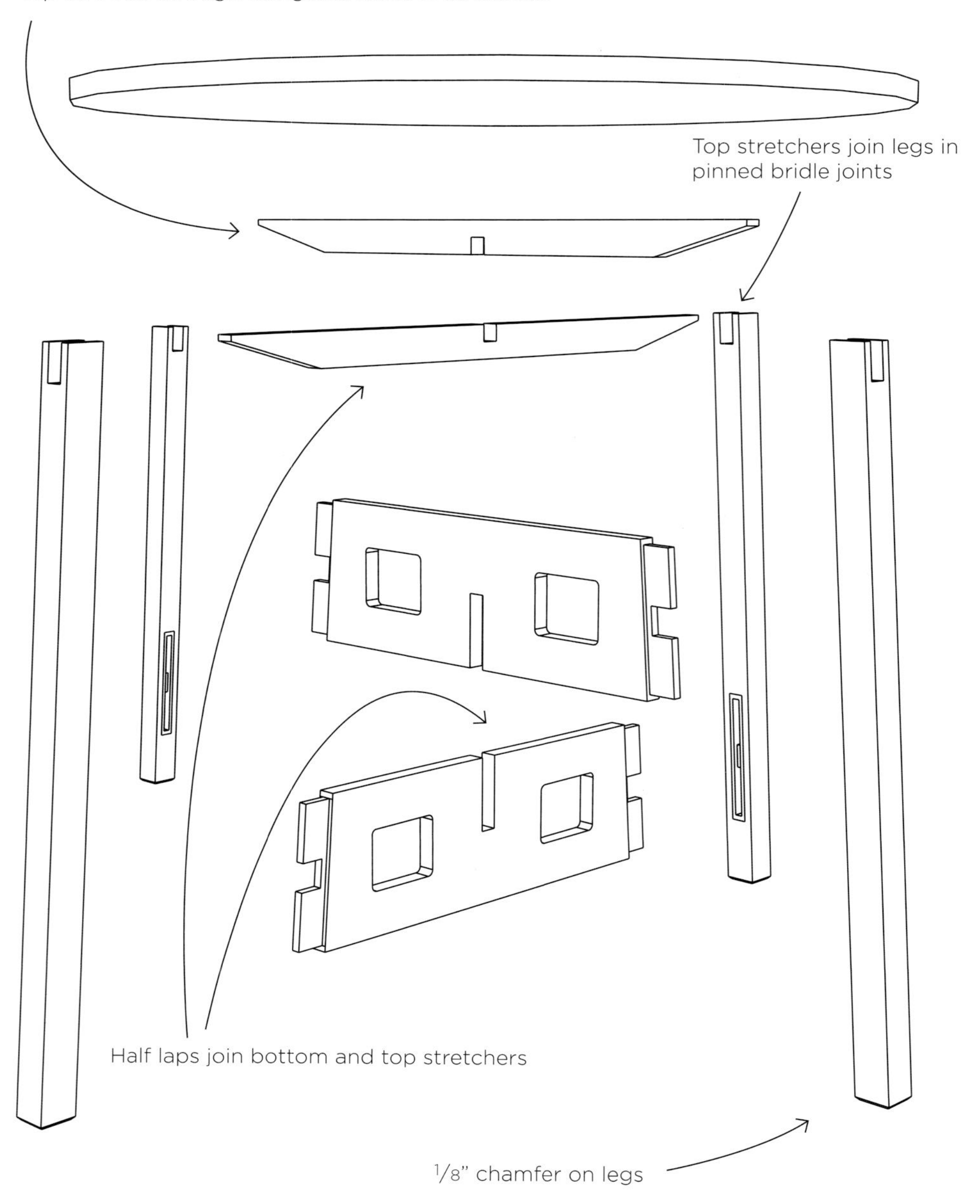

Top screwed through elongated holes in stretchers
Top stretchers join legs in pinned bridle joints
Half laps join bottom and top stretchers
1/8" chamfer on legs

PART LIST

Qty	Description	Length	Width	Thickness
2	bottom stretcher	21 1/2"	6 3/4"	3/4"
4	leg	29 5/16"	1 1/2"	1 1/2"
1	top	30"	30"	3/4"
2	top stretcher	28	1 1/2"	3/4"

TOP STRETCHER SIDE VIEW

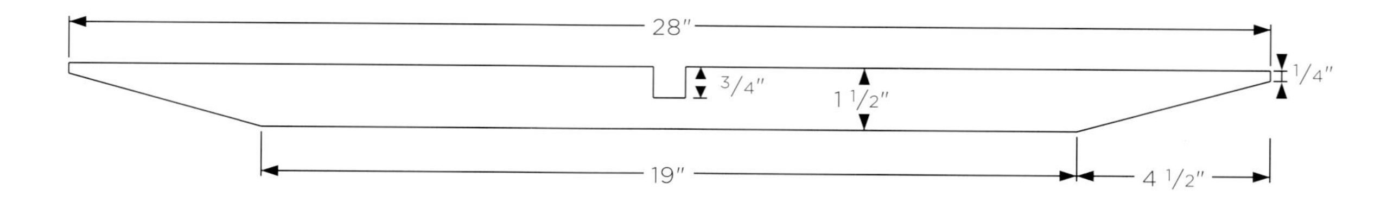

SIDE VIEW

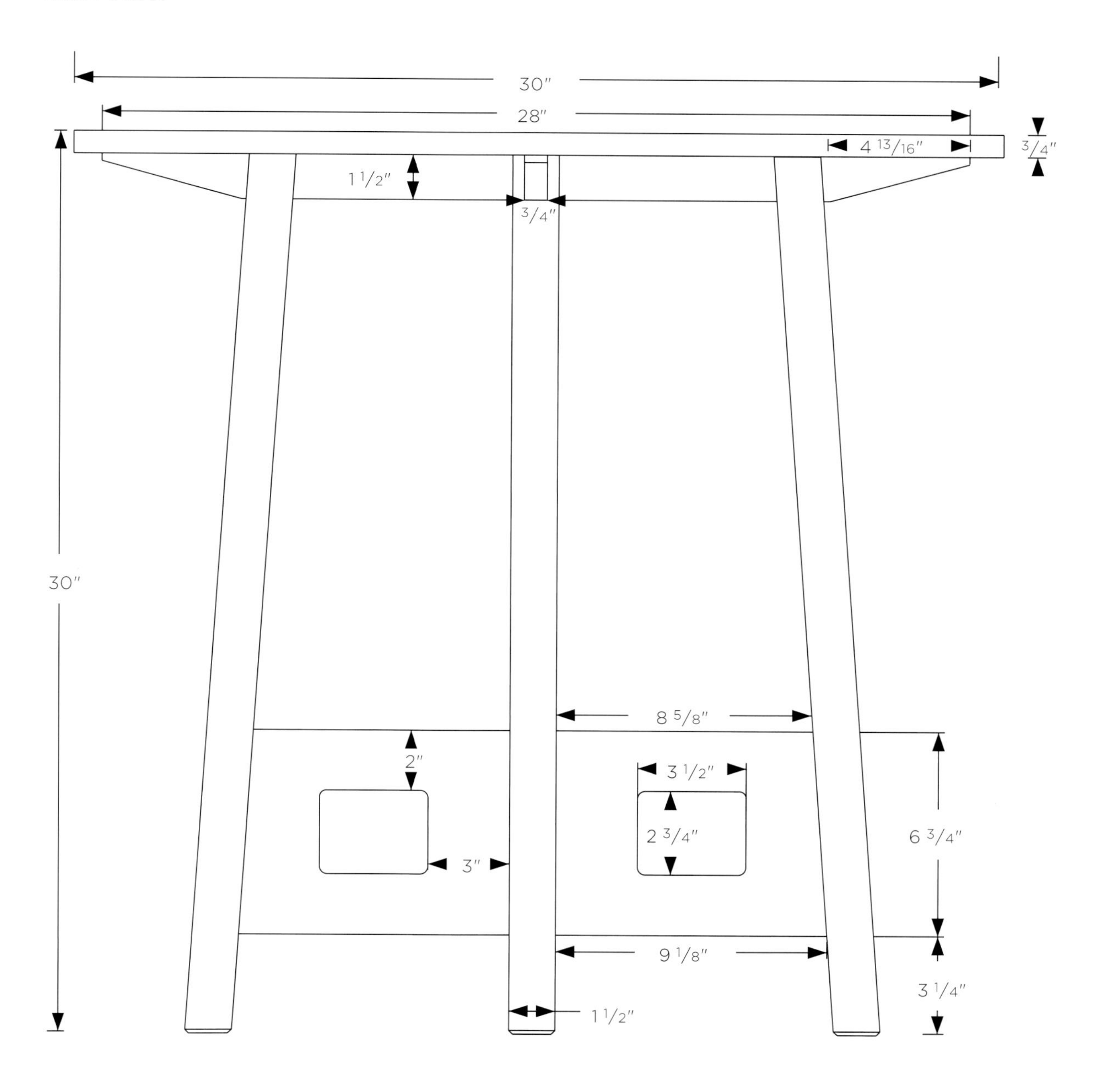

TOP SECTION VIEW

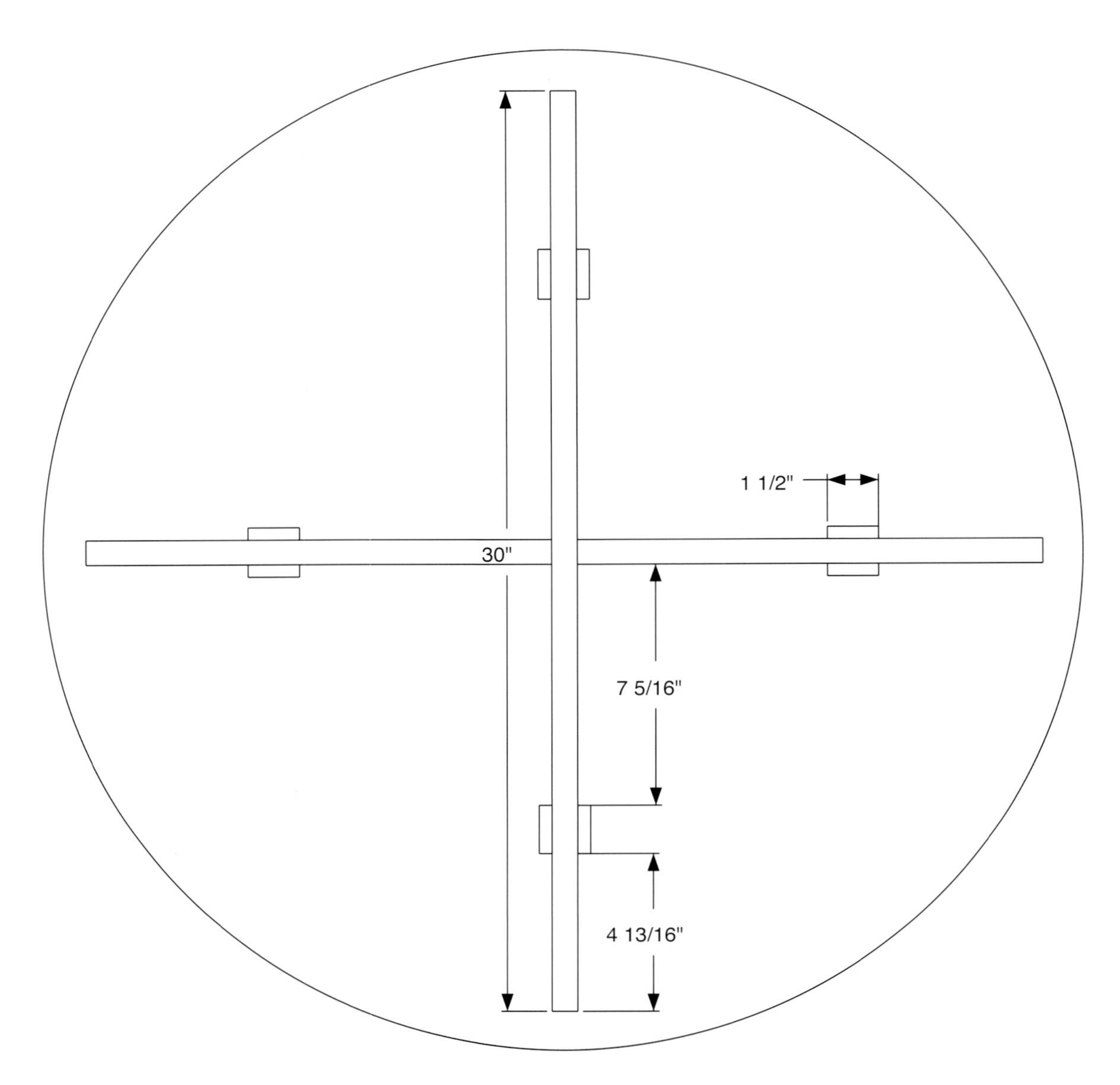

BOTTOM STRETCHER SIDE VIEW

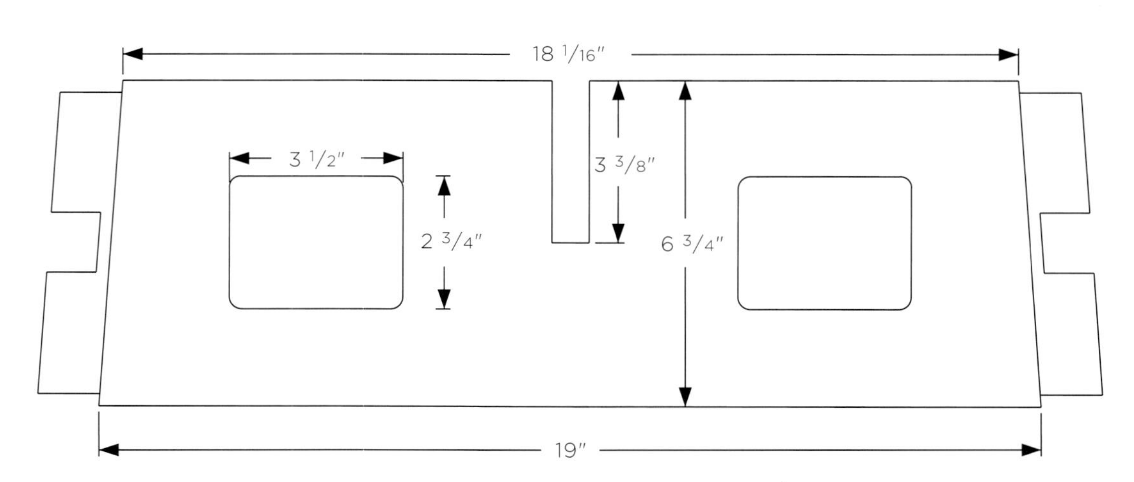

No. 164

PAGODA TABLE

30″ high x 33 1/2″ wide x 33 1/2″ deep

The number of pieces required for each side and the large interior shelf may make the No. 164 the most complex expression of the tapered-column form produced by the Limbert Company. Yet the same strategies that work for building less complicated examples of the form apply here. Work with subassemblies, building first the individual sides and gluing two pairs of sides together, then wrap the sides around the shelf to form the base. Finally top the table. The result is a distinctive table that shows a synthesis of east and west.

EXPLODED VIEW

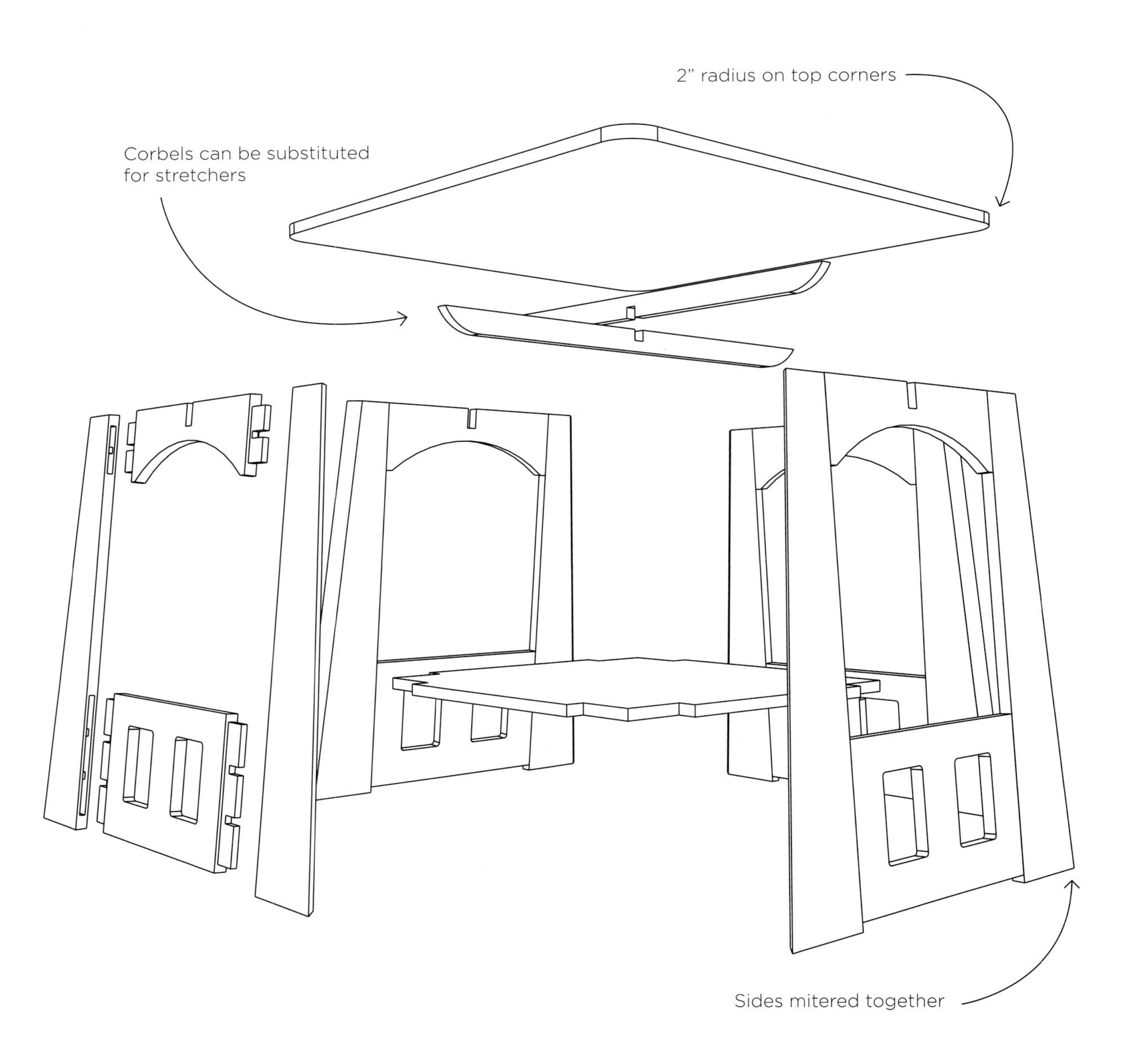

PART LIST

Qty	Description	Length	Width	Thickness
4	bottom rail	18"	9 1/2"	3/4"
8	stile	29 7/8"	5 1/2"	3/4"
1	shelf	25 3/16"	25 3/16"	3/4"
2	stretcher	31 1/2"	1 1/2"	3/4"
1	top	33 1/2"	33 1/2"	3/4"
4	top rail	18"	5"	3/4"

FRONT VIEW

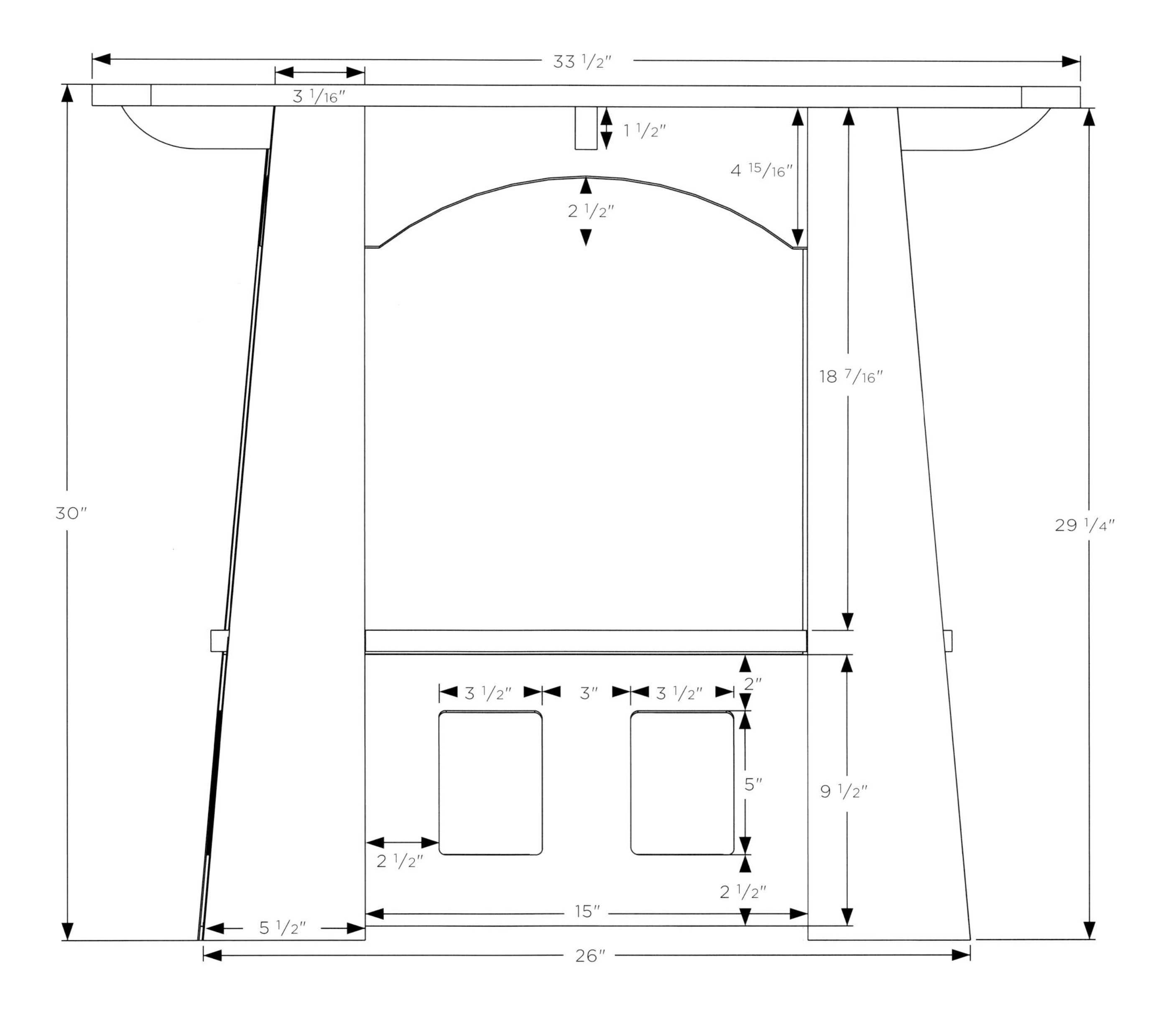

33 1/2"
3 1/16"
1 1/2"
4 15/16"
2 1/2"
18 7/16"
30"
29 1/4"
3 1/2"
3"
3 1/2"
2"
5"
9 1/2"
2 1/2"
2 1/2"
15"
5 1/2"
26"

TOP SECTION VIEW

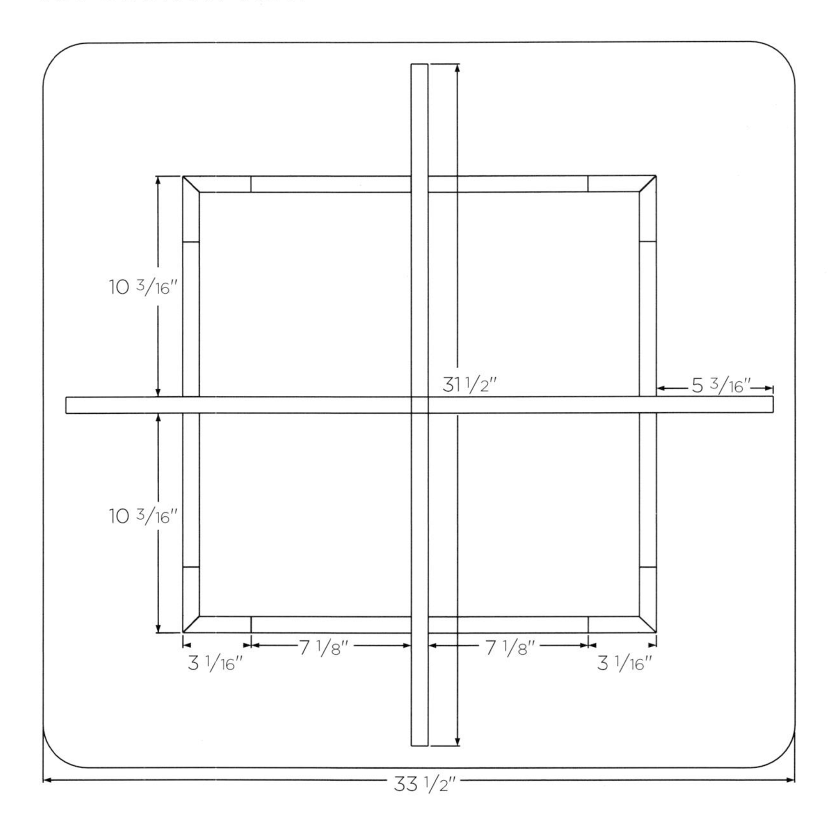

SHELF TOP VIEW

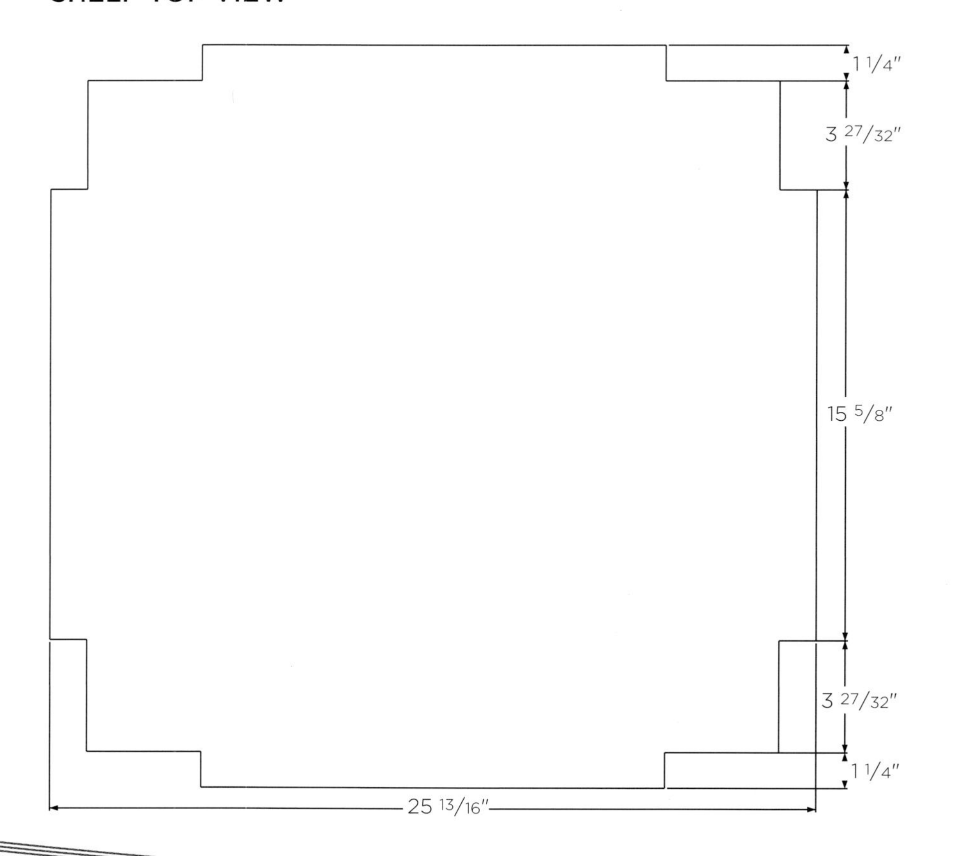

No. 407

DINING TABLE

30″ high x 72″ wide x 50″ deep — $40.00 (1903)

While most of the pieces in the 1903 catalog are almost whimsical interpretations of cottage forms (an effect amplified by use of line drawings instead of photographs to illustrate the furniture), a few, like the No. 47 and No. 700, show the Japanese influence on Limbert design. The size of the table, bulk of the thick legs, and position of the stretcher make it a less refined piece, but the reverse taper and overhanging top anticipate more polished work to come.

Even if you could find stock large enough for the legs, consider building them as hollow columns. This allows you to produce legs with attractive grain on all sides. The drawings do not illustrate the expansion mechanism in the original. It could extend to ten feet with extra leaves.

EXPLODED VIEW

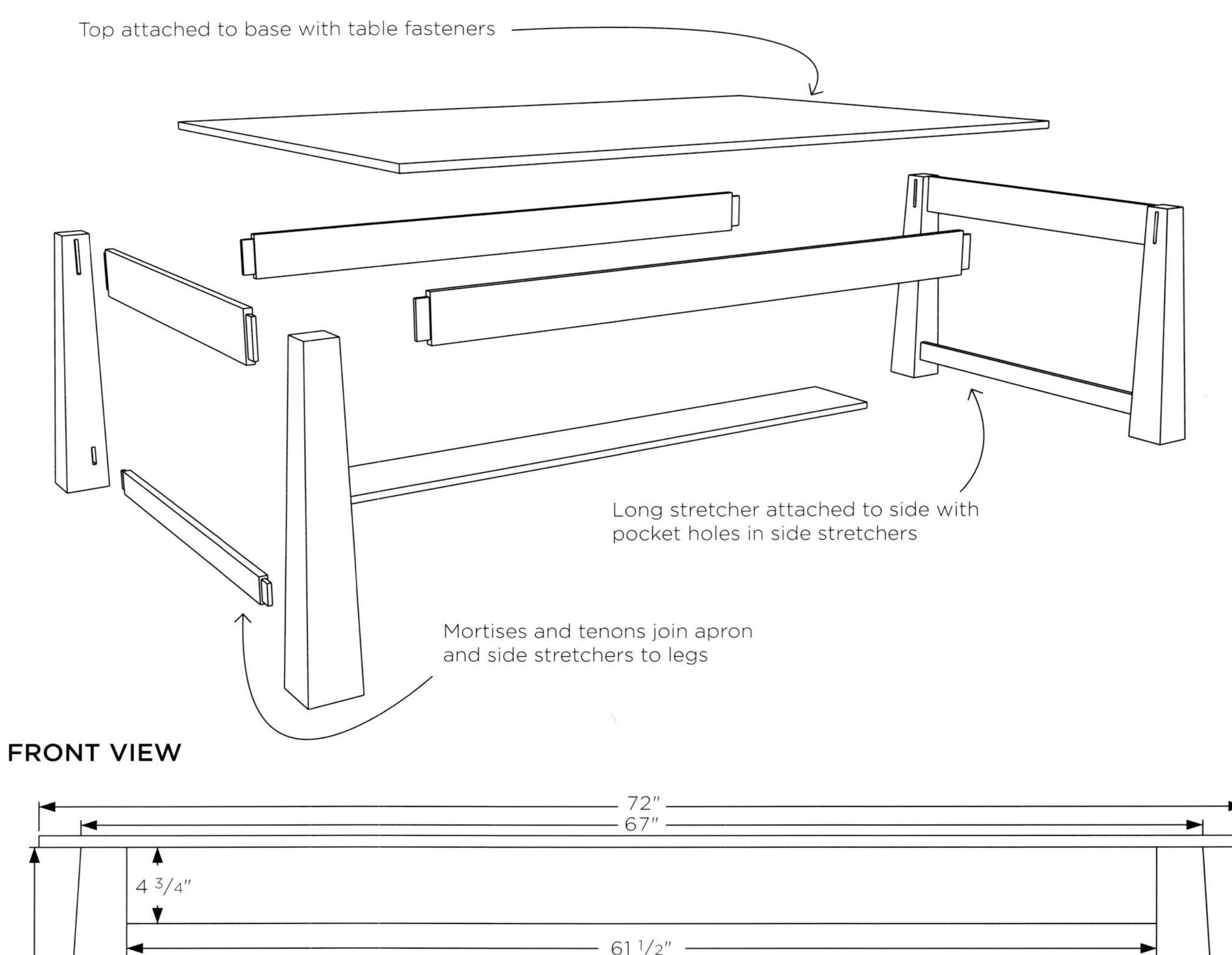
Top attached to base with table fasteners
Long stretcher attached to side with pocket holes in side stretchers
Mortises and tenons join apron and side stretchers to legs

FRONT VIEW

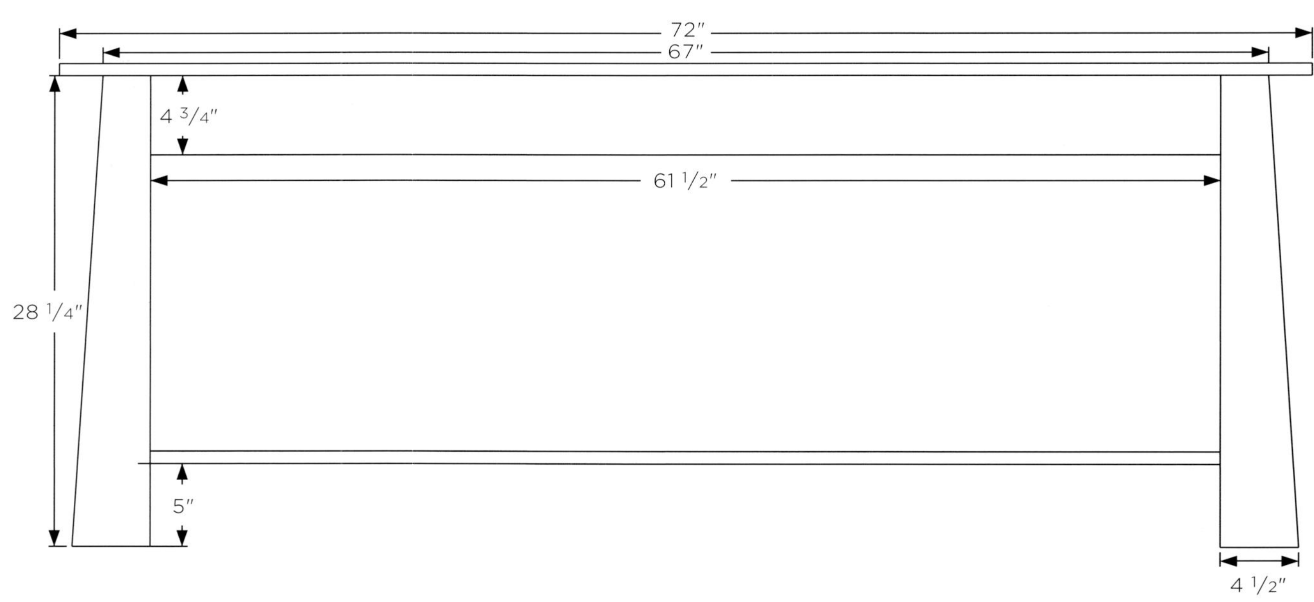
72″
67″
4 3/4″
61 1/2″
28 1/4″
5″
4 1/2″

PART LIST

Qty	Description	Length	Width	Thickness
4	leg	28 1/4″	4 1/2″	4 1/2″
2	long apron	64″	4 3/4″	3/4″
1	long stretcher	65″	9″	3/4″
2	short apron	38 1/4″	4 3/4″	3/4″
2	short stretcher	38 1/2″	2 1/2″	3/4″
1	top	72″	50″	3/4″

SIDE VIEW

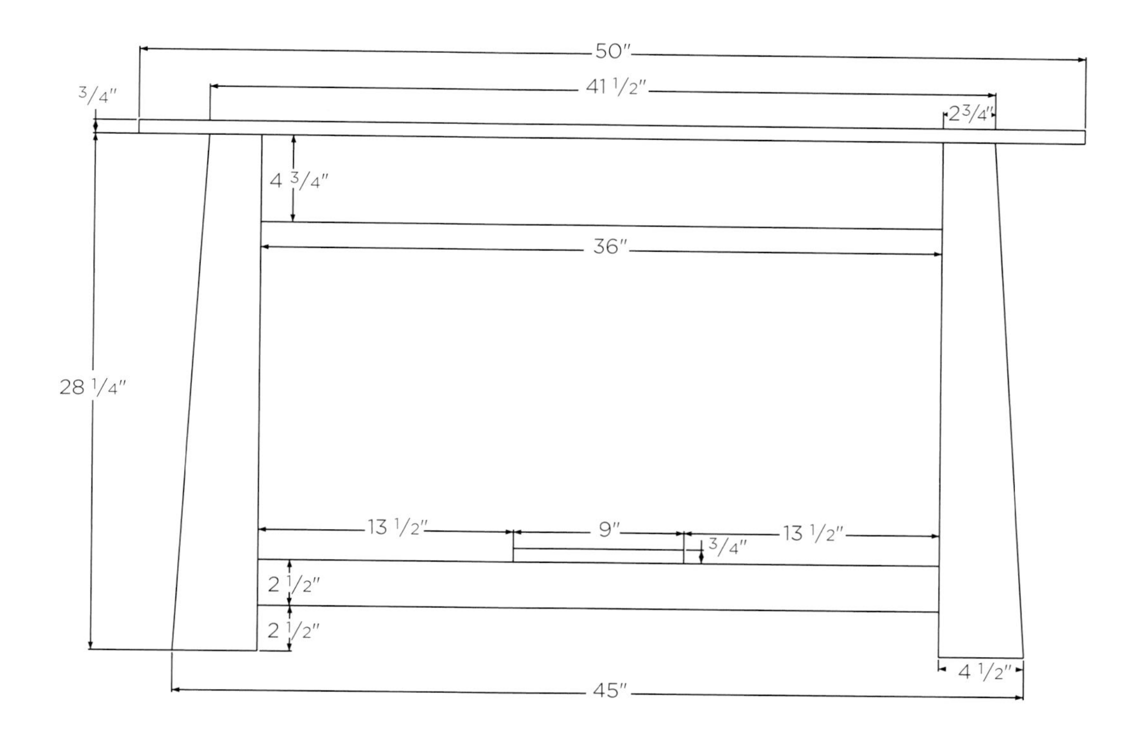

TOP SECTION VIEW

No. 416

CHINA CABINET

55″ high x 35″ wide x 16″ deep — $35.00 (1903)

The No. 416 china cabinet shares with several other pieces the tapered sides and overhanging top which show the Japanese influence on Limbert's work. While the tapered sides present some challenges—the shelves will require angled cuts on the ends—construction is not as complicated as some of Limbert's other tapered forms since the sides join the front and back at a 90 degree angle and the door opening is square. The false divided lights on the doors and sides also minimize complexity. The middle shelves are removable. You can drill a set of holes for each set of shelf brackets, or you can drill a series to make them adjustable. If you're not going to make them adjustable, wait until the door is installed before drilling for the brackets. Doing so ensures you can align the shelves precisely with the false muntins on the door front and sides.

EXPLODED VIEW

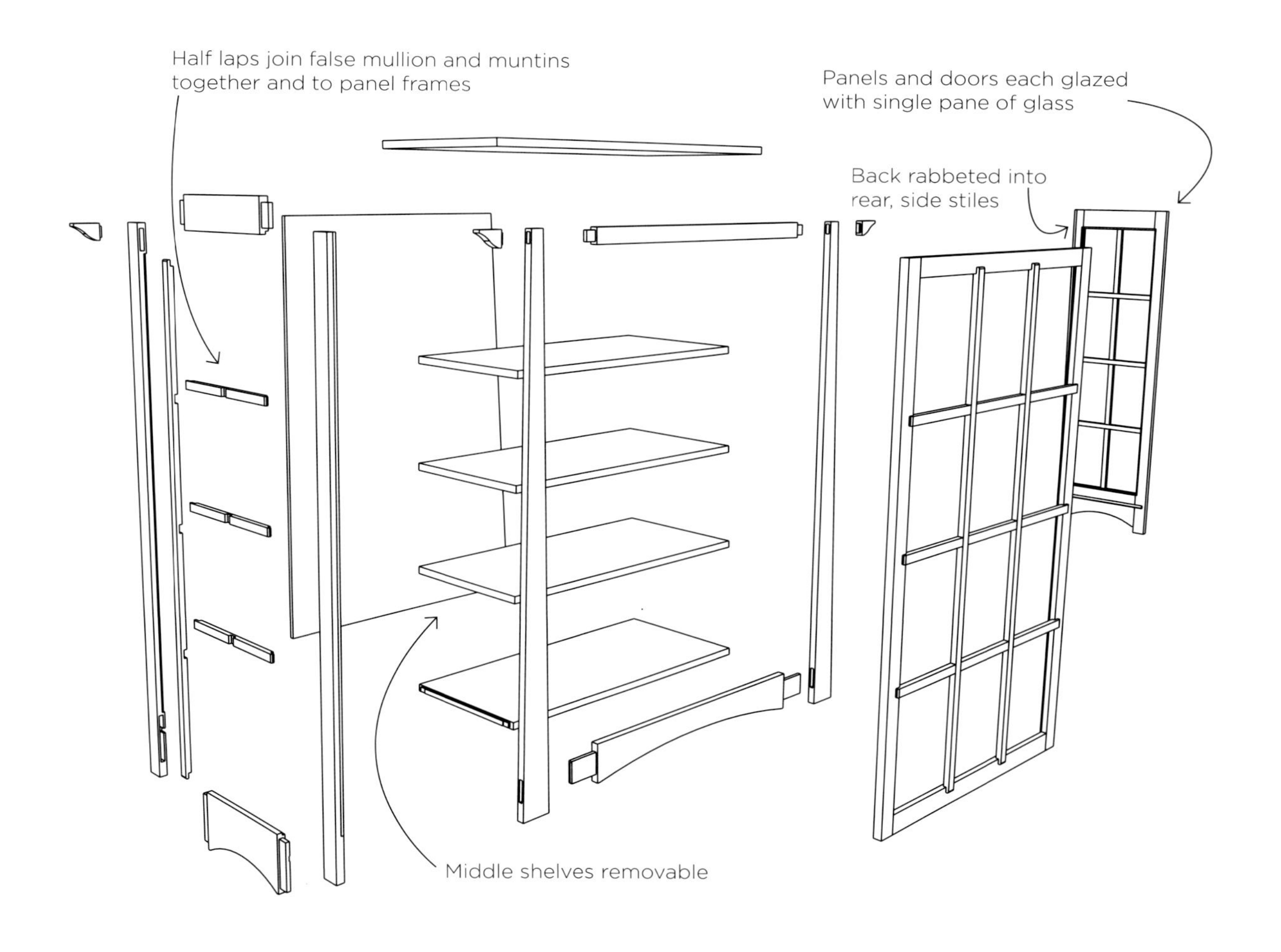
Half laps join false mullion and muntins together and to panel frames
Panels and doors each glazed with single pane of glass
Back rabbeted into rear, side stiles
Middle shelves removable

PART LIST

Qty	Description	Length	Width	Thickness
1	back	49″	31 23/32″	1/2″
1	bottom shelf	31 23/32″	14 3/4″	3/4″
4	corbel	2 1/2″	1 1/2″	3/4″
1	door bottom rail	26″	1 3/4″	3/4″
2	door mullion	44 1/2″	3/4″	1/2″
3	door muntin	25″	3/4″	1/2″
2	door stile	46 3/4″	1 1/2″	3/4″
1	door top rail	26″	1 1/2″	3/4″
1	front bottom rail	33 3/8″	4″	3/4″
2	front stile	53 1/4″	3″	3/4″
1	front top rail	29″	1 1/2″	3/4″
1	lower middle shelf	30 3/8″	14 3/4″	3/4″
2	side bottom rail	13 3/4″	5 3/4″	3/4″
2	side mullion	44 1/2″	3/4″	1/2″
6	side muntin	12 3/4″	3/4″	1/2″
4	side stile	53 1/4″	2 1/2″	3/4″
2	side top rail	13 3/4″	3″	3/4″
1	top	35″	16 1/2″	3/4″
1	top shelf	28 59/64″	14 3/4″	3/4″
1	upper middle shelf	29 21/32″	14 3/4″	3/4″

FRONT VIEW

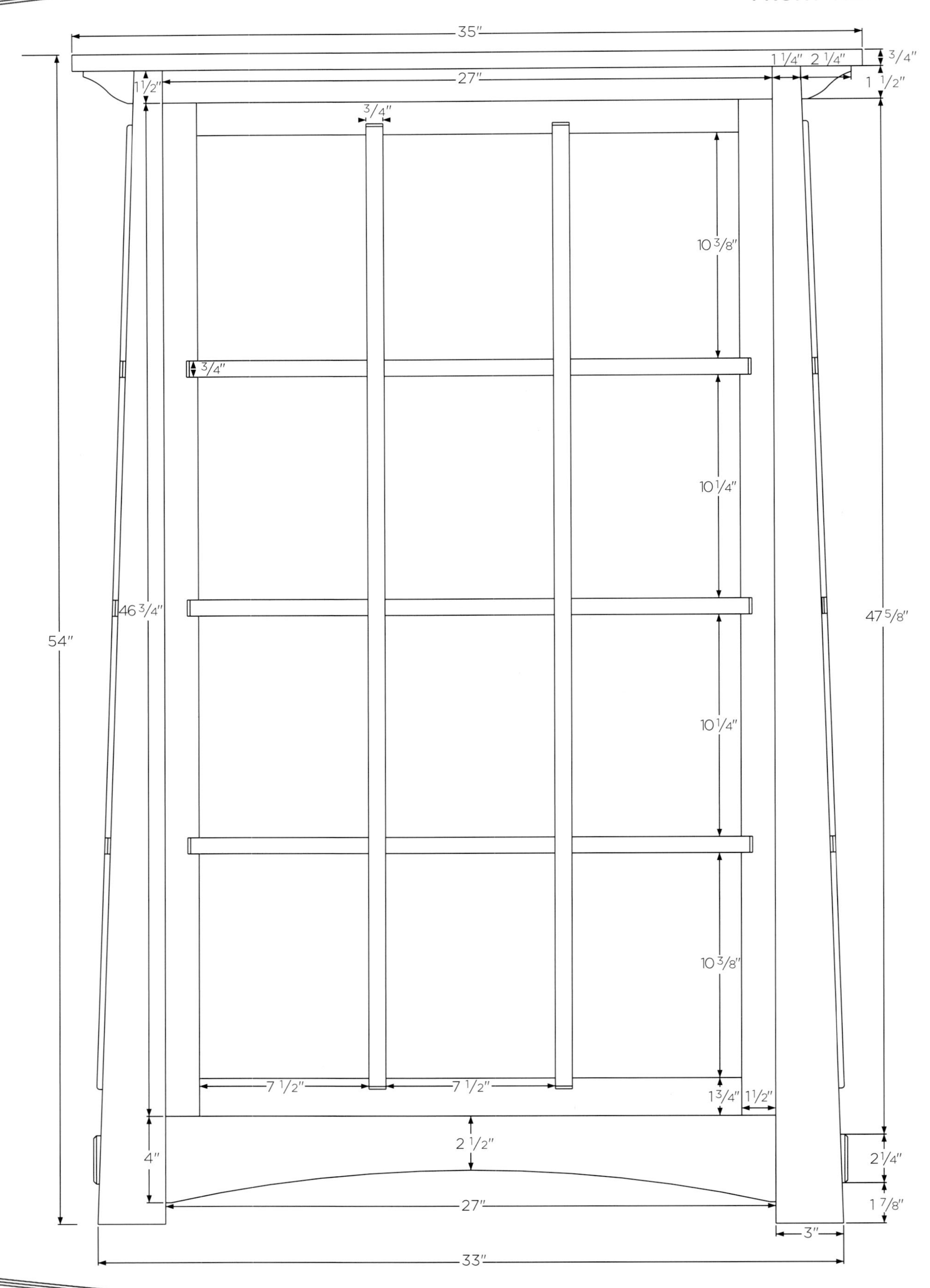

35″
3/4″
1 1/4″
2 1/4″
1 1/2″
27″
1 1/2″
3/4″
10 3/8″
3/4″
10 1/4″
46 3/4″
54″
47 5/8″
10 1/4″
10 3/8″
7 1/2″
7 1/2″
1 3/4″
1 1/2″
2 1/2″
4″
2 1/4″
27″
1 7/8″
3″
33″

SIDE VIEW

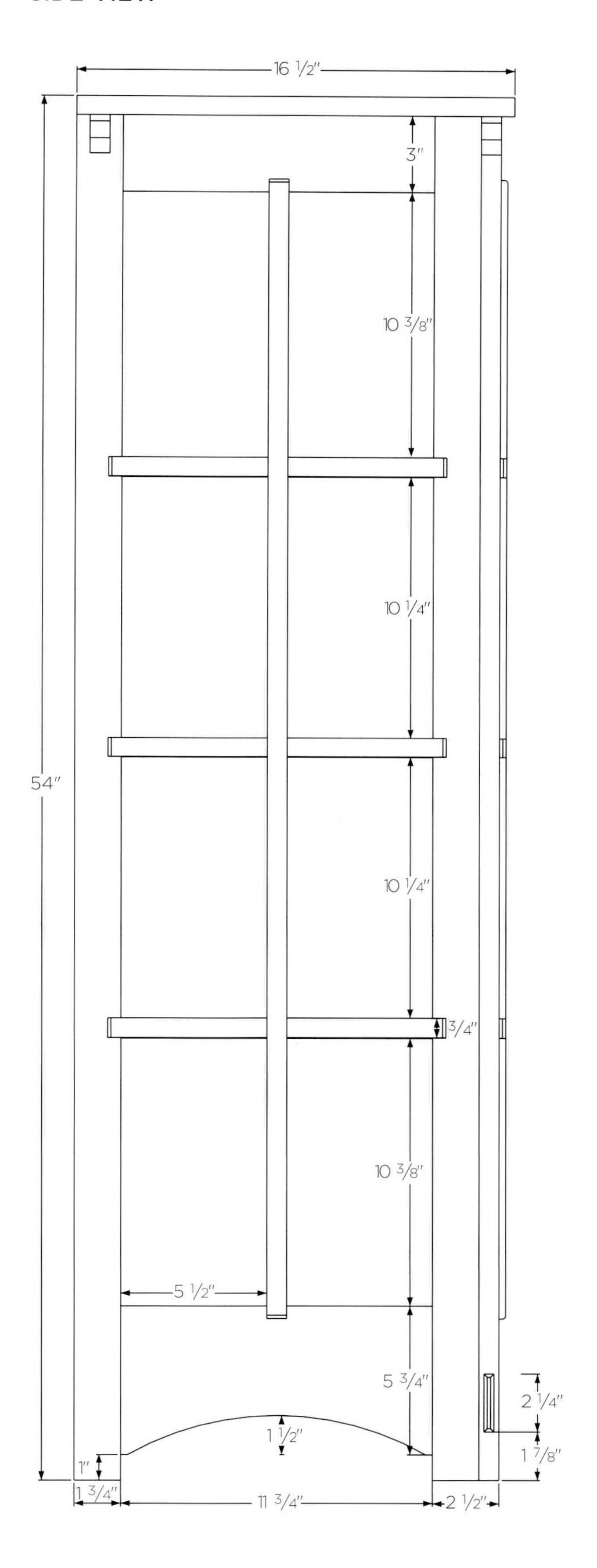
16 1/2″
3″
10 3/8″
10 1/4″
10 1/4″
3/4″
54″
10 3/8″
5 1/2″
5 3/4″
2 1/4″
1 1/2″
1 7/8″
1″
1 3/4″
11 3/4″
2 1/2″

No. 458-1/2

BUFFET

44″ high x 48″ wide x 19″ deep

The arches and rectilinear lines of this buffet would not be out of place on a piece by Stickley. The size of the piece works in smaller spaces, but smaller scale doesn't mean simpler. The buffet shares the same complexity as larger examples of the form.

EXPLODED VIEW

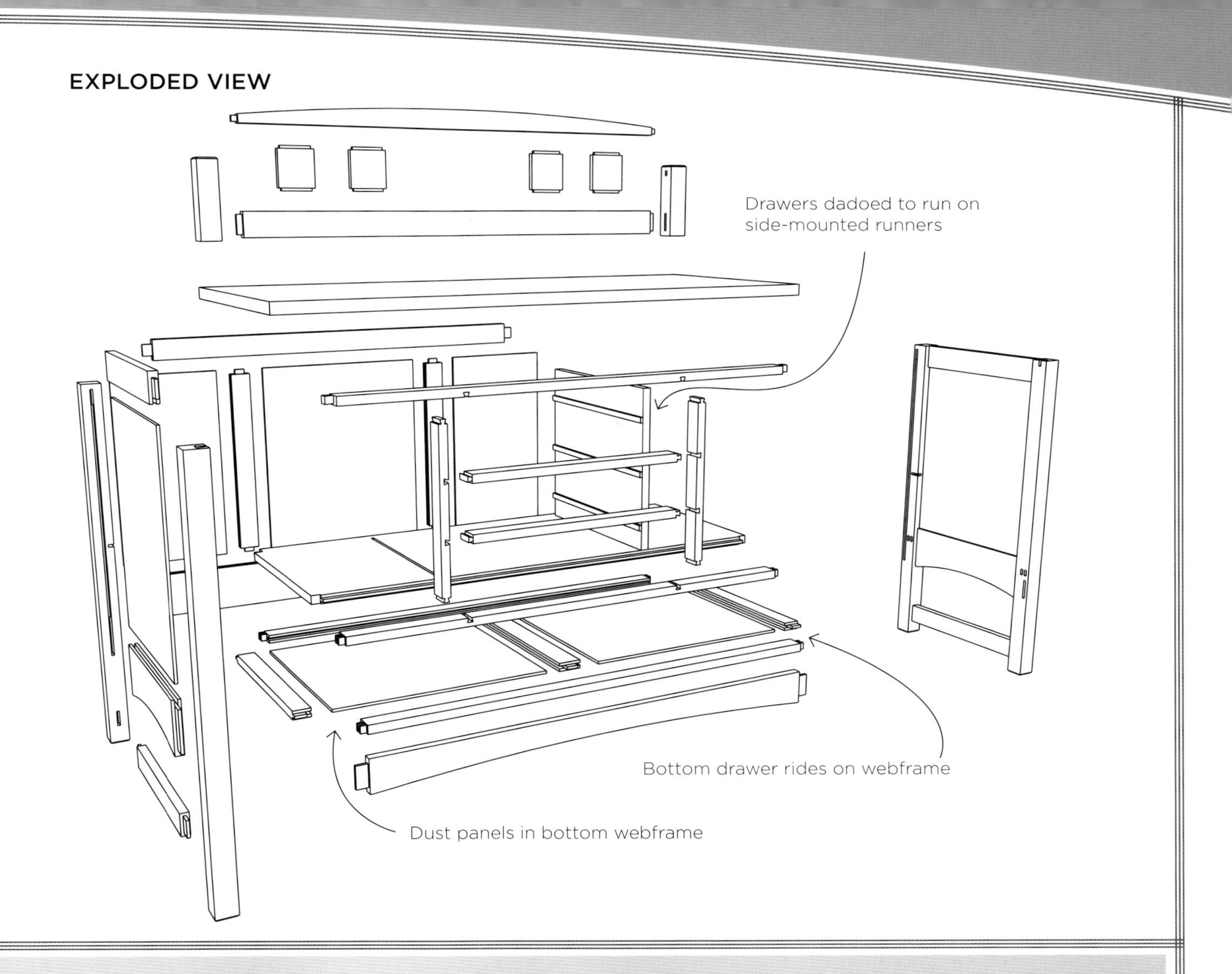

PART LIST

Qty	Description	Length	Width	Thickness
1	back bottom rail	42 1/2"	4 3/4"	3/4"
1	back long panel	20 3/4"	17 1/2"	1/4"
2	back panel stile	20 3/4"	2"	3/4"
2	back short panel	20 3/4"	11"	1/4"
1	back top rail	42 1/2"	2 1/4"	3/4"
2	bottom dust panel	18 3/4"	16 3/16"	1/4"
2	door bottom rail	7 1/2"	2"	3/4"
2	door panel	11 1/2"	7 1/2"	1/4"
4	door stile	14 1/4"	1 3/4"	3/4"
2	door top rail	7 1/2"	1 3/4"	3/4"
2	drawer dividers	14 1/4"	1 1/2"	3/4"
1	front top rail	42"	1 1/2"	3/4"
1	large drawer bottom	40"	16"	1/4"
2	large drawer frame rail	16 3/16"	1 1/2"	3/4"
1	large drawer front	40 1/2"	7 1/4"	3/4"
2	large drawer side	16 1/2"	7 1/4"	1/2"
1	lg. drawer webframe center stile	16 3/16"	2"	3/4"
4	leg	35 3/4"	1 3/4"	1 3/4"
1	long bottom stretcher	42 1/2"	3"	3/4"
2	long drawer rail	41 1/2"	1 1/2"	3/4"
1	long webframe back rail	41 1/2"	1 1/2"	3/4"
1	plate rail bottom rail	41 1/2"	2 1/4"	3/4"
2	plate rail pillar	7"	1 3/4"	1 3/4"
4	plate rail slat	3 7/8"	3 1/4"	1/2"
1	plate rail top rail	41 1/2"	1 3/4"	3/4"
1	shelf	42"	17 3/16"	3/4"
2	short drawer rail	19"	1 1/2"	3/4"
2	side bottom stretcher	17 1/2"	2"	3/4"
2	side middle stretcher	17 1/2"	4 3/4"	3/4"
2	side panel	20 1/2"	16 1/2"	1/4"
2	side top stretcher	17 1/2"	2 1/2"	3/4"
3	small drawer back	19"	4 1/4"	1/2"
3	small drawer bottom	18 1/2"	16"	1/4"
3	small drawer front	19"	4 1/4"	3/4"
5	small drawer side	16 1/2"	4 1/4"	1/2"
1	top	48"	20"	1"

FRONT VIEW

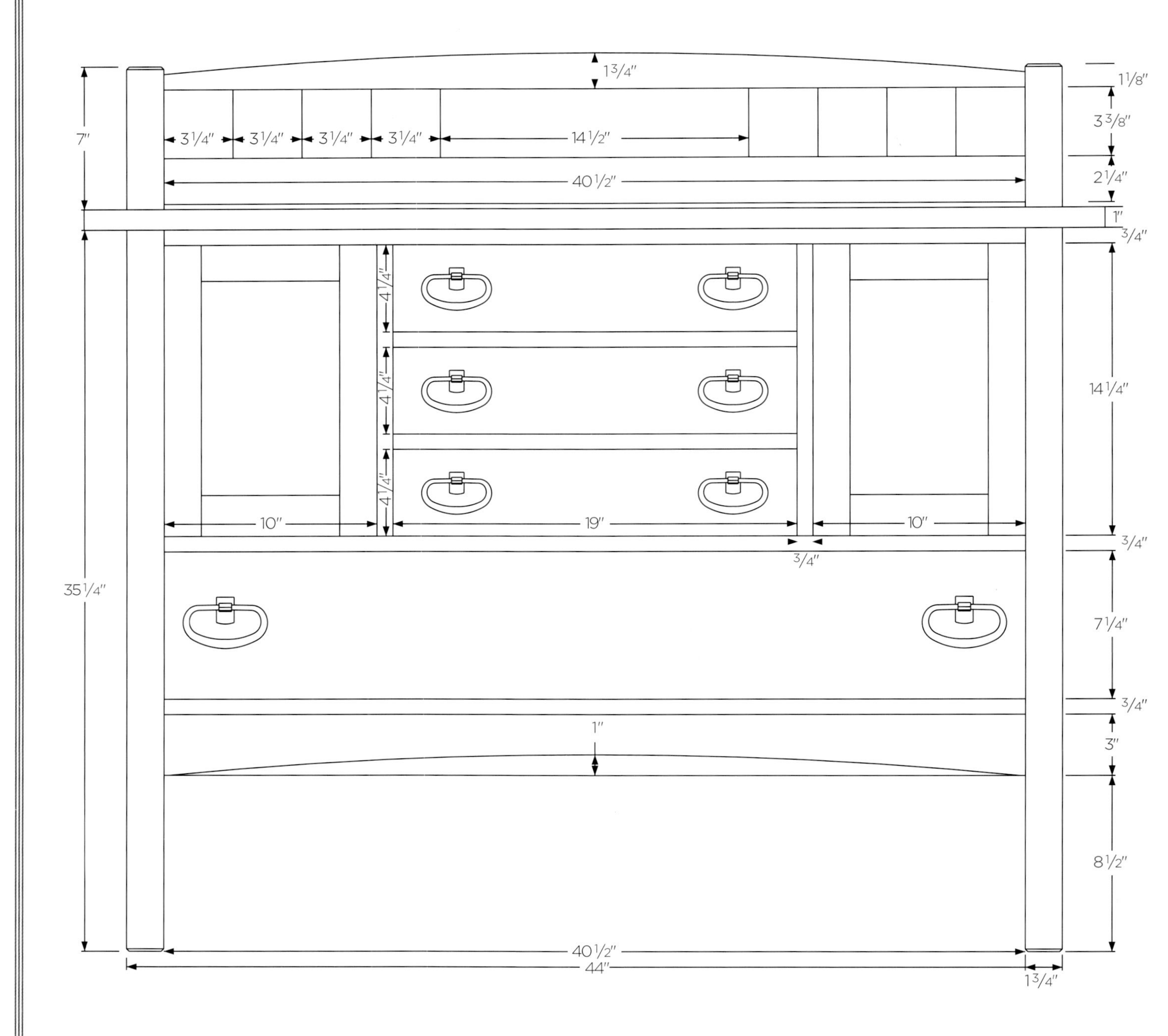

1 3/4"
1 1/8"
3 3/8"
7"
3 1/4"
3 1/4"
3 1/4"
3 1/4"
14 1/2"
40 1/2"
2 1/4"
1"
3/4"
4 1/4"
4 1/4"
4 1/4"
14 1/4"
10"
19"
10"
3/4"
3/4"
35 1/4"
7 1/4"
3/4"
1"
3"
8 1/2"
40 1/2"
44"
1 3/4"

SIDE VIEW

7″

20″

1″

2 1/2″

19 1/2″

3 3/4″

4 3/4″

5″

2″

1 1/2″

15 1/2″

1 3/4″

TOP SECTION VIEW

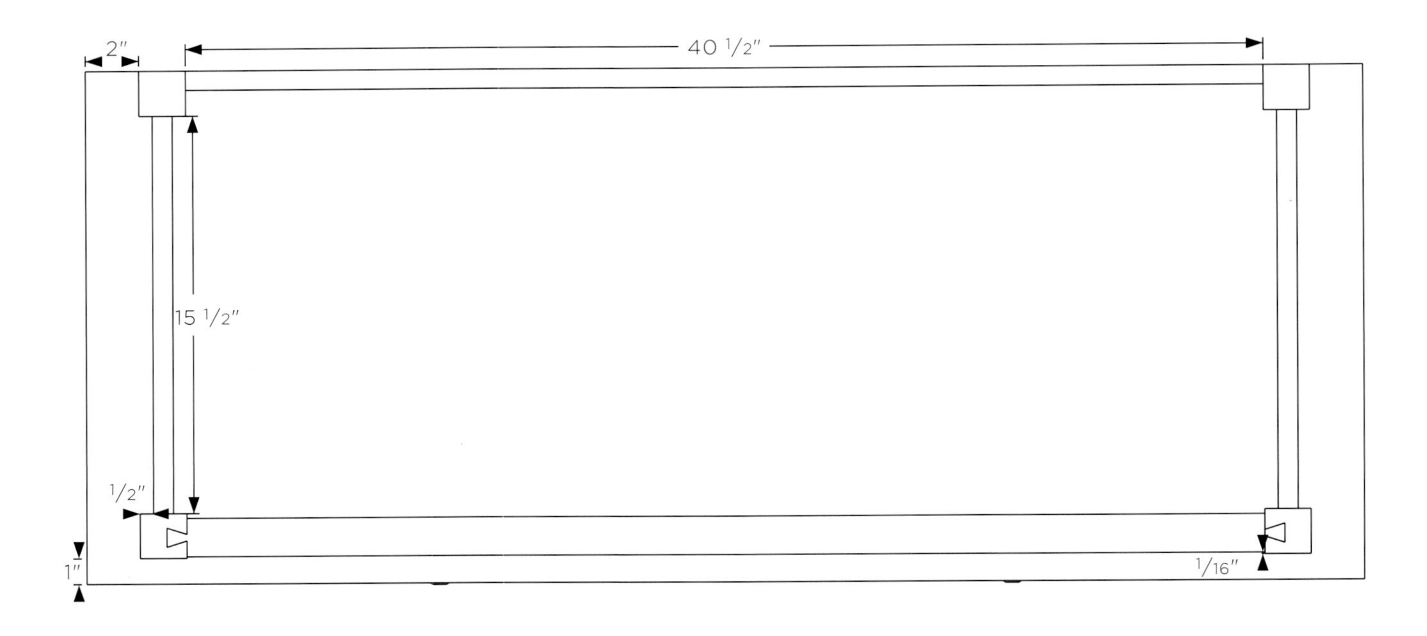

TOP VIEW

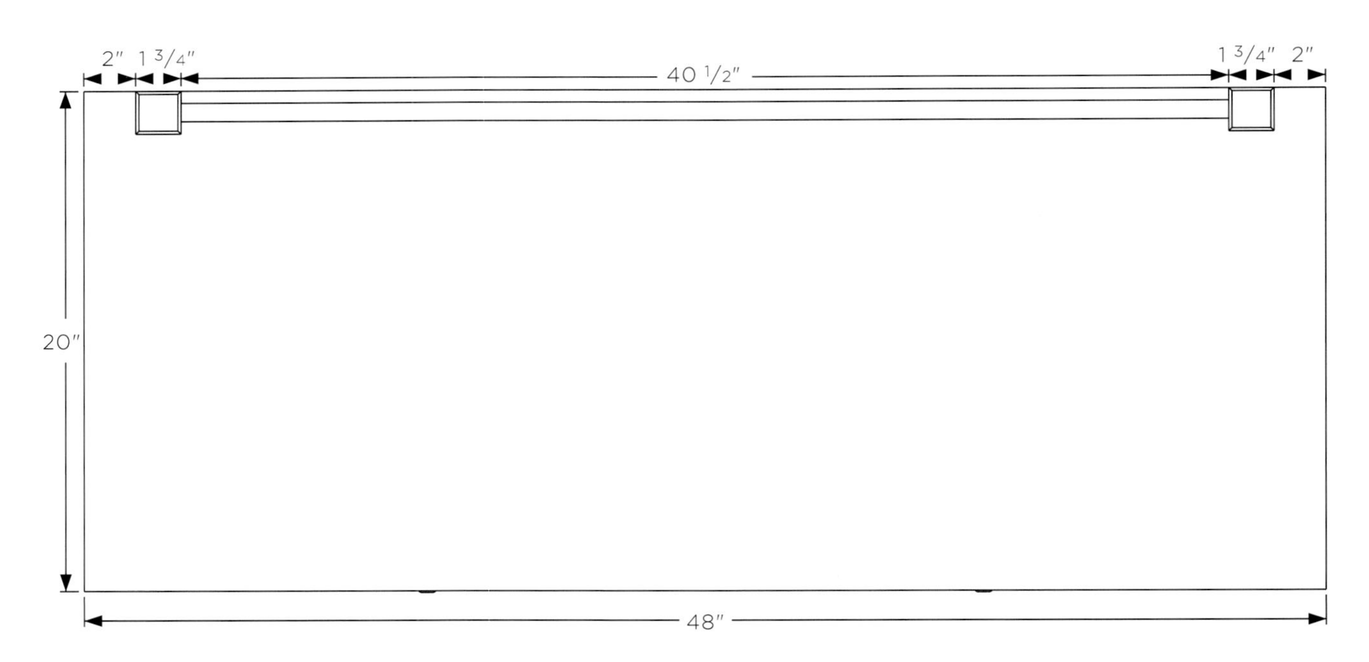

No. 602

CELLARETTE

36″ high x 34″ wide x 14″ deep — $15.00 (1905)

The No. 602 is one of the few pieces to appear both in the 1903 catalog and in later catalogs as the company transitioned from folk-influenced designs. It provides a convenient place for storing and mixing drinks. With the addition of an extra shelf, it could serve in the place of a larger sideboard in a small dining room. The original featured a spinning rack for bottles and a wire rack at the top, inside of the door for holding bar implements. One modern interpretation of the piece features a backsplash and copper-lined top to allow serving hot dishes.

EXPLODED VIEW

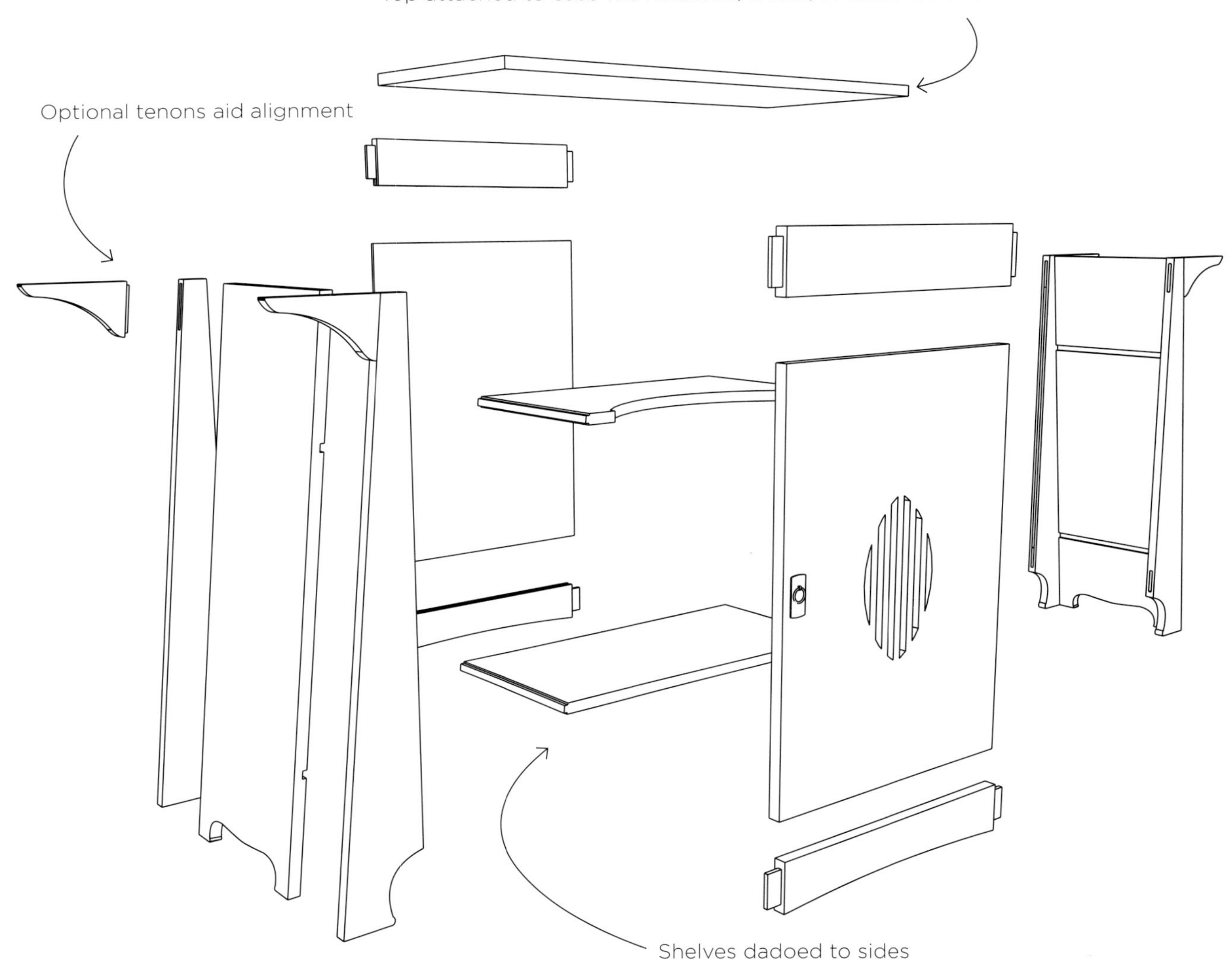

PART LIST

Qty	Description	Length	Width	Thickness
1	back bottom rail	19 1/2"	3"	3/4"
1	back panel	25 3/4"	18 1/2"	1/4"
2	back stile	35 1/4"	5"	3/4"
1	back top rail	19"	3 1/2"	3/4"
1	bottom shelf	25 5/64"	12"	3/4"
4	corbel	6 15/32"	3 1/2"	3/4"
1	door	24 3/4"	17 1/2"	3/4"
1	front bottom rail	19 1/2"	3"	3/4"
2	front stile	35 1/4"	5"	3/4"
1	front top rail	19"	3 1/2"	3/4"
2	side	35 11/64"	12"	3/4"
1	top	34"	14"	3/4"
1	top shelf	21 9/32"	12"	3/4"

FRONT VIEW

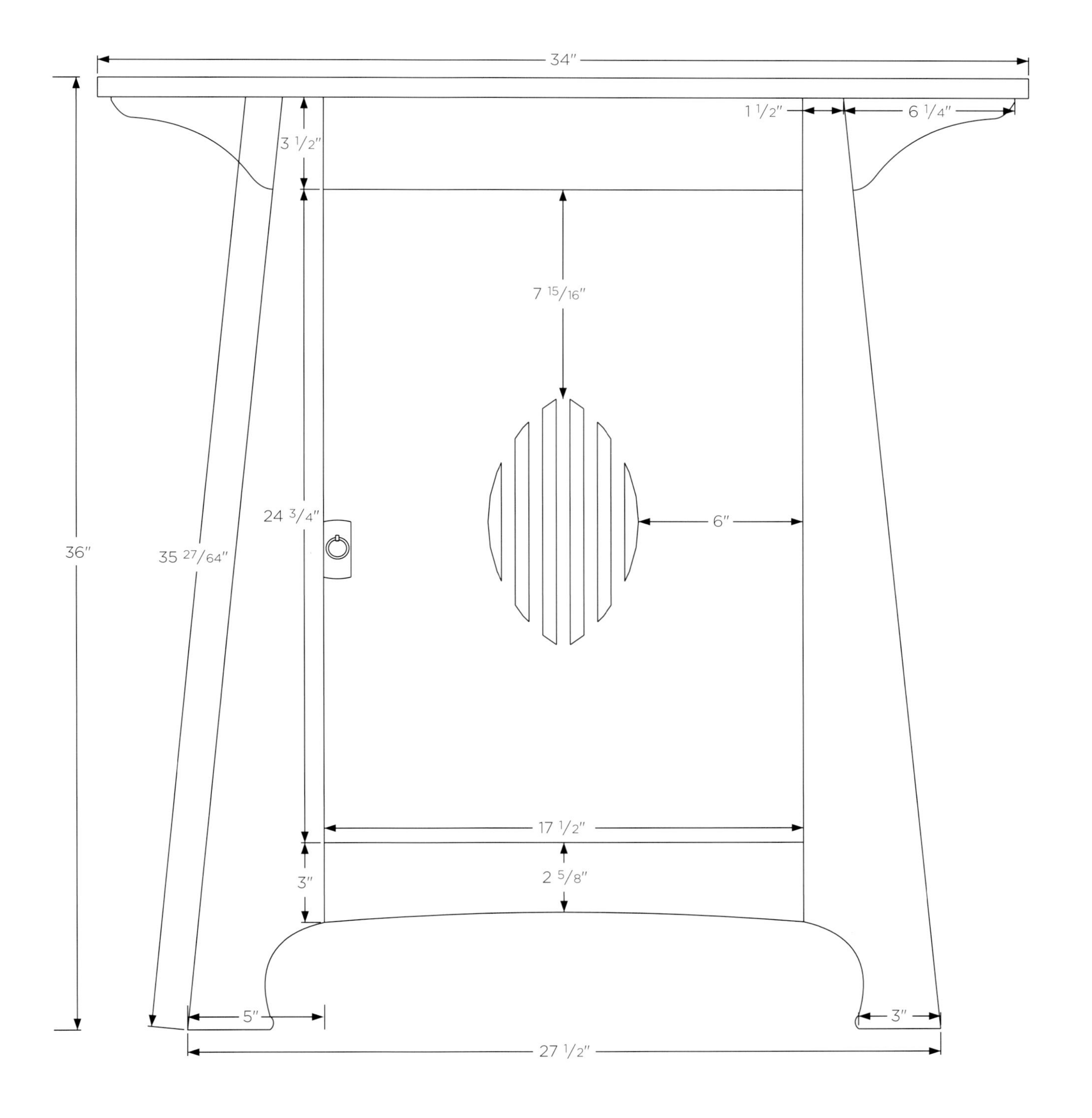

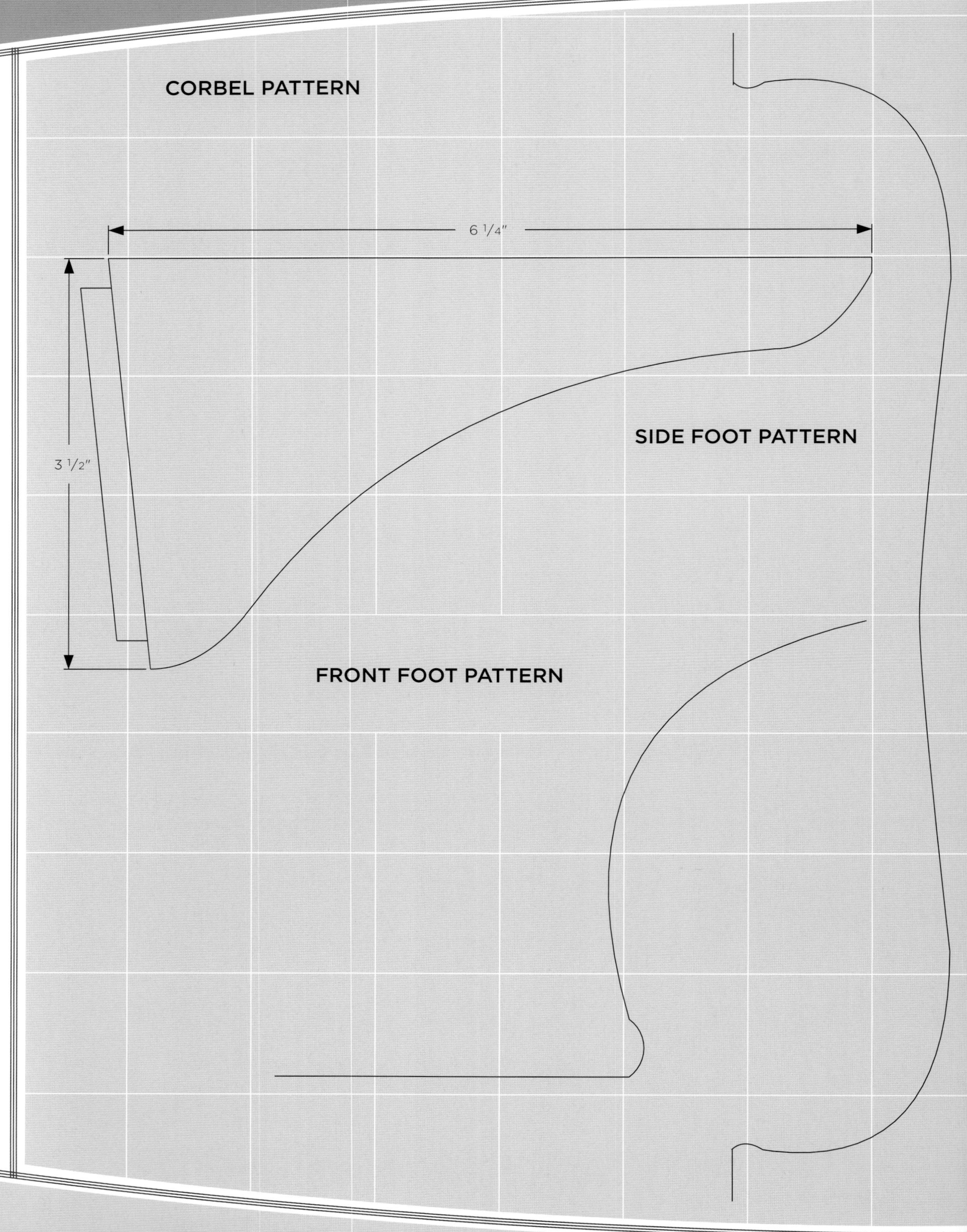
CORBEL PATTERN
6 1/4"
3 1/2"
SIDE FOOT PATTERN
FRONT FOOT PATTERN

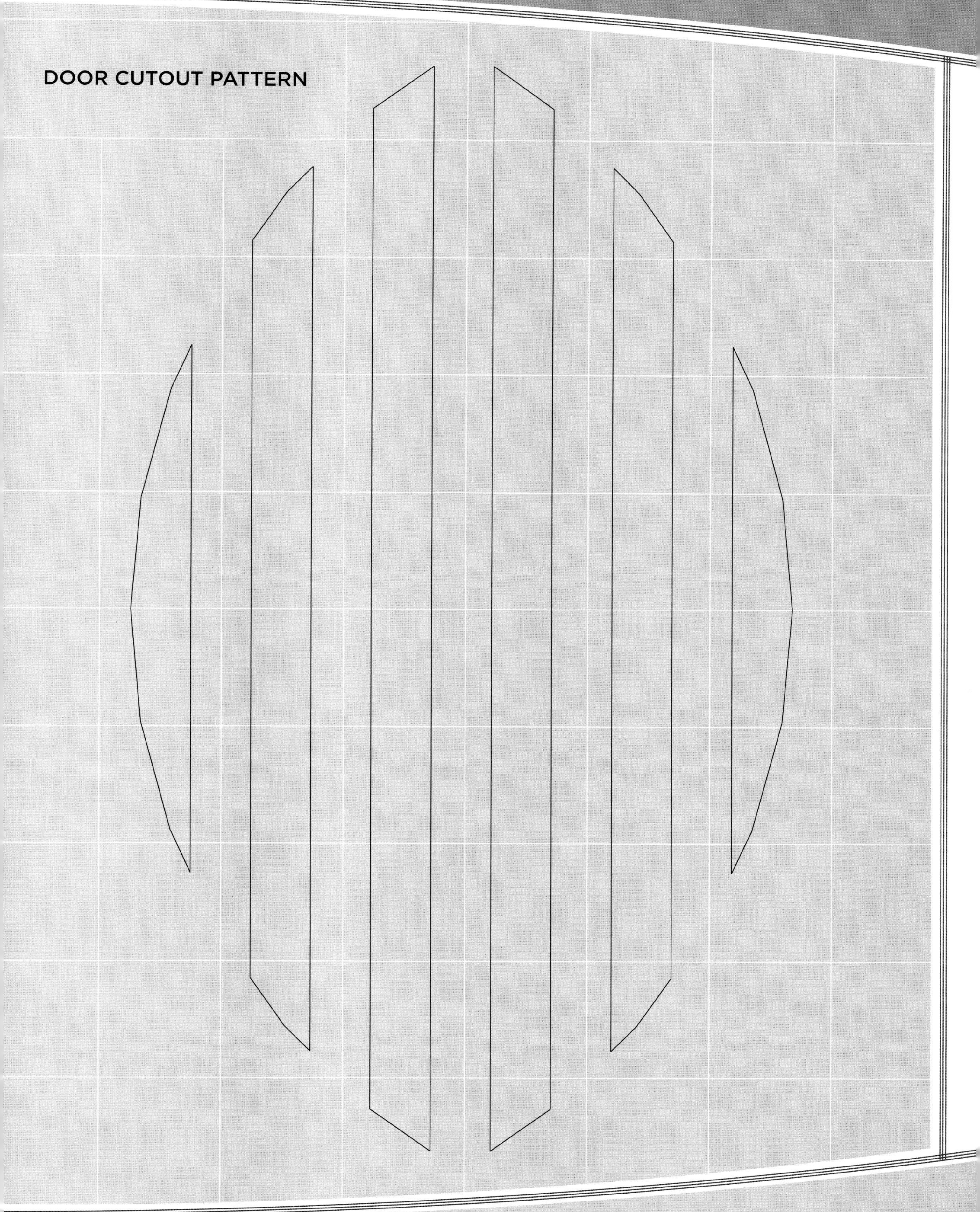
DOOR CUTOUT PATTERN

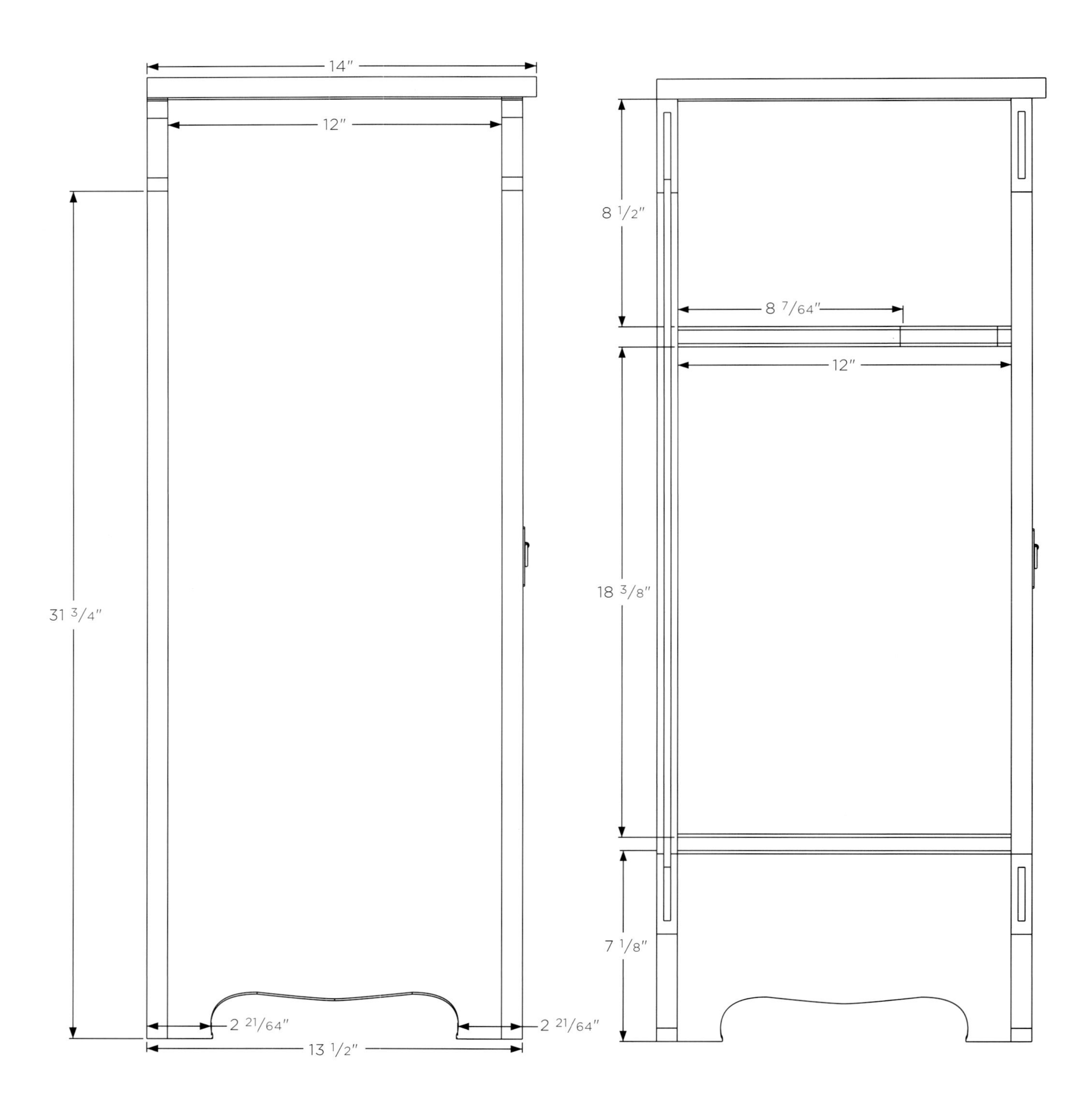
SIDE VIEW
SIDE SECTION VIEW
14″
12″
31 3/4″
2 21/64″
2 21/64″
13 1/2″
8 1/2″
8 7/64″
12″
18 3/8″
7 1/8″

No. 911

DINING CHAIR

37″ high x 17″ wide x 17″ deep

Since the chair seat tapers back to front, the side stretchers meet the front and back legs at an angle with the tenon cut so that it meets the leg at 90 degrees. The original featured a slip seat, but a solid seat is a simple substituion.

EXPLODED VIEW

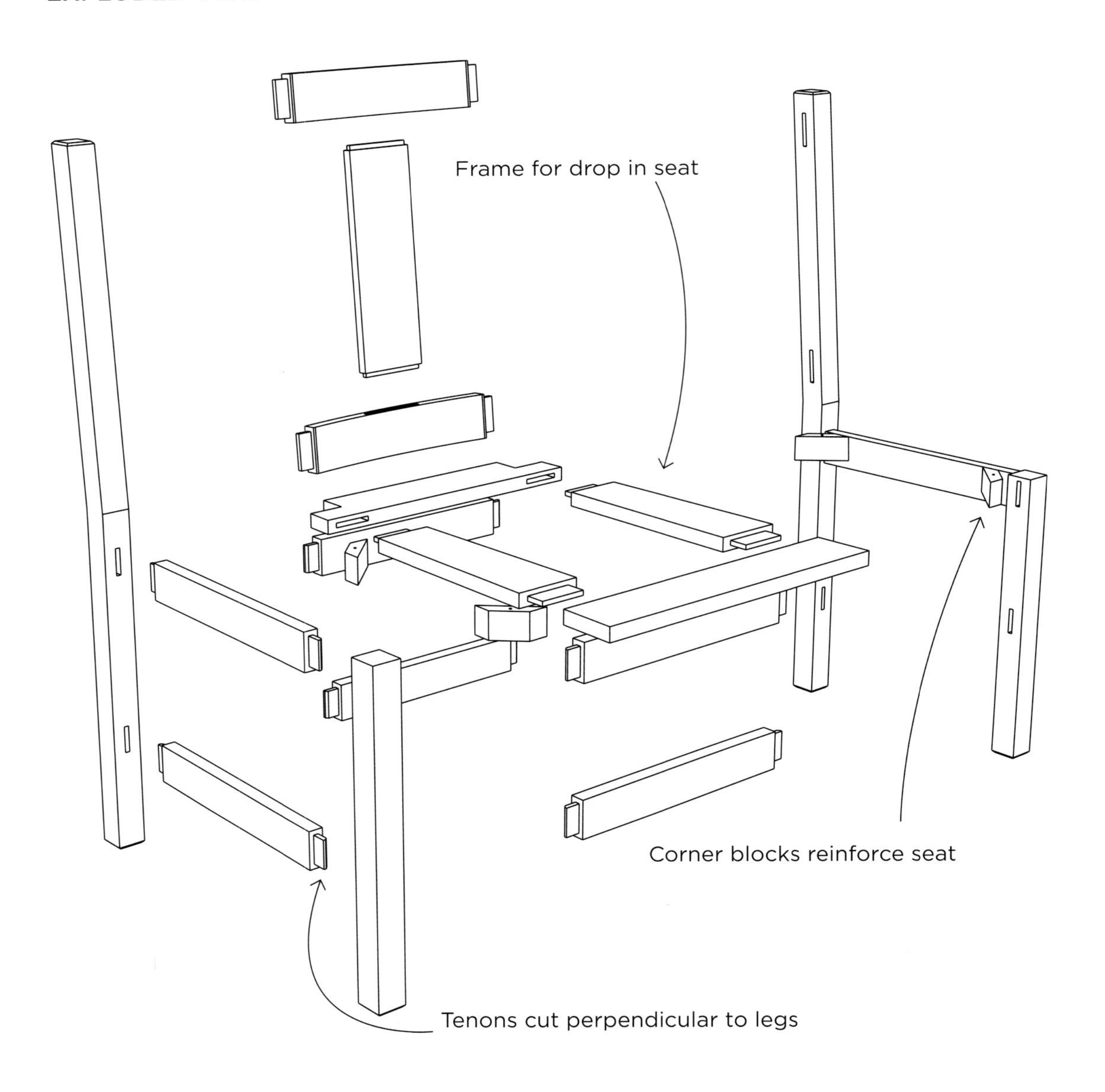

PART LIST

Qty	Description	Length	Width	Thickness
2	back leg	38"	2 63/64"	1 1/2"
2	back rail	12 55/64"	2 1/2"	1 1/4"
1	back slat	12 1/2"	3 3/4"	1/2"
2	back stretcher	12 55/64"	2"	3/4"
2	front corner block	2 25/64"	2 11/32"	1 1/2"
2	front leg	17 1/4"	1 1/2"	1 1/2"
2	front stretcher	14"	2"	3/4"
2	rear corner block	2 9/32"	2 7/32"	1 1/2"
1	seat back rail	15 1/4"	3"	3/4"
1	seat front rail	16 13/32"	3"	3/4"
2	seat stile	12 5/8"	3 13/32"	3/4"
4	side stretcher	14 3/4"	2"	3/4"

FRONT VIEW

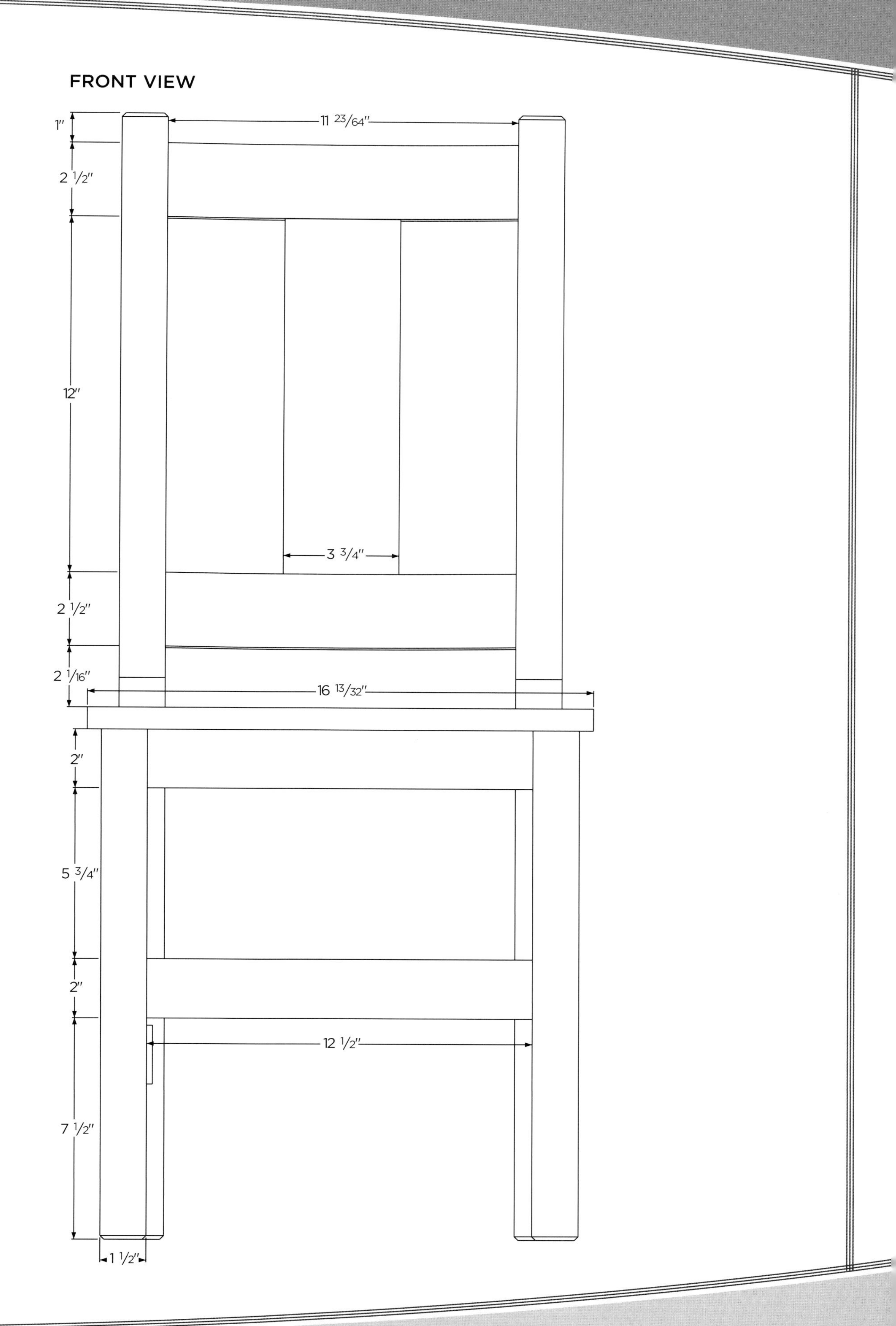

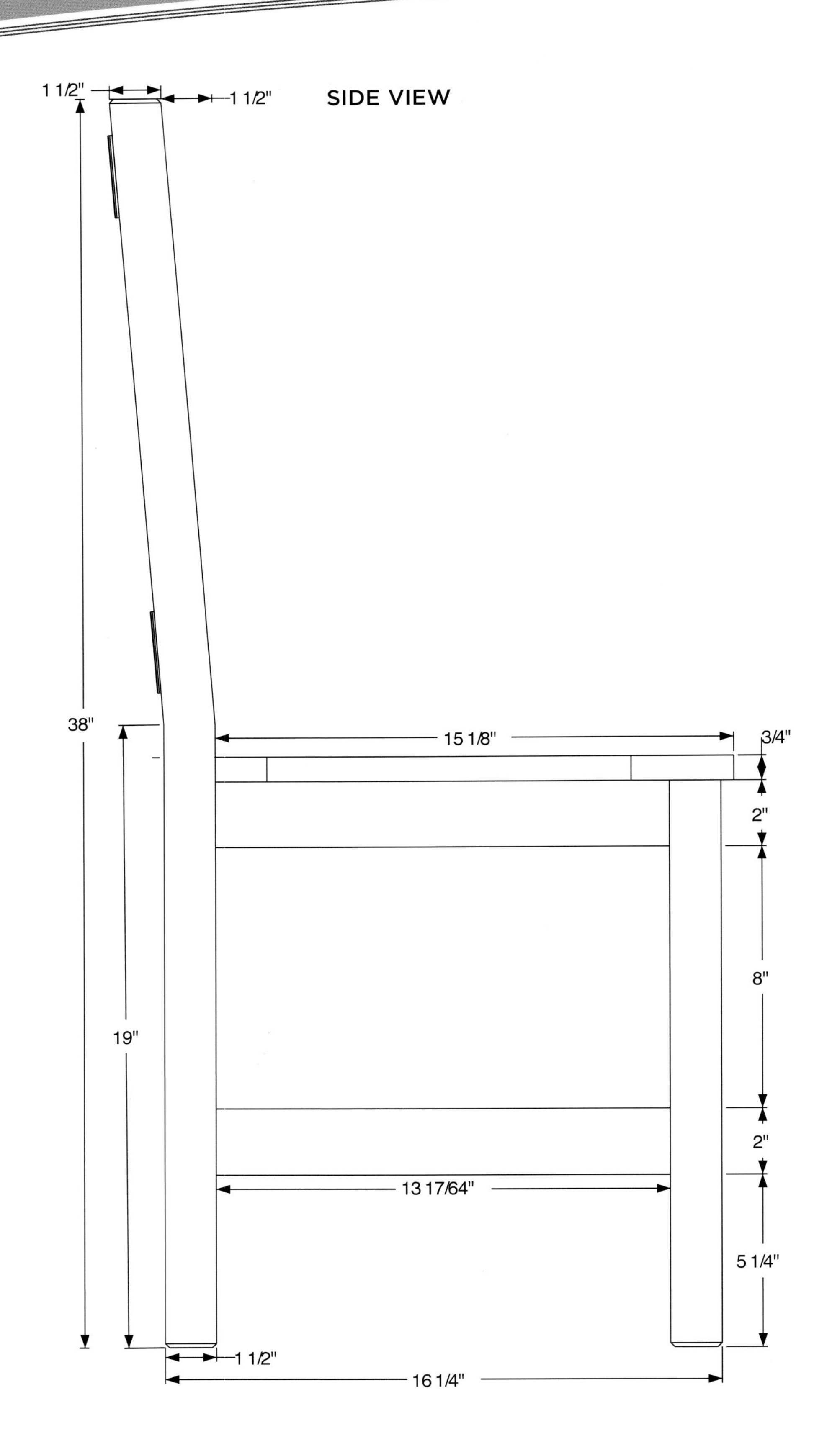
SIDE VIEW
1 1/2"
1 1/2"
38"
19"
15 1/8"
3/4"
2"
8"
2"
13 17/64"
5 1/4"
1 1/2"
16 1/4"

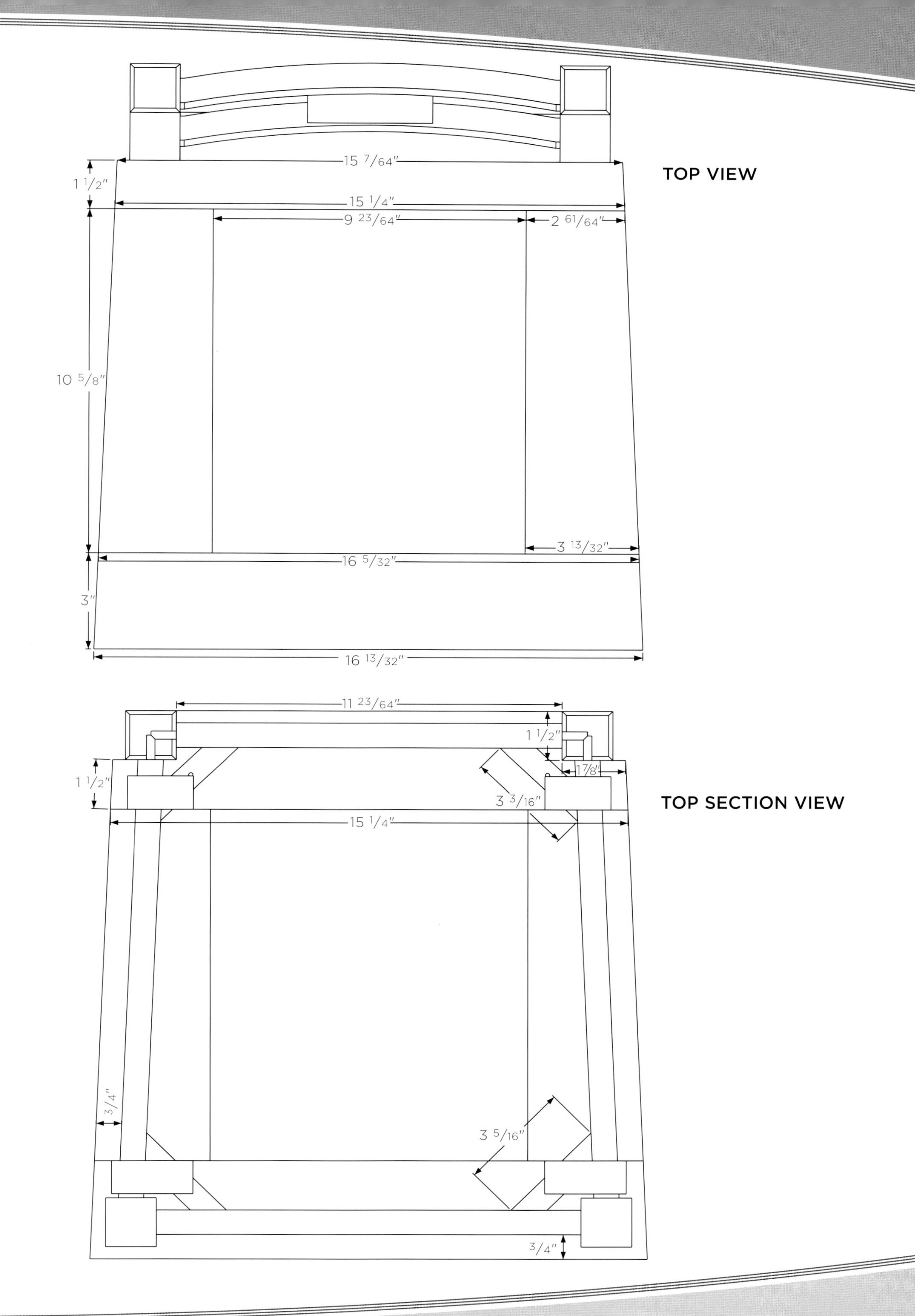
15 7/64"
TOP VIEW
1 1/2"
15 1/4"
9 23/64"
2 61/64"
10 5/8"
3 13/32"
16 5/32"
3"
16 13/32"
11 23/64"
1 1/2"
1 1/2"
1 7/8"
3 3/16"
TOP SECTION VIEW
15 1/4"
3/4"
3 5/16"
3/4"

No. 258

BOOK RACK

11″ high x 22″ wide x 10″ deep

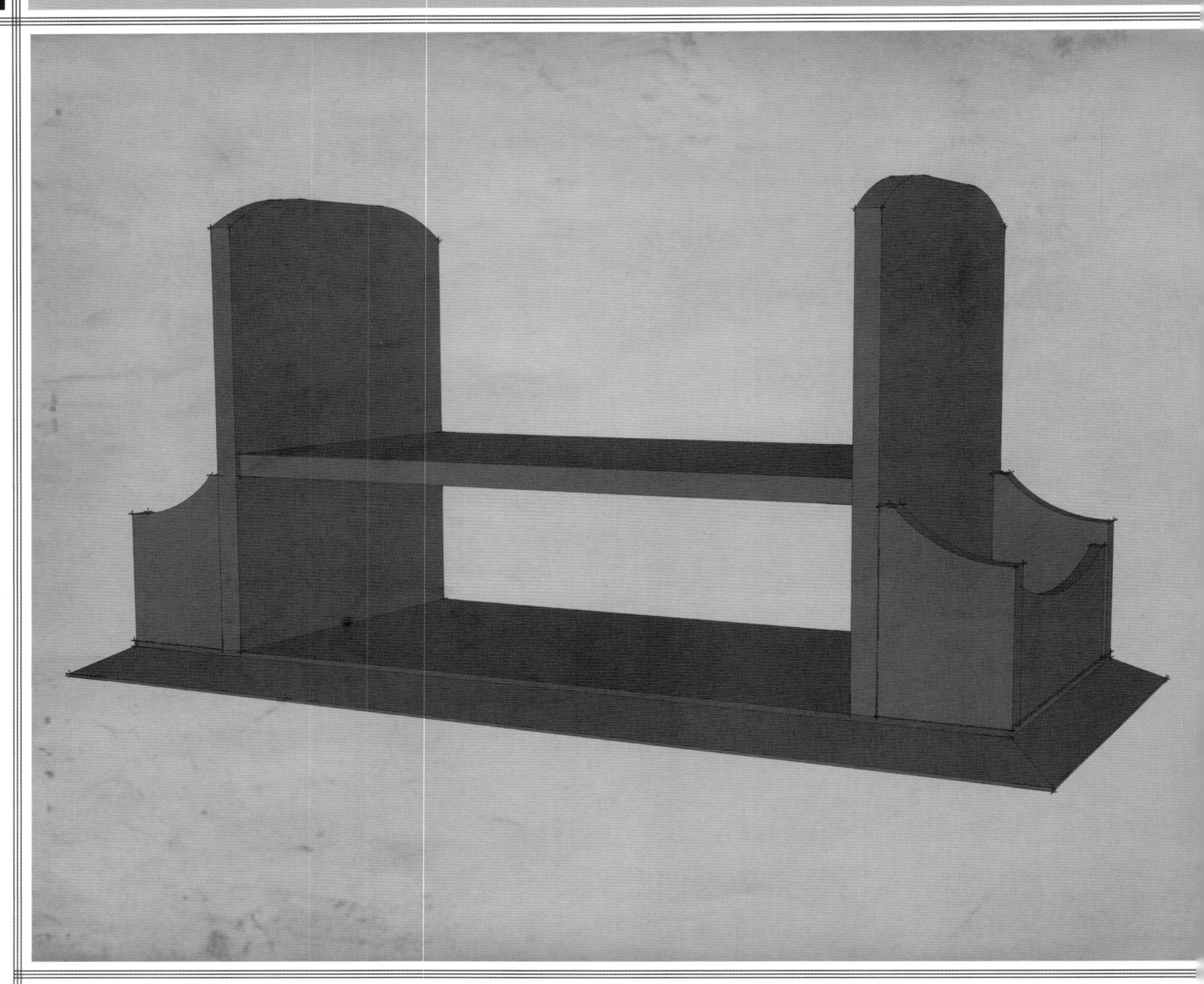

This simple piece provides additional space on a desk or transforms a table into a desk. A drawer could be added easily to the bottom shelf for increased utility.

EXPLODED VIEW

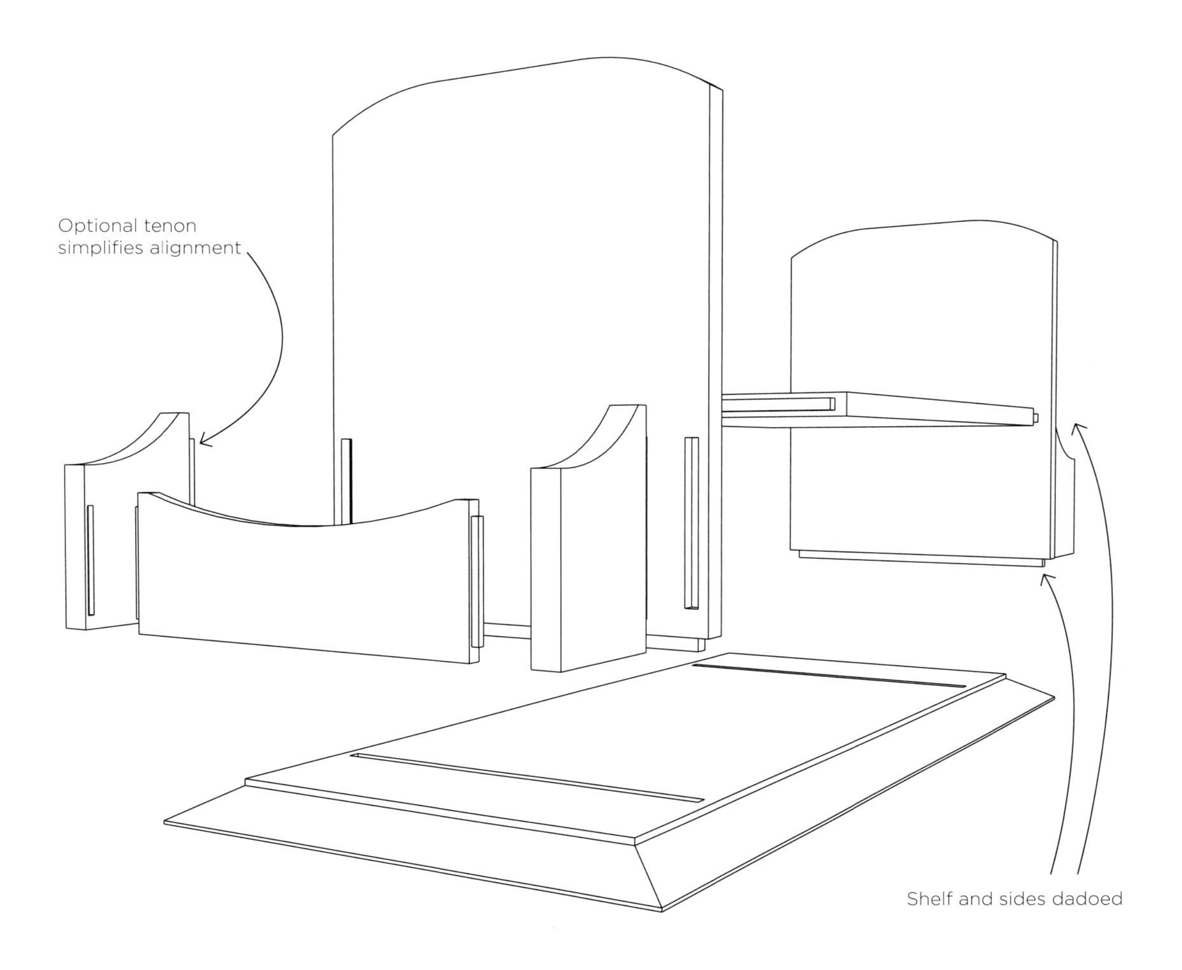

PART LIST

Qty	Description	Length	Width	Thickness
1	base	22″	10″	3/4″
2	letter front	7 1/8″	2 1/2″	1/4″
4	letter side	4″	2 3/4″	1/2″

Qty	Description	Length	Width	Thickness
1	shelf	14 3/8″	7 7/8″	1/2″
2	side	10 1/2″	8″	1/2″

SIDE VIEW

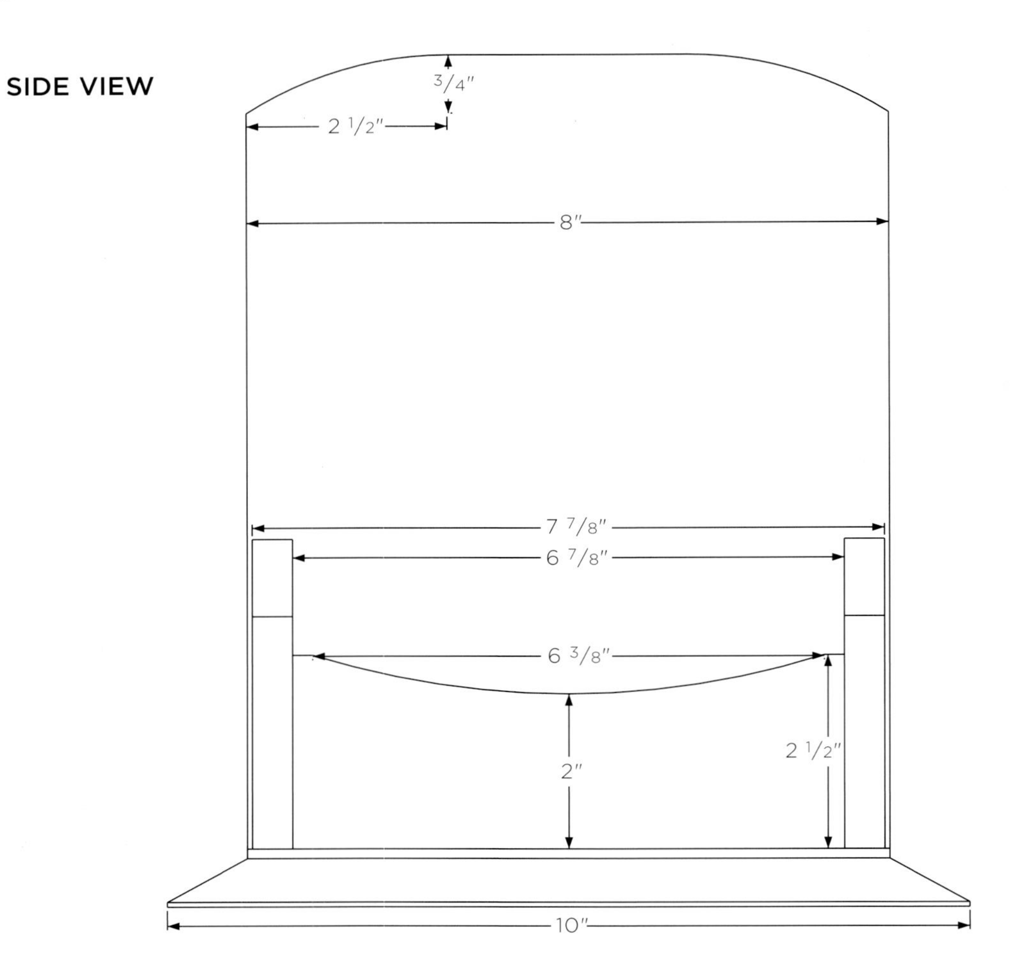

FRONT VIEW

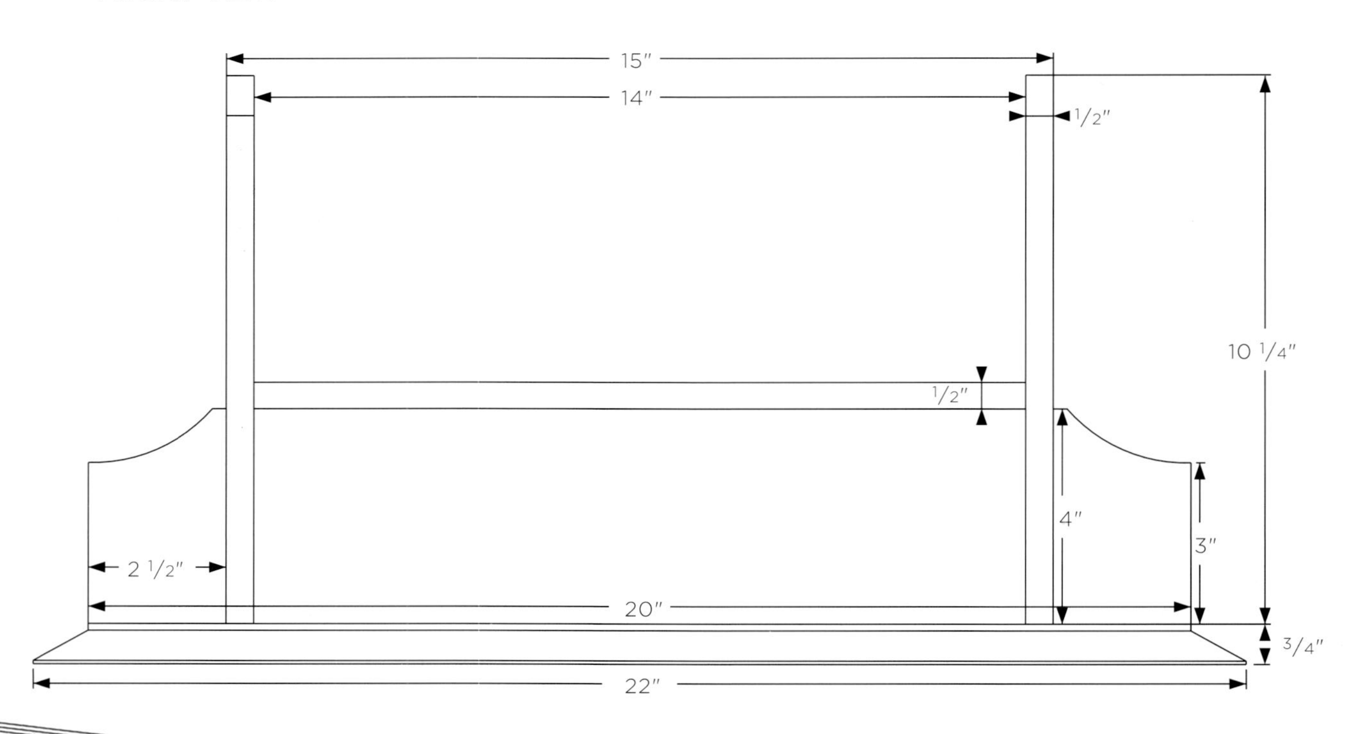

No. 346

MAGAZINE STAND

40″ high x 24″ wide x 14″ deep

The Morris chair is often regarded as signature piece of the Arts & Crafts movement, but you could make a strong argument for the magazine stand instead. All of the major manufacturers featured at least one model. Limbert's Fall 1906 catalog included six variations alone. Its size and utility make the magazine stand a flexible piece at home wherever you need a little additional storage.

The trapezoidal form and double cutouts distinguishes the 346 from more pedestrian iterations of the stand, but they do complicate construction. Substitute plugged screws through the sides or pocket holes in the shelves for the dadoes and construction becomes a lot easier.

EXPLODED VIEW

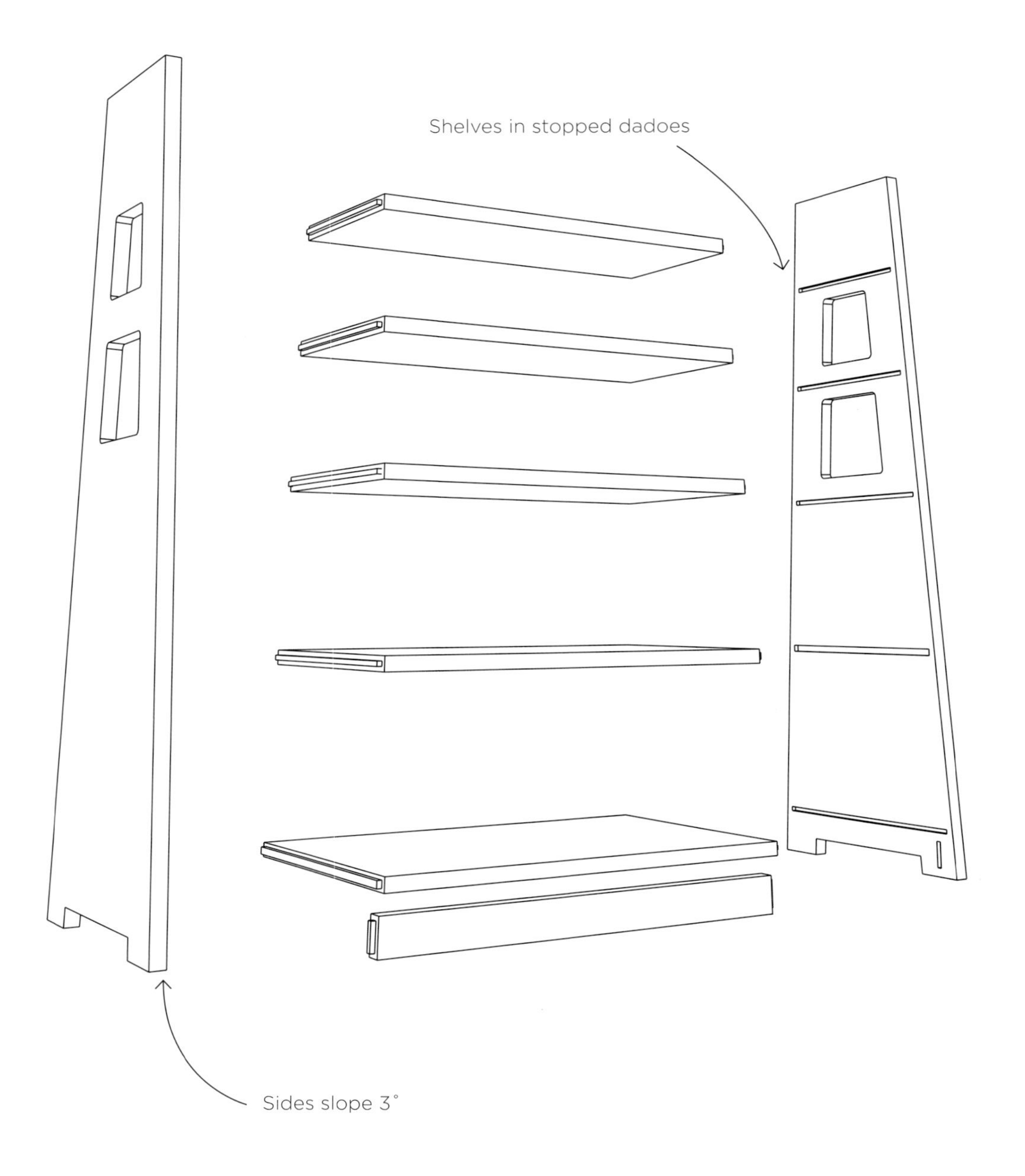

PART LIST

Qty	Description	Length	Width	Thickness
1	shelf 1 *	20 25/64"	8"	3/4"
1	shelf 2 *	20 27/32"	8 7/8"	3/4""
1	shelf 3 *	21 25/64"	9 15/16"	3/4"
1	shelf 4 *	22 1/32"	11 5/16"	3/4"
1	shelf 5 *	22 51/64"	12 13/16"	3/4"
2	Side	40"	1' 1 1/2"	3/4"
1	toe kick	22 15/16"	2"	3/4"

* length includes 1/4"-long tenon on both ends

FRONT VIEW

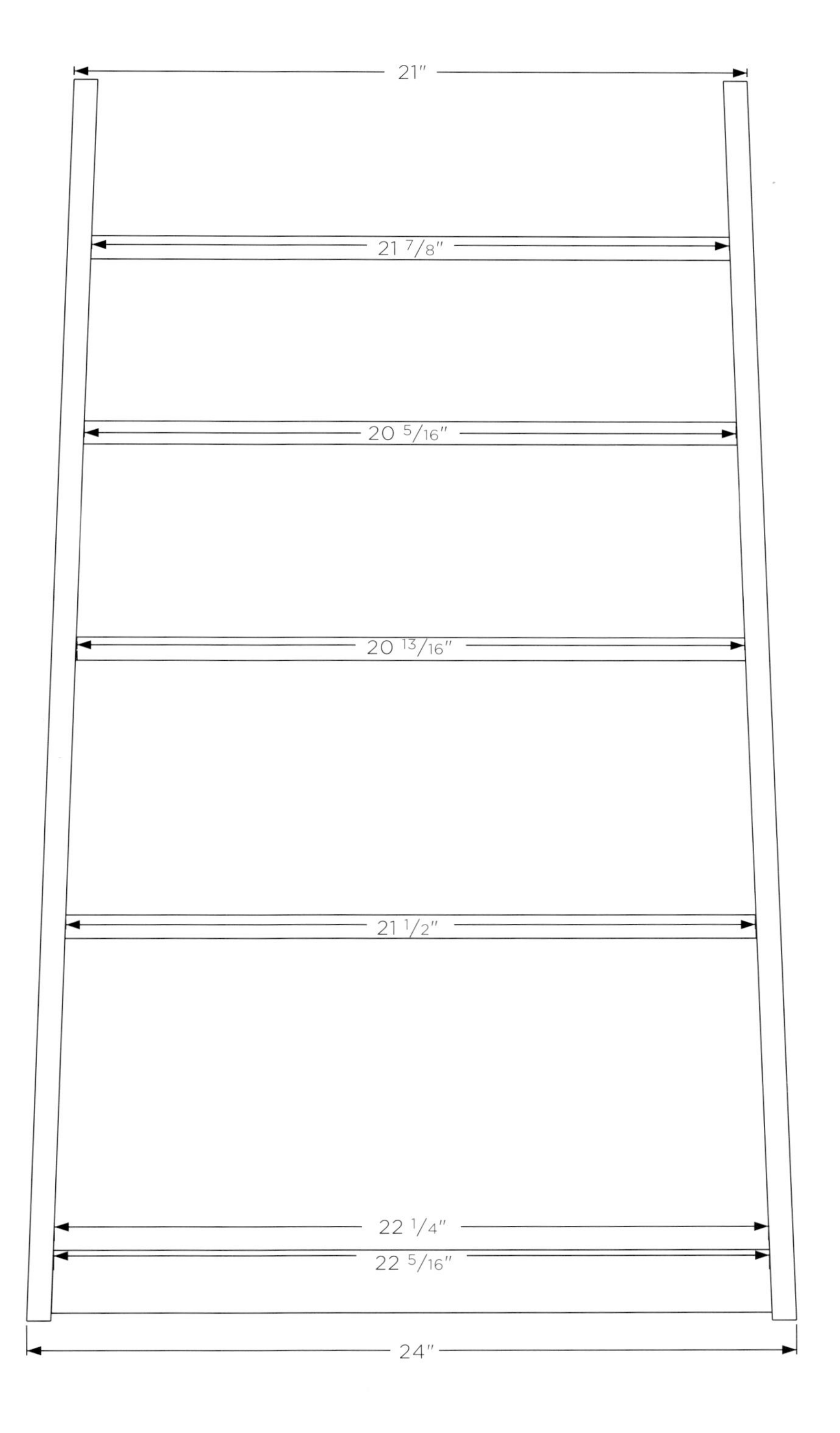

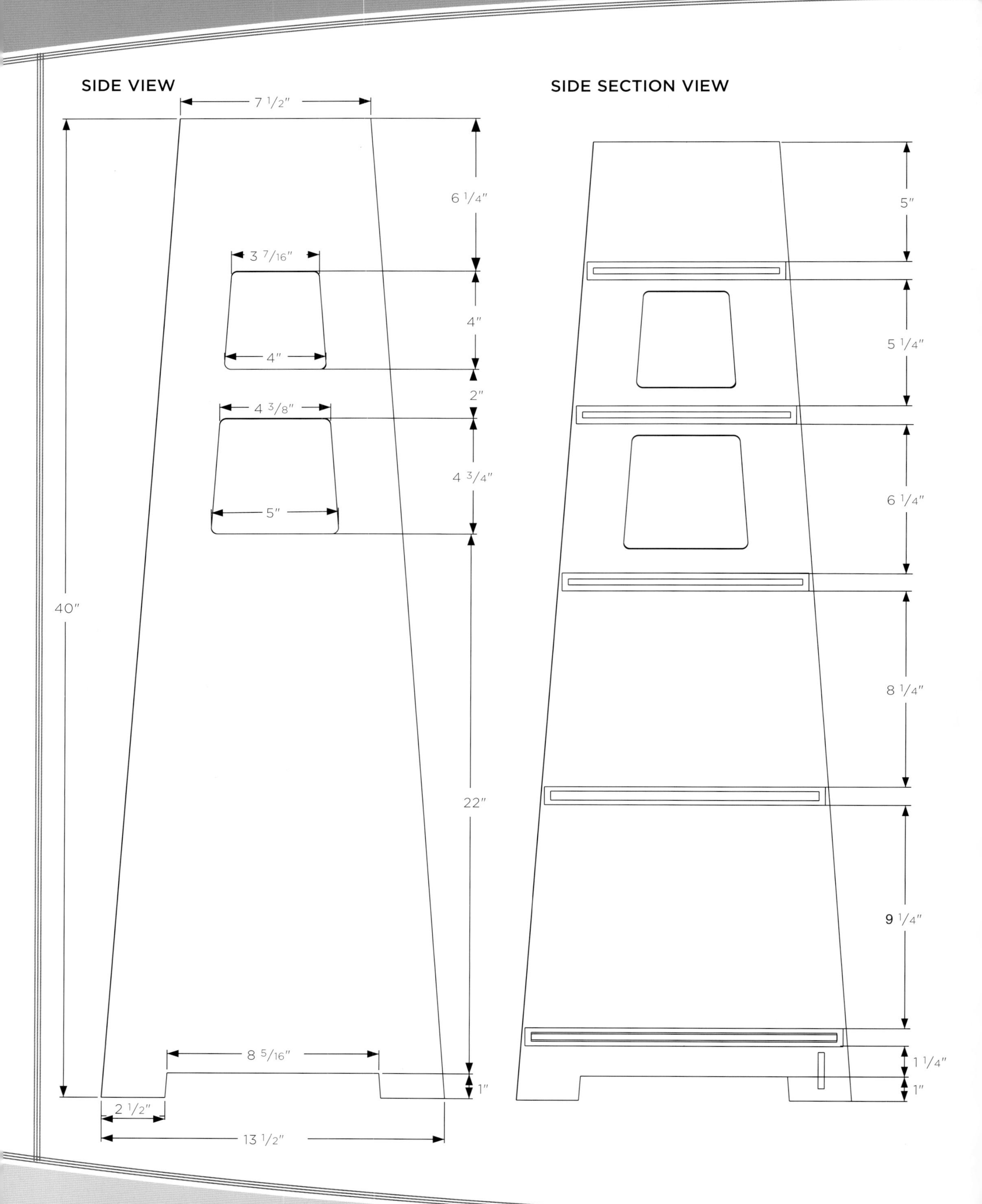
SIDE VIEW
7 1/2"
6 1/4"
3 7/16"
4"
4"
2"
4 3/8"
4 3/4"
5"
40"
22"
8 5/16"
1"
2 1/2"
13 1/2"
SIDE SECTION VIEW
5"
5 1/4"
6 1/4"
8 1/4"
9 1/4"
1 1/4"
1"

No. 355

BOOKCASE

48″ high x 33″ wide x 12″ deep — $24.00 (1905)

The sloping sides, organiform cutouts and wing shelves mark this as a Limbert piece. Those traits also help drive popular demand—one example fetched $12,500 at auction. A double-wide, double-door version, the No. 356 sold for $36,000 in 1999. You can have your own for substantially less, and further economize by using plainsawn wood for the sides and shelves if desired.

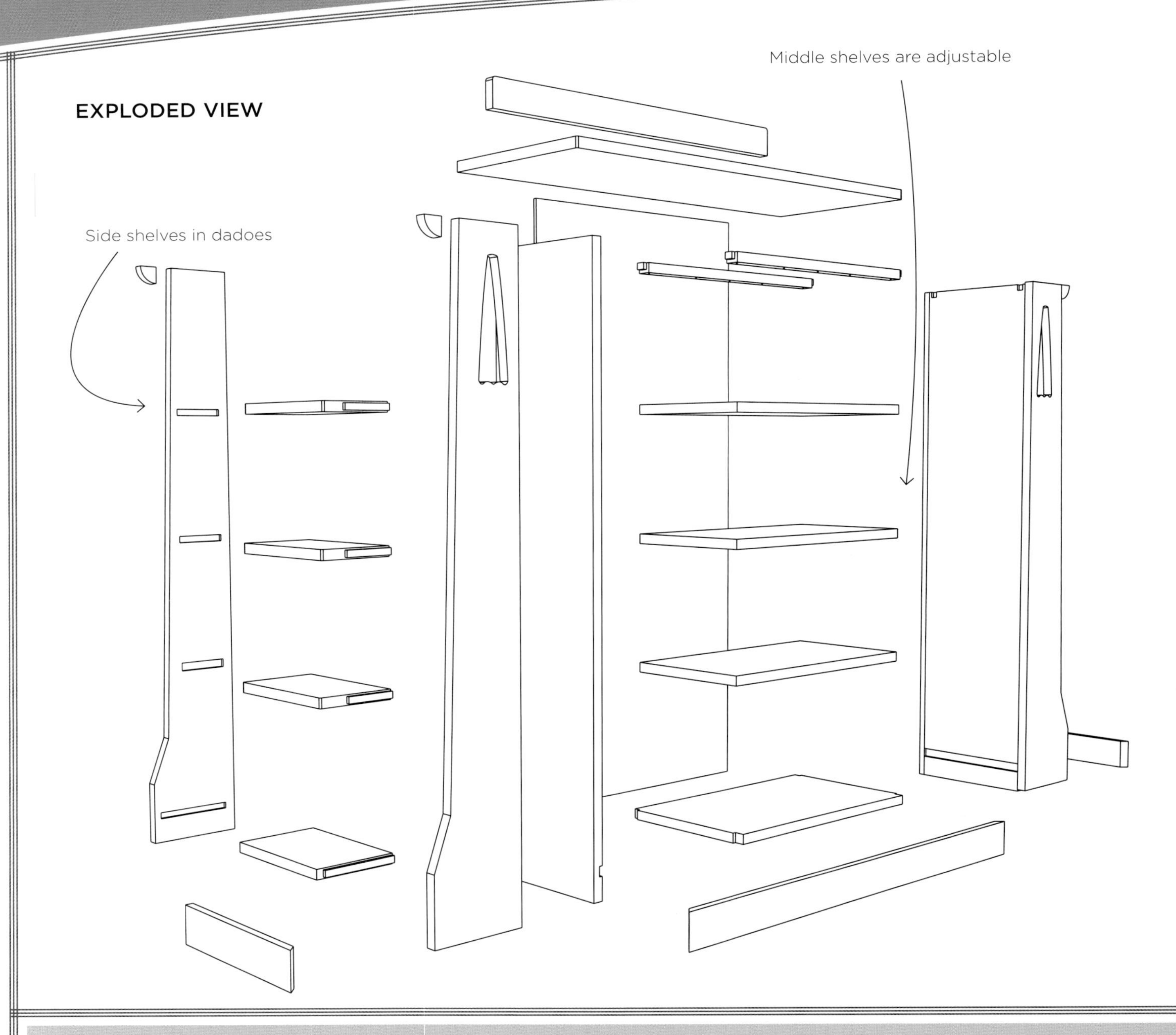

PART LIST

Qty	Description	Length	Width	Thickness
1	back	45"	19 51/64"	1/4"
1	back splash	28"	2 1/4"	3/4"
1	bottom shelf	19 1/16"	11"	3/4"
4	corbel	1 1/4"	1 1/4"	3/4"
2	door panel	9 1/2"	7 21/32"	1/8"
1	front trim	33 1/16"	2 1/2"	1/2"
1	door lower rail	17 1/16"	2"	3/4"
1	door mullion	39 1/2"	1 1/4"	3/4"
3	door muntin	16 1/16"	1 1/4"	3/4"
2	door stile	42 1/2"	1 3/4"	3/4"
1	door upper rail	17 1/16"	2"	3/4"

Qty	Description	Length	Width	Thickness
4	leg	45"	6 3/4"	3/4"
3	shelf	18 35/64"	9 3/4"	3/4"
2	side	45"	9 3/4"	3/4"
2	side self 1	10 1/4"	5 1/32"	3/4"
2	side shelf 2	10 1/4"	5 19/64"	3/4"
2	side shelf 3	10 1/4"	5 9/16"	3/4"
2	side shelf 4	10 1/4"	6"	3/4"
2	side trim	11 3/4"	2 1/2"	1/2"
2	subtop rail	19 5/16"	1"	3/4"
1	top	33"	12"	3/4"

DOOR EXPLODED VIEW

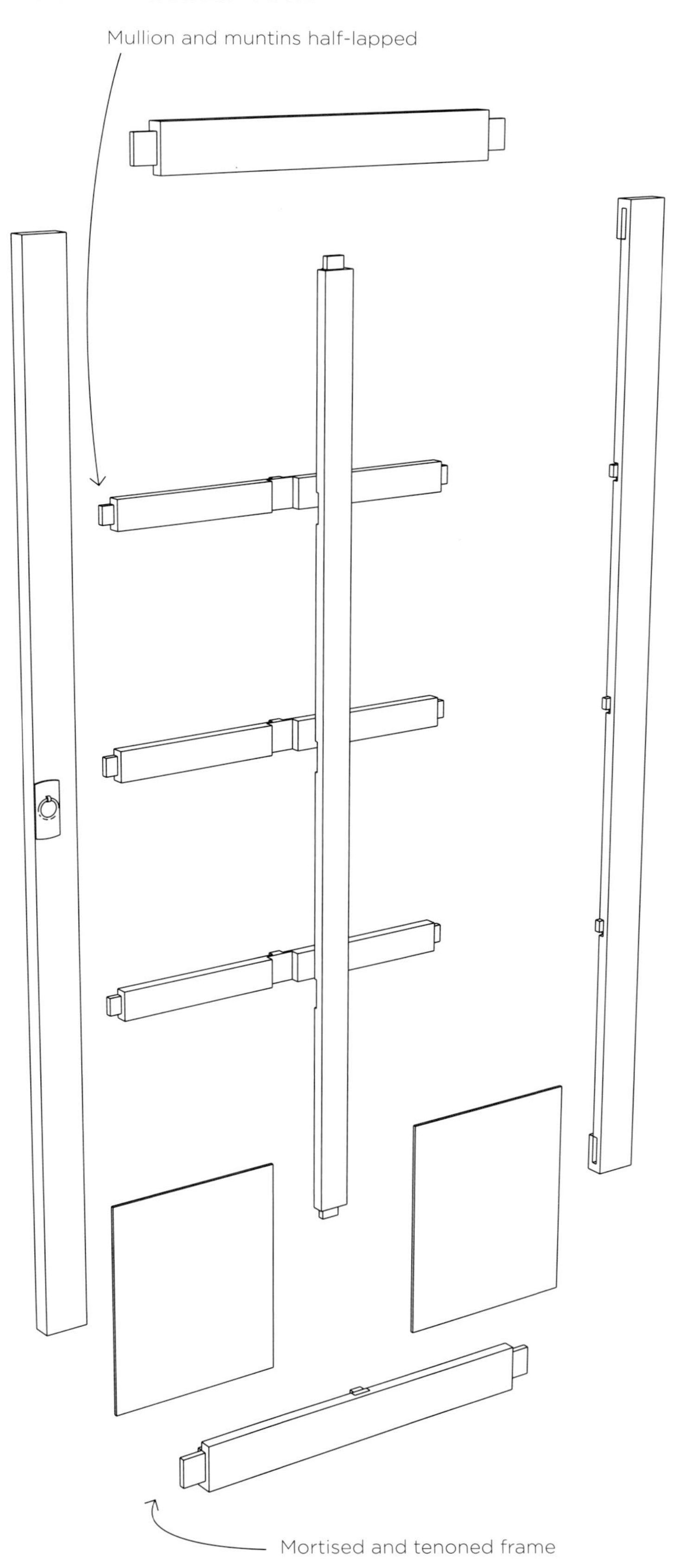

TOP VIEW

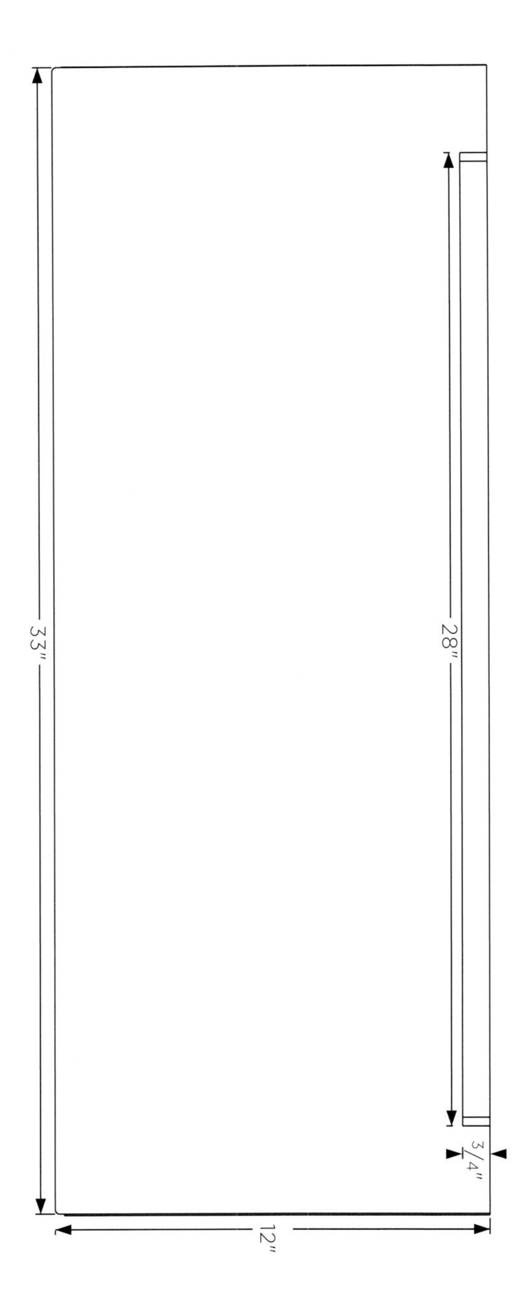

SIDE VIEW

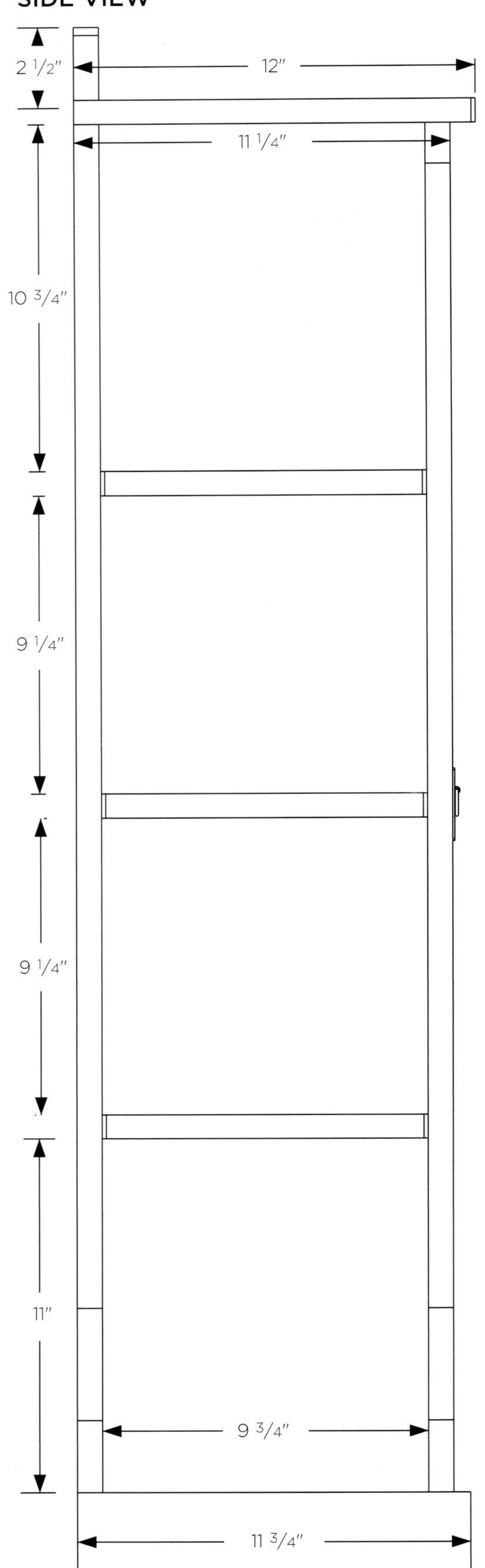

FRONT VIEW

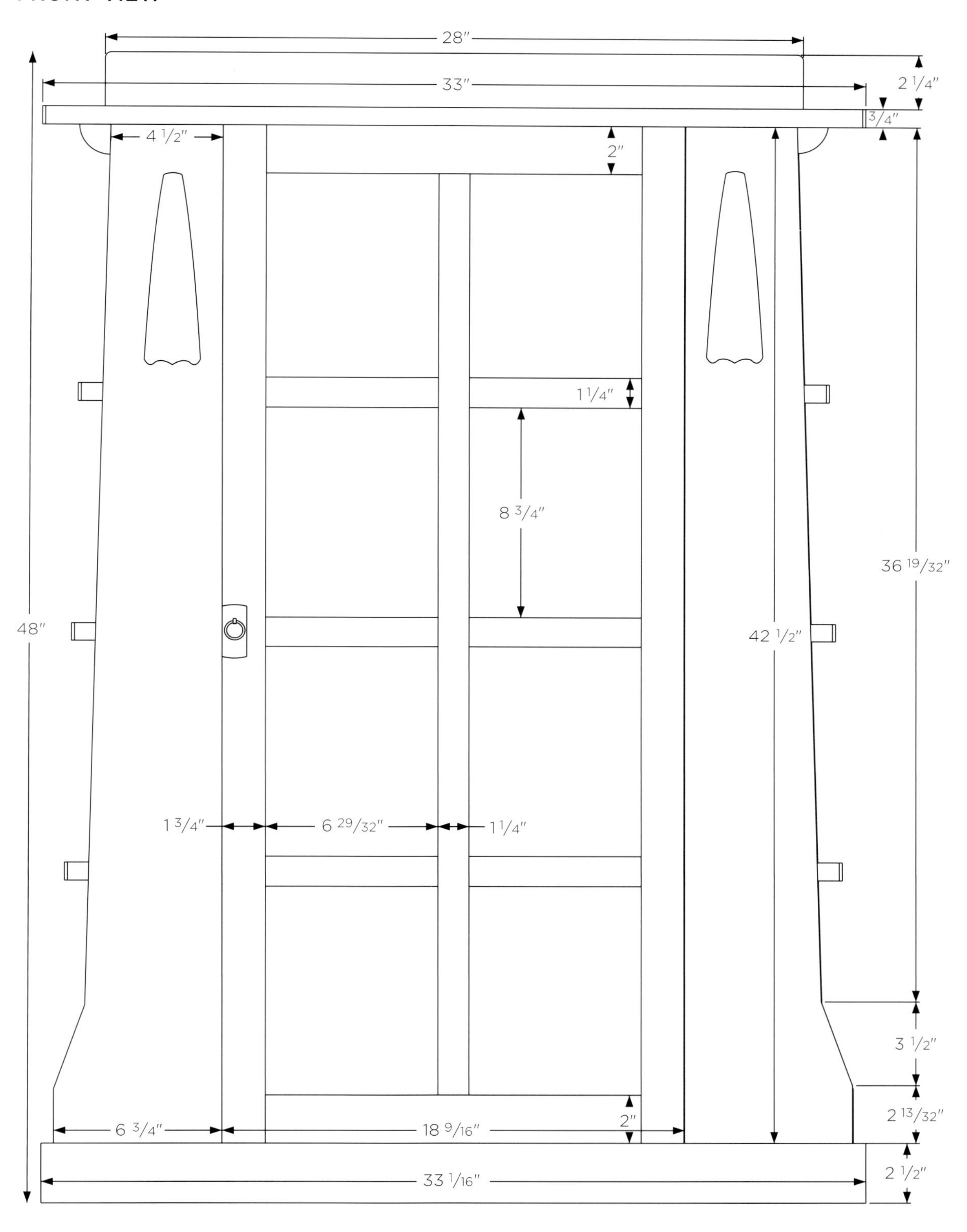

28″
33″
2 1/4″
3/4″
4 1/2″
2″
1 1/4″
8 3/4″
36 19/32″
48″
42 1/2″
1 3/4″
6 29/32″
1 1/4″
3 1/2″
2 13/32″
6 3/4″
18 9/16″
2″
2 1/2″
33 1/16″

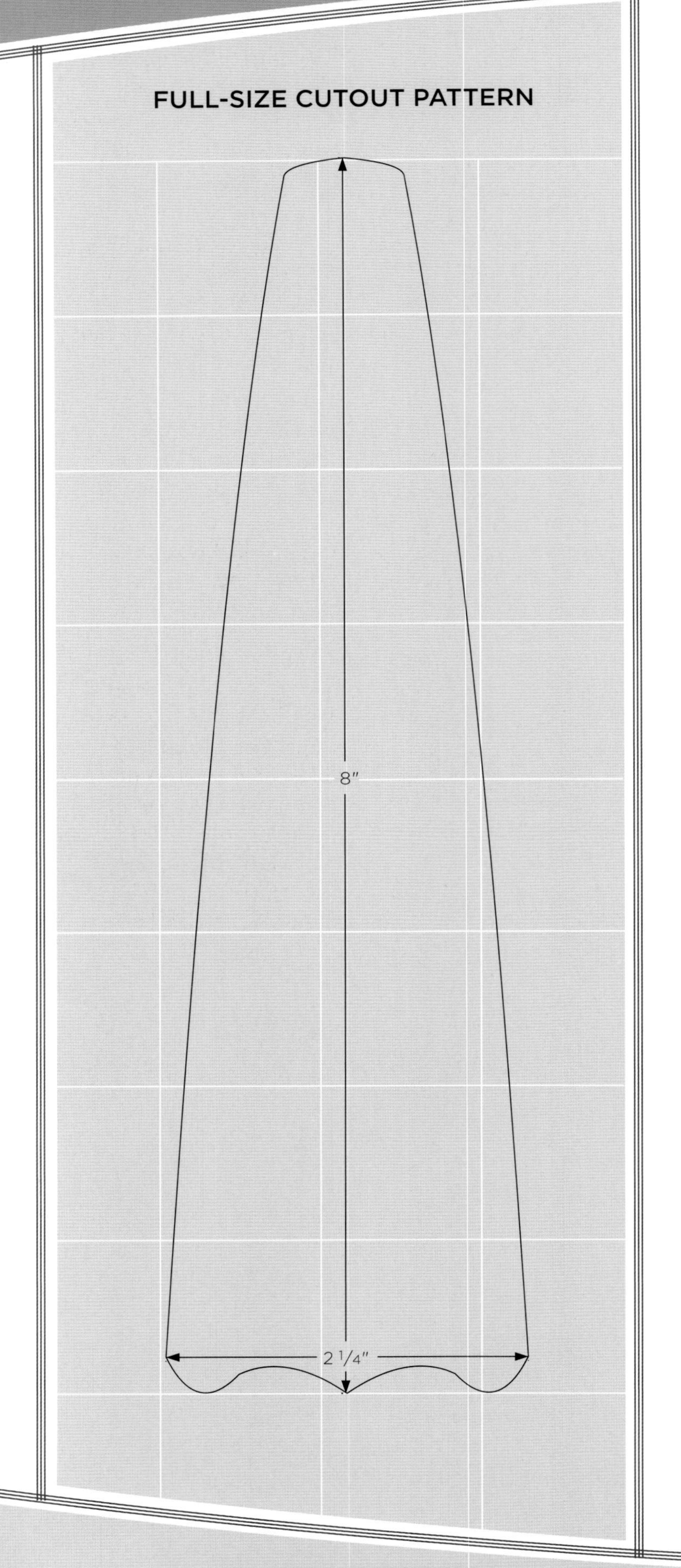
FULL-SIZE CUTOUT PATTERN
8″
2 1/4″

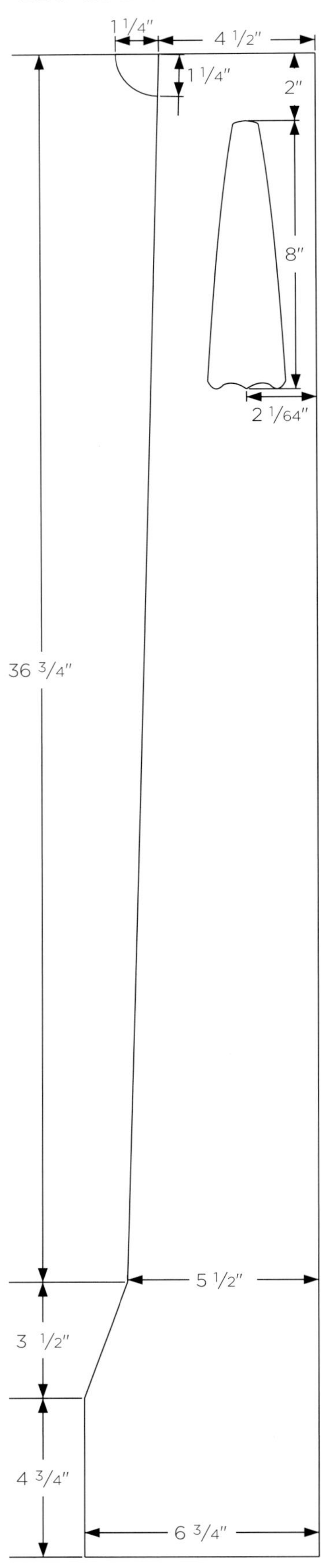
LEG SIDE VIEW
1 1/4″
4 1/2″
1 1/4″
2″
8″
2 1/64″
36 3/4″
5 1/2″
3 1/2″
4 3/4″
6 3/4″

No. 357

BOOKCASE

57″ high x 3″ wide x 14″ deep — $18.00 (1905)

The No. 357 Book Case is perhaps less distinctly Limbert than the No. 355, but it remains an attractive form. As with many other bookcases produced by the company, this one was available in double- and triple-width versions. It would serve just as well as a display case. Consider adding an inch or two of depth if display is its intended use.

EXPLODED VIEW

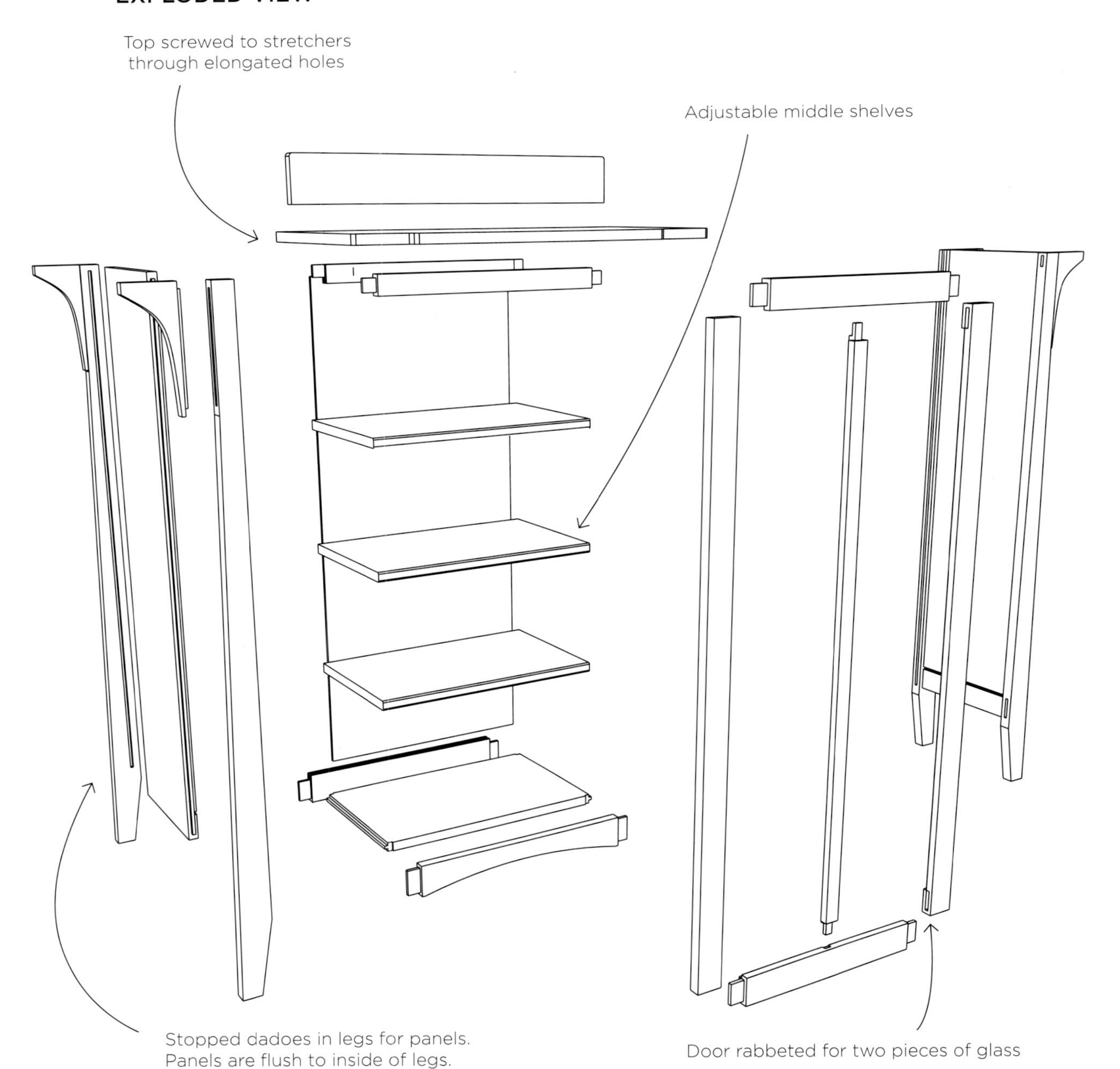

Top screwed to stretchers through elongated holes
Adjustable middle shelves
Stopped dadoes in legs for panels. Panels are flush to inside of legs.
Door rabbeted for two pieces of glass

PART LIST

Qty	Description	Length	Width	Thickness
3	adjustable shelf	17 3/4"	11"	3/4"
1	back	42 3/4"	18"	1/4"
1	back bottom stretcher	19"	2 1/2"	3/4"
1	backsplash	27"	3 3/4"	3/4"
1	bottom stretcher	19"	2 1/2"	3/4"
4	corbel	8 3/4"	3 1/2"	3/4"
1	door bottom rail	15 1/2"	2"	3/4"
1	door muntin	40"	1"	3/4"
2	door stile	41 3/4"	1 3/4"	3/4"
1	door top rail	15 1/2"	1 3/4"	3/4"
4	leg	52 1/2"	2 1/2"	1"
1	shelf	18 1/4"	11 9/32"	3/4"
2	side	45 3/4"	11 1/2"	3/4"
1	top	29"	14"	3/4"
2	top stretcher	19"	1 1/2"	3/4"

FRONT VIEW

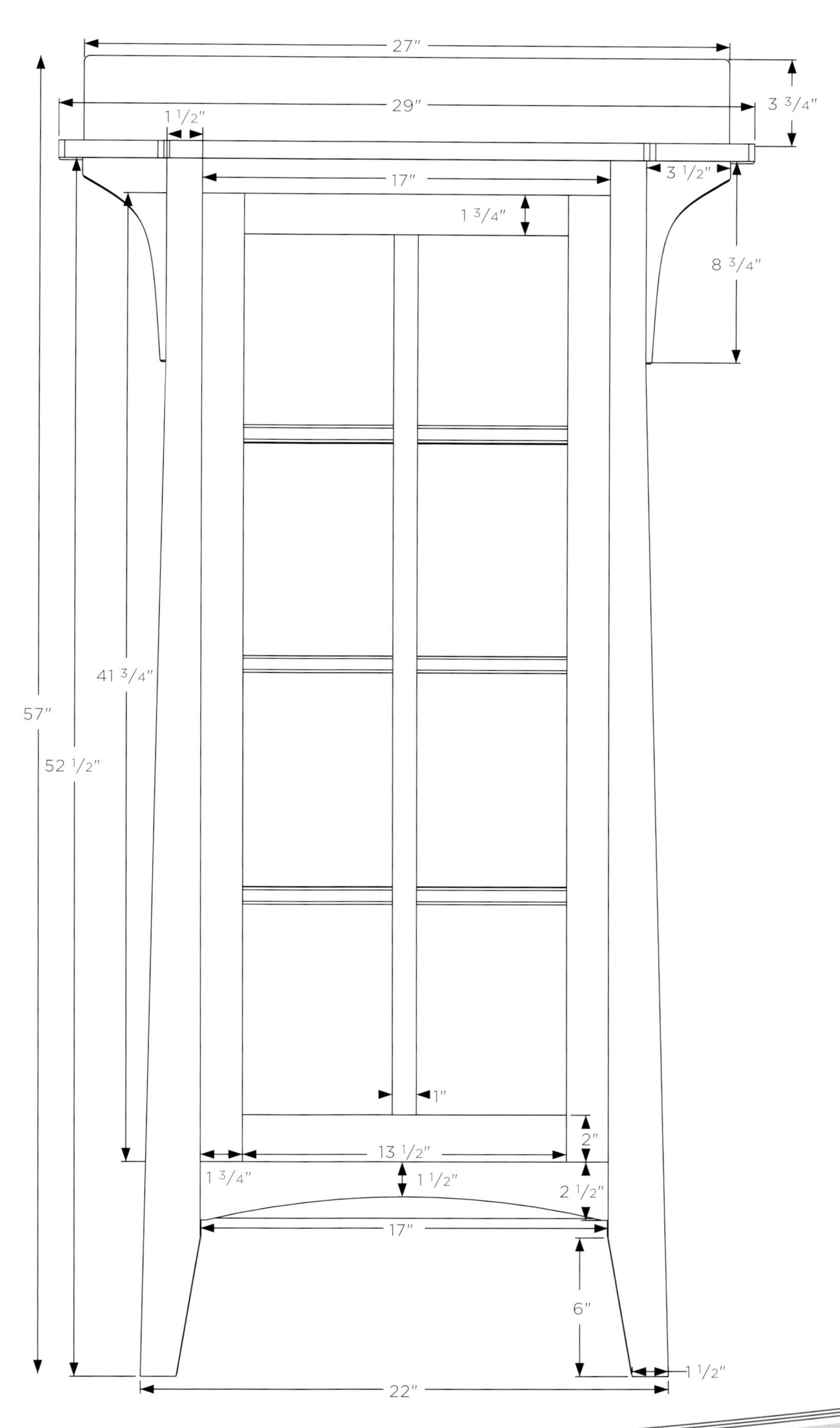

27″
29″
3 3/4″
1 1/2″
3 1/2″
17″
1 3/4″
8 3/4″
41 3/4″
57″
52 1/2″
1″
2″
13 1/2″
1 3/4″
1 1/2″
2 1/2″
17″
6″
1 1/2″
22″

SIDE VIEW
3 3/4″
14″
3/4″
57″
11″
1″
13″

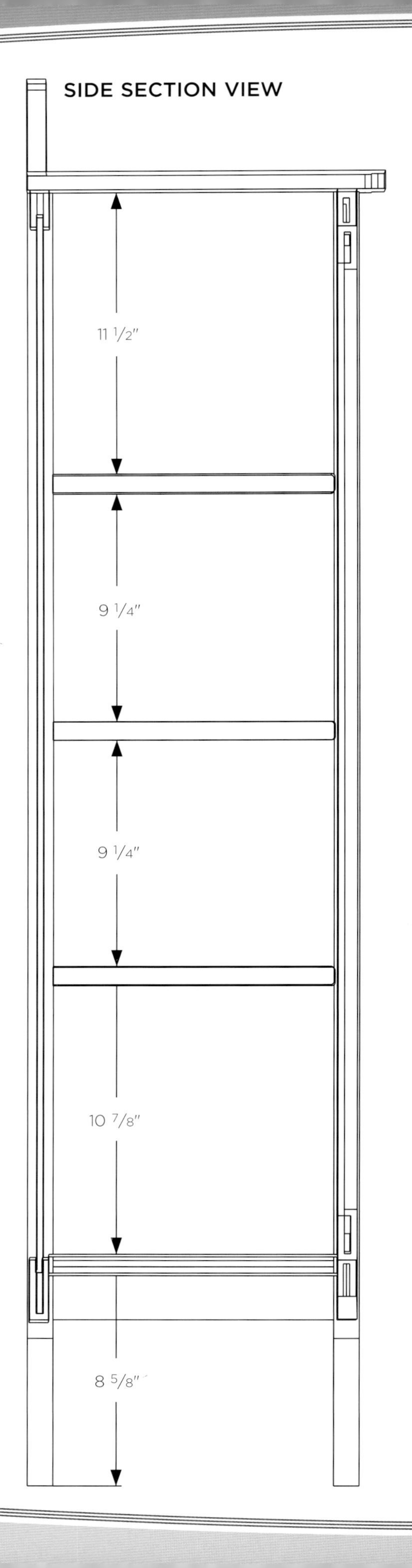
SIDE SECTION VIEW
11 1/2″
9 1/4″
9 1/4″
10 7/8″
8 5/8″

TOP VIEW

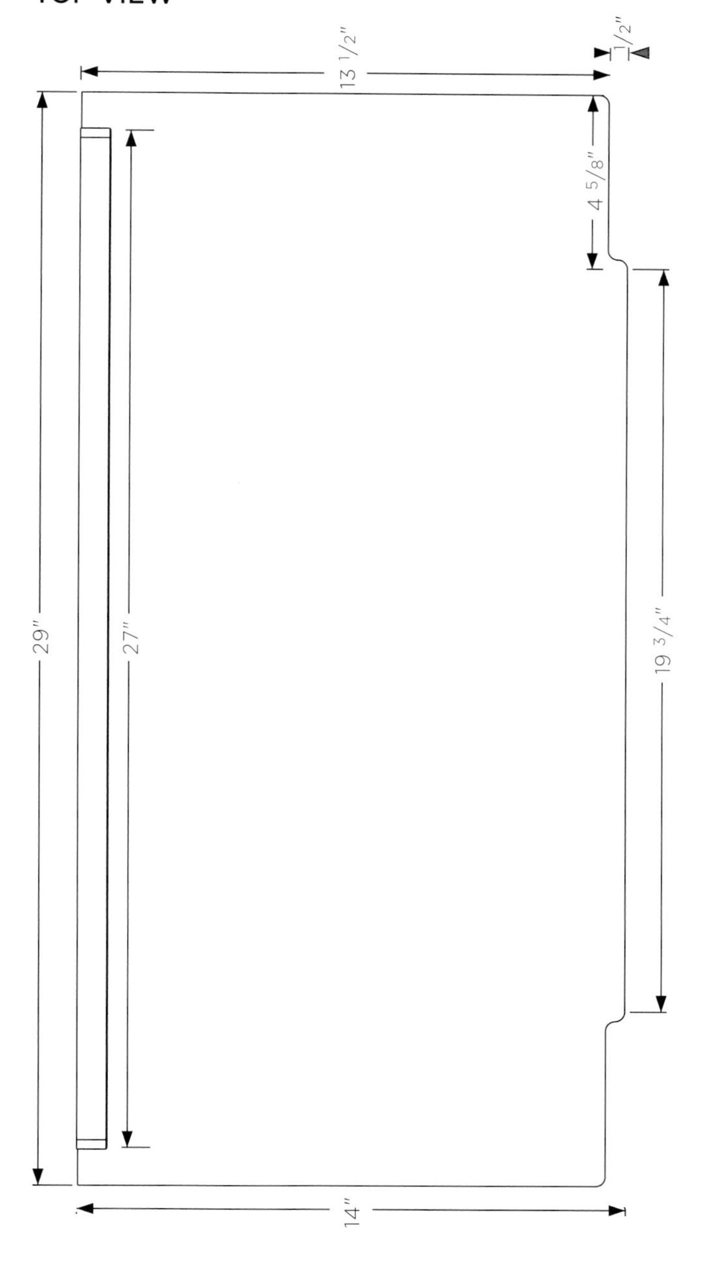

No. 367

BOOKCASE

50″ high x 30″ wide x 12″ deep

The gallery shelf and cutouts distinguish the No. 367 from other Limbert bookcases. The two full-depth fixed shelves stand slightly proud of the case sides and liven the front of the case. Stopped and through dadoes make construction straightforward. Since the back is visible through the doors, a shiplapped back or frame and panel will look better than the simple veneered panel of the original.

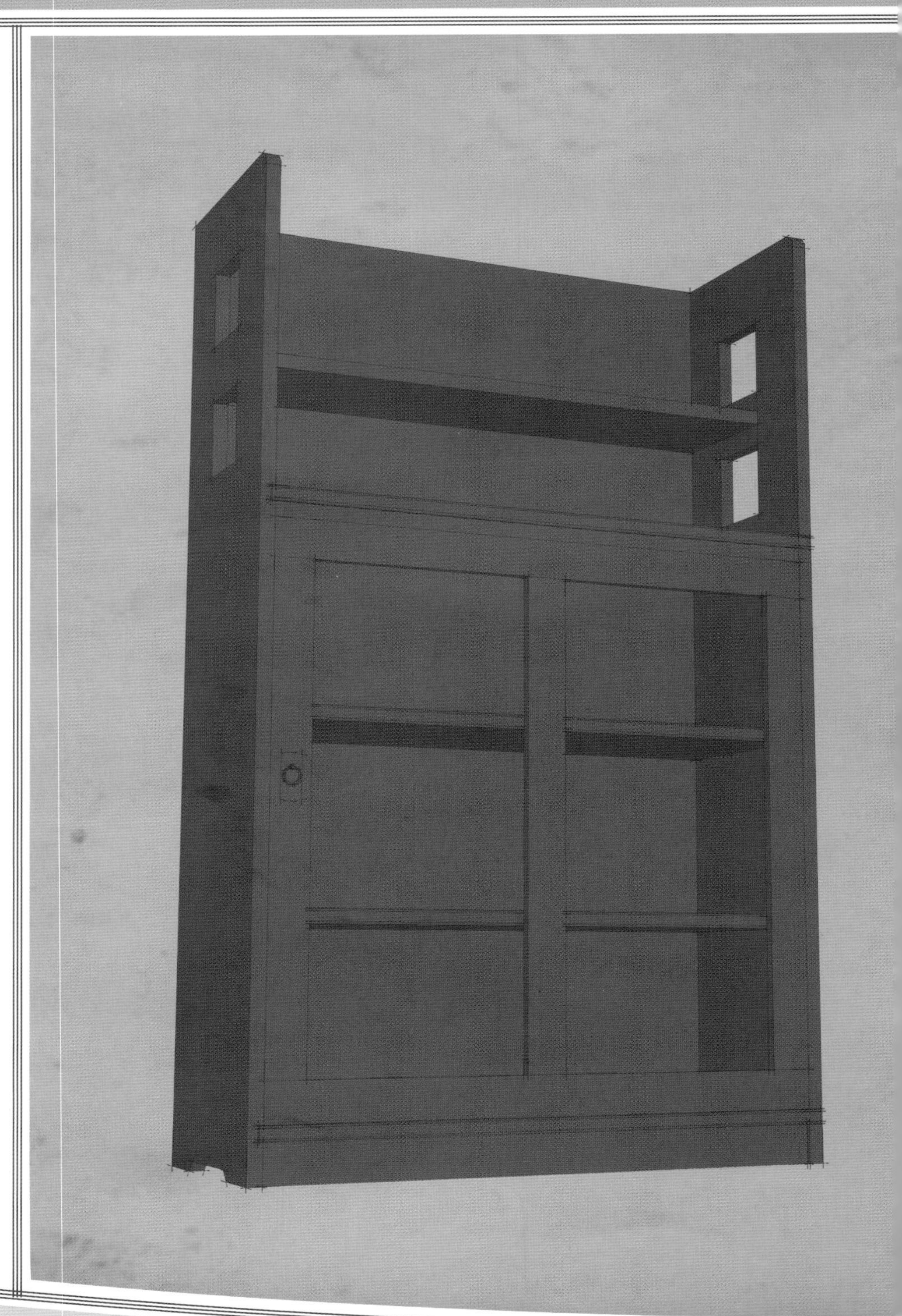

EXPLODED VIEW

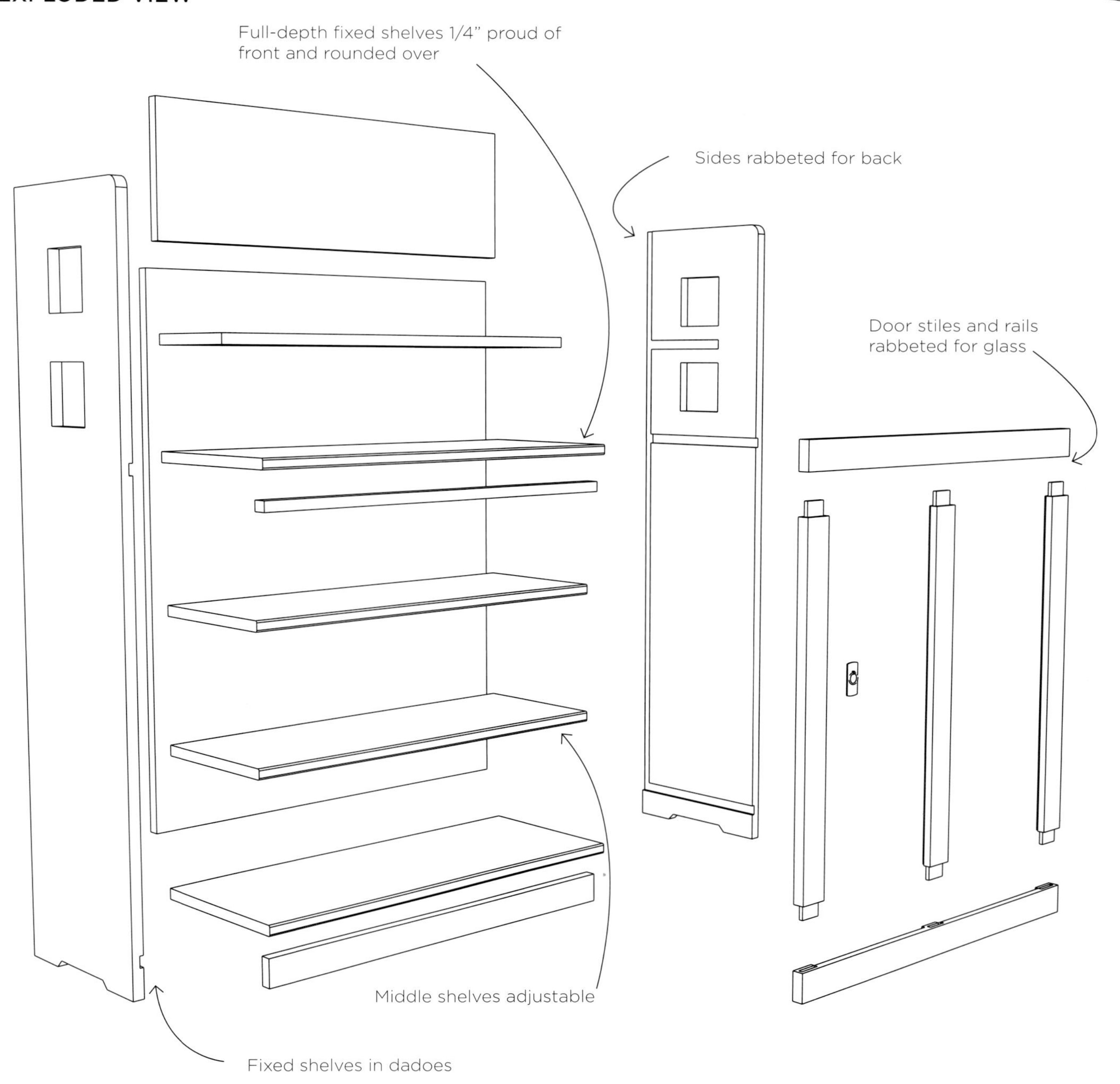

PART LIST

Qty	Description	Length	Width	Thickness
2	adjustable shelf	28 1/2"	10 1/4"	3/4"
1	back panel	38 1/2"	29"	3/4"
1	back rail	29"	9 1/2"	3/4"
1	door frame stop	28 1/2"	1"	3/4"
2	door rail	28 1/2"	2"	3/4"
2	fixed shelf	29 1/4"	11 1/2"	3/4"
1	middle door stile	26 3/4"	2"	3/4"
2	outer door stile	26 3/4"	2"	3/4"
2	side	50"	12"	3/4"
1	toe kick	28 1/2"	2"	3/4"
1	upper shelf	29 1/4"	7 1/4"	3/4"

FRONT VIEW

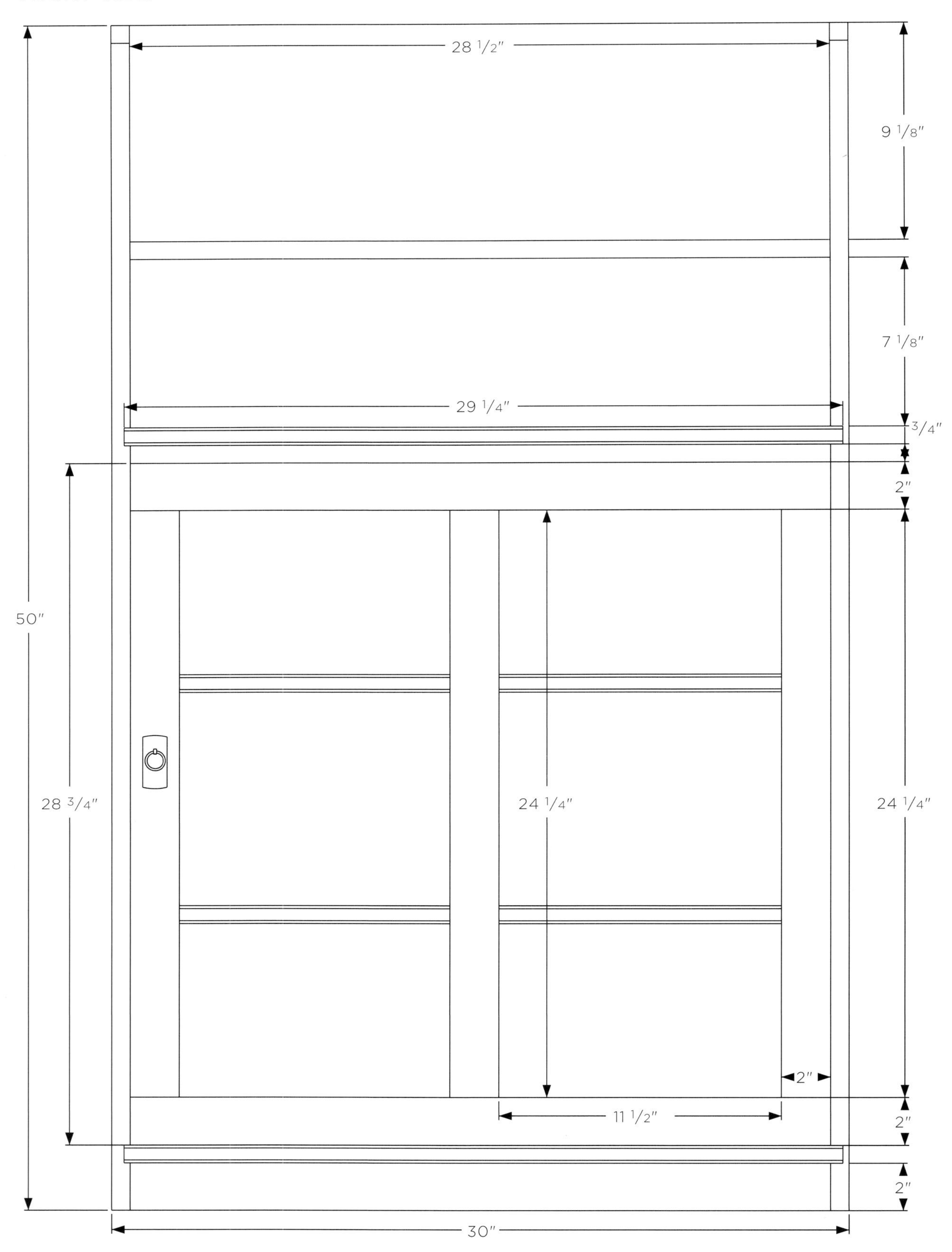

SIDE VIEW

TOP VIEW

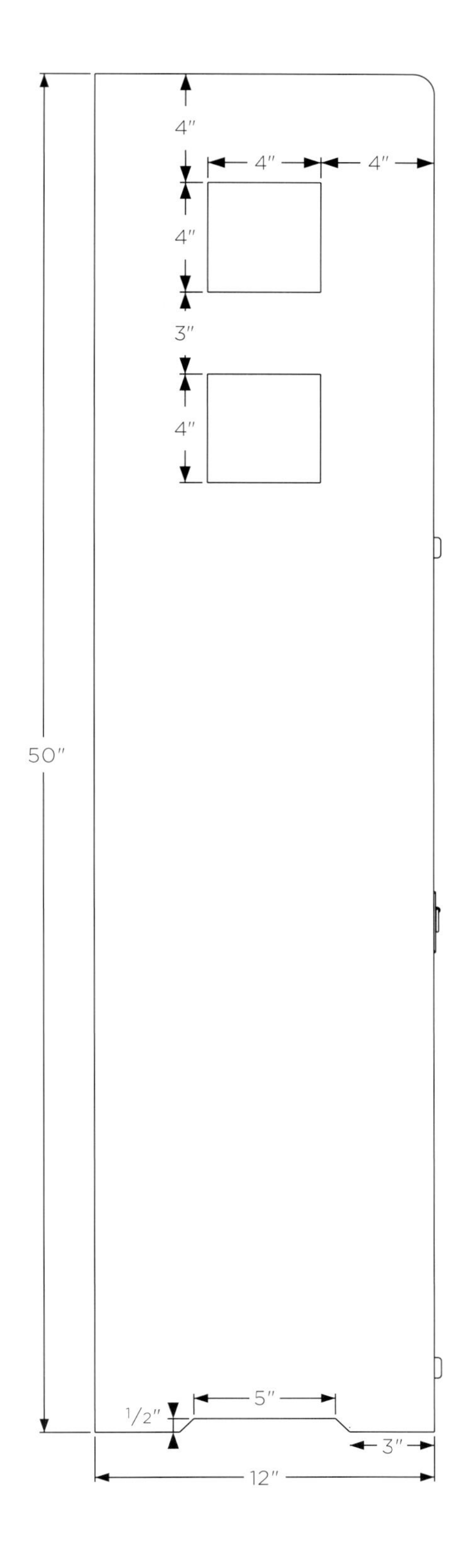

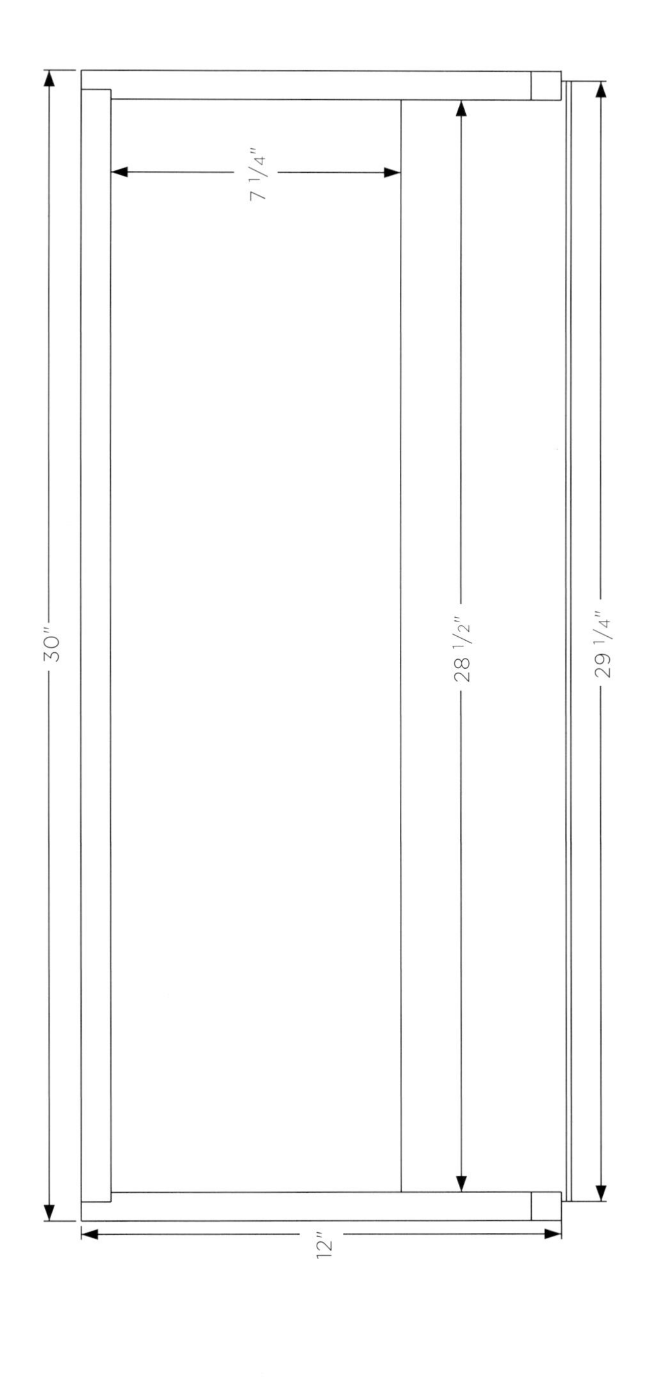

No. 519

MORRIS CHAIR

38″ high x 32″ wide x 39 1/2″ deep — $40.00 (1905)

The 1905 catalogue featured numerous variations on the Morris Chair. These different versions of an Arts and Crafts staple ranged from heavy, rectilinear forms in the style of Stickley to the more inspired. Definitely the latter, the No. 519 makes a virtue of material constraints — it conserves material and simplifies manufacturing by using only thinner stock — and its sloping legs and cutouts distinguish it from its more traditional peers. These characteristics also make it a desirable collector's item. One sold at auction for $6,250 in 2012.

Substitute the right bed hardware for the joints connecting the front and back stretchers to the sides, and you could create a knockdown version.

EXPLODED VIEW

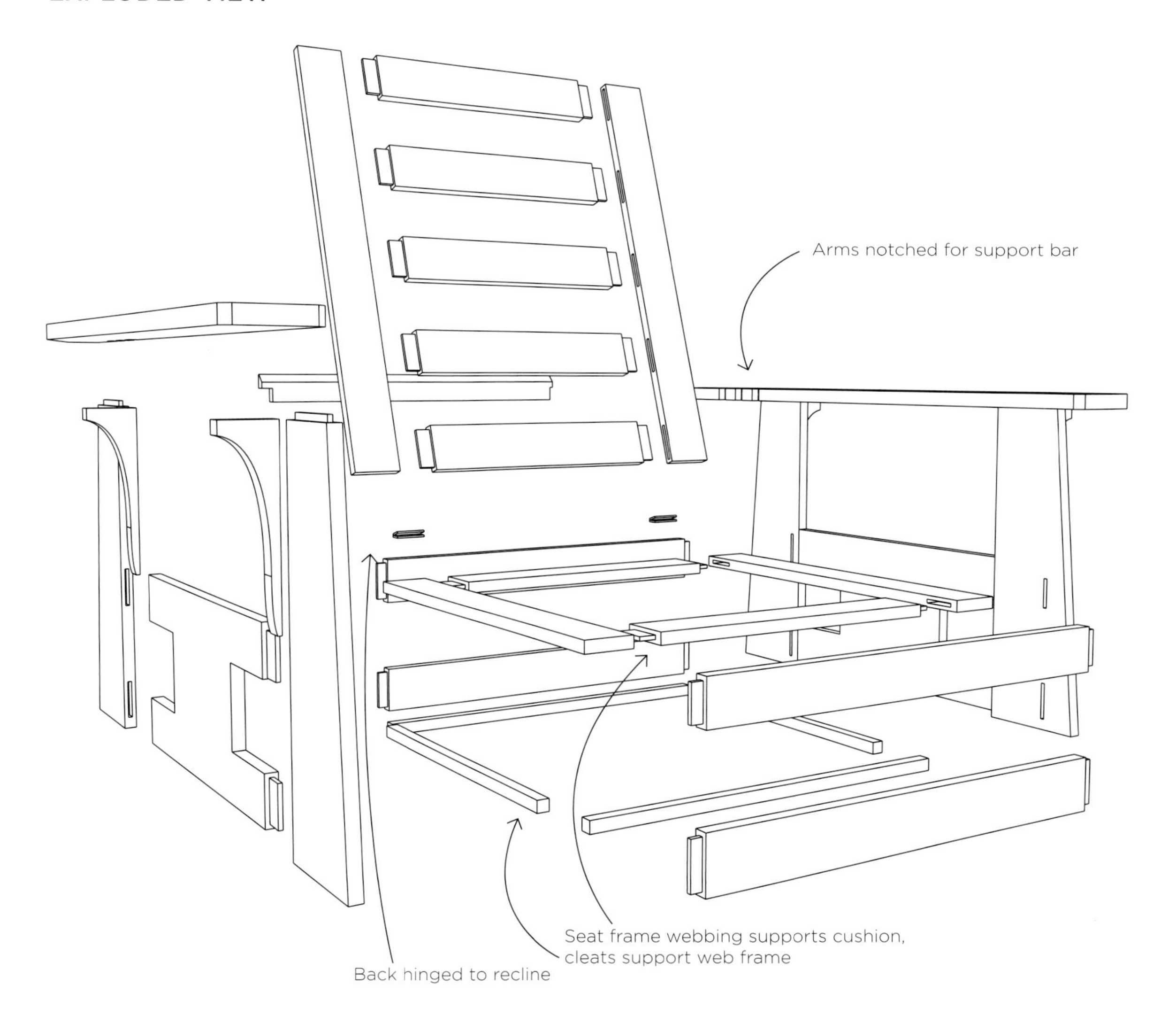

PART LIST

Qty	Description	Length	Width	Thickness
2	arm	43"	5"	1"
5	back rail	19"	3 1/4"	3/4"
1	back rod	26 3/8"	2 1/4"	3/4"
2	back stiles	32"	3 1/4"	3/4"
2	bottom stretcher	25 3/4"	3"	3/4"
4	corbel	10 3/4"	3 1/4"	1"
4	leg	22 3/8"	6 3/4"	3/4"
2	seat cleats	to fit	3/4"	3/4"
2	seat frame rail	20 1/2"	3"	3/4"
2	seat frame stile	25"	3"	3/4"
2	side	22 1/2"	11"	3/4"
2	top stretcher	25 3/4"	2 1/2"	3/4"

FRONT VIEW

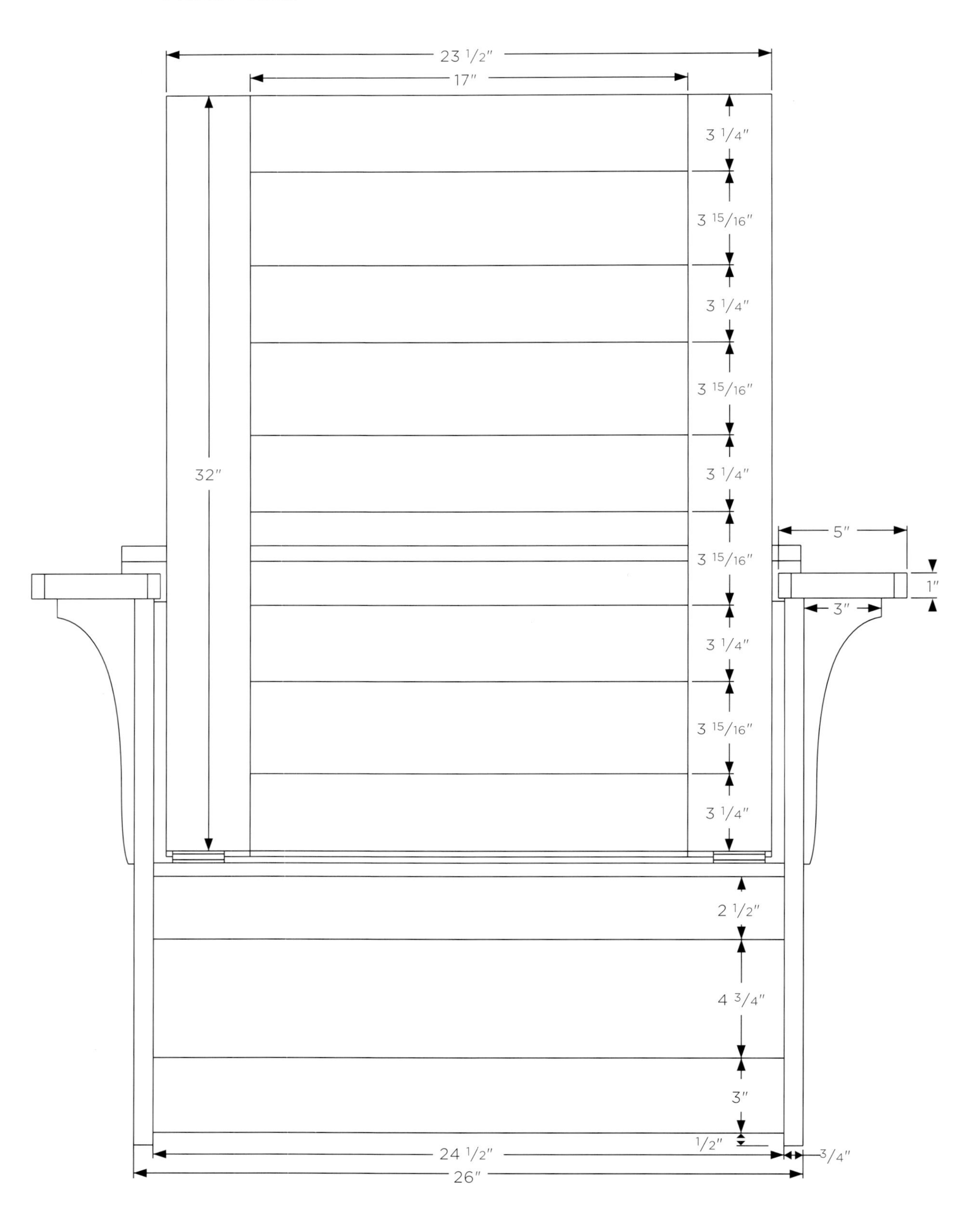

23 1/2"
17"
32"
3 1/4"
3 15/16"
3 1/4"
3 15/16"
3 1/4"
3 15/16"
3 1/4"
3 15/16"
3 1/4"
5"
1"
3"
2 1/2"
4 3/4"
3"
1/2"
24 1/2"
3/4"
26"

SIDE VIEW

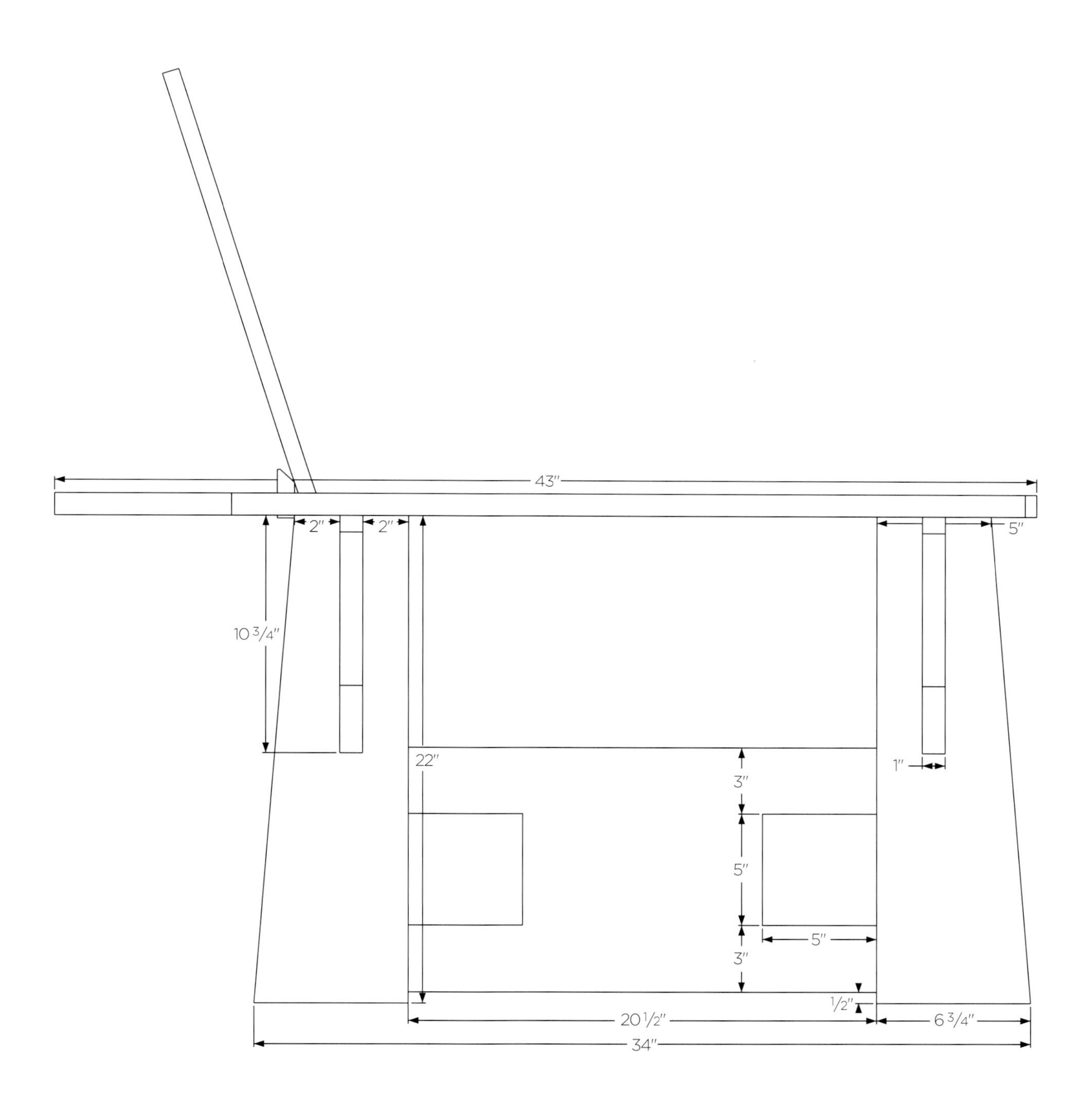
43″
2″
2″
5″
10 3/4″
22″
1″
3″
5″
5″
3″
1/2″
20 1/2″
6 3/4″
34″

TOP VIEW

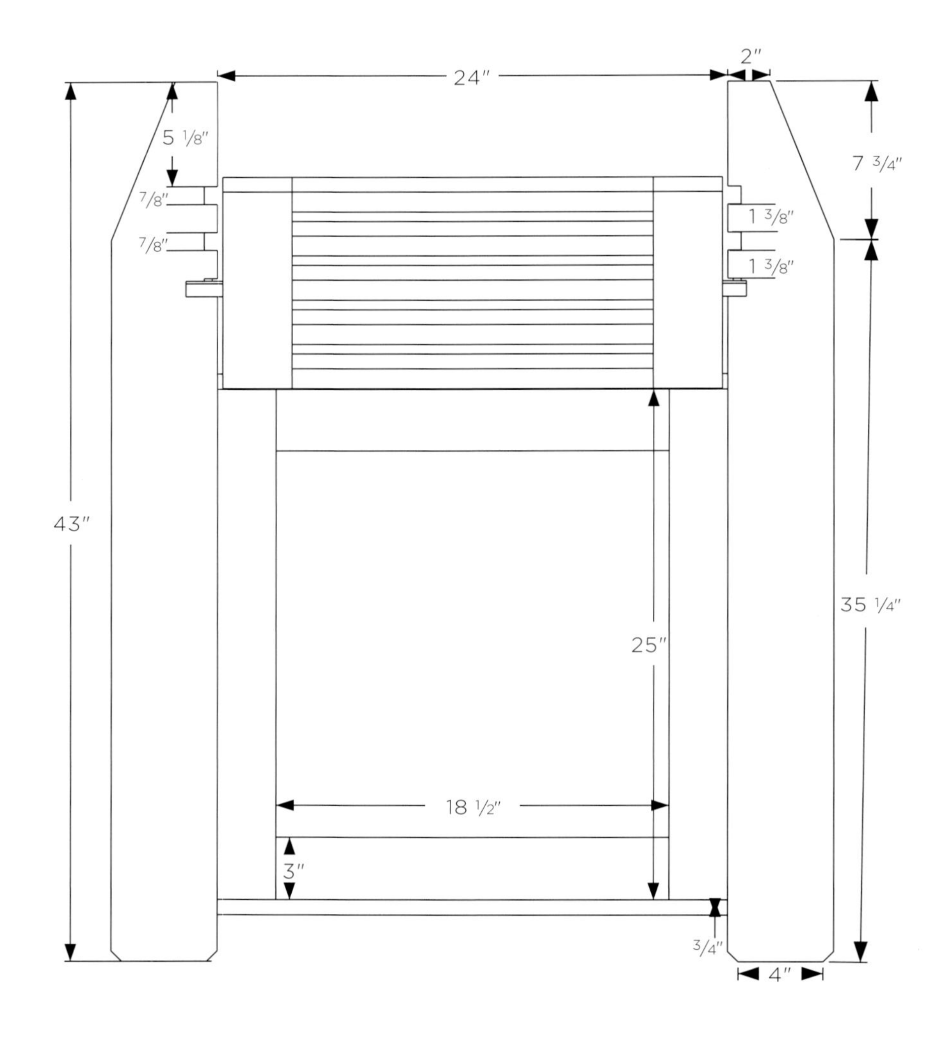

No. 676

ROCKER

36″ high x 28″ wide x 24″ deep

The Morris Chair tends to overshadow the Arts and Crafts rocker, but makers produced a surprising number, the Limbert Furniture Company included. The 1905 catalog alone featured 46, and that doesn't include those meant for children. Distinctly Limbert in style, the No. 676 features cutouts in the front legs and wide back slat. The design also makes it an approachable project since the joinery is straightforward and the rockers are cut rather than bent to produce the curve. You could substitute a solid seat for the frame and webbing shown here to simplify construction, but that comes at some cost to comfort. A cushion on webbing is surprisingly more comfortable to sit in than the same cushion on a solid seat.

EXPLODED VIEW

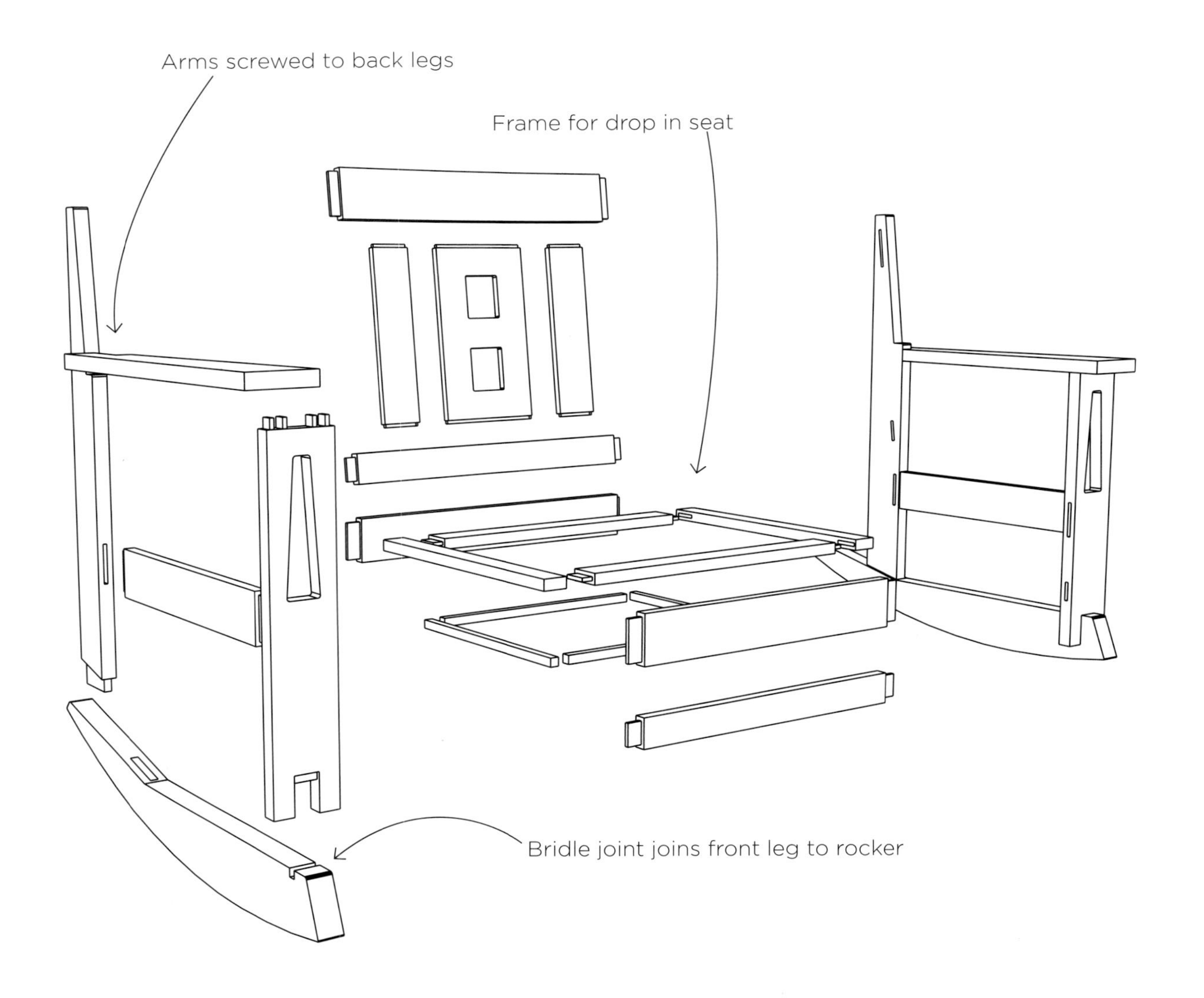

PART LIST

Qty	Description	Length	Width	Thickness
2	Arm	24 1/2"	4 1/2"	1"
1	back bottom rail	24 9/32"	2 1/4"	3/4"
2	back leg	32 15/16"	3 1/2"	1"
2	back narrow slat	13 3/8"	3"	1/2"
1	back stretcher	24 5/32"	3 1/4"	3/4"
1	back top rail	24 9/32"	3 3/4"	3/4"
1	back wide slat	13 3/8"	7 1/2"	1/2"
2	front & back seat cleat	19 3/8"	3/4"	3/4"
1	front bottom stretcher	21 3/8"	2"	3/4"
2	front leg	22 3/8"	4"	1"
1	front top stretcher	21 25/32"	3 1/4"	3/4"
2	runner	33 27/32"	6 55/64"	1 1/2"
2	seat frame end	21 9/32"	2"	3/4"
2	seat frame side	18 23/64"	1 5/8"	3/4"
2	seat frame cleat	18 15/64"	3/4"	3/4"
2	side stretcher	19 25/32"	3 1/4"	3/4"

FRONT VIEW

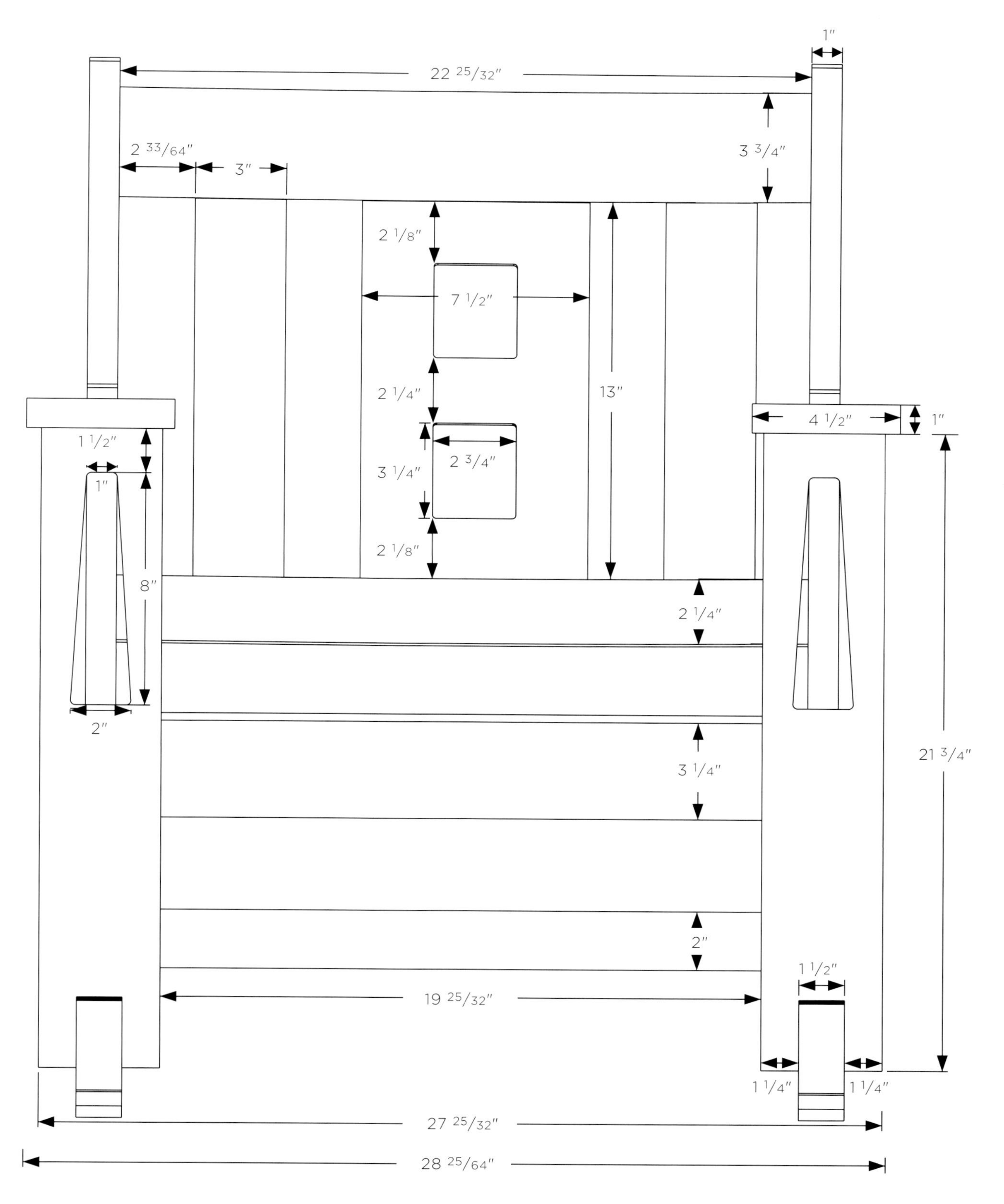

1″
22 25/32″
3 3/4″
2 33/64″
3″
2 1/8″
7 1/2″
13″
2 1/4″
4 1/2″
1″
1 1/2″
1″
3 1/4″
2 3/4″
2 1/8″
8″
2 1/4″
2″
21 3/4″
3 1/4″
2″
1 1/2″
19 25/32″
1 1/4″
1 1/4″
27 25/32″
28 25/64″

SIDE VIEW

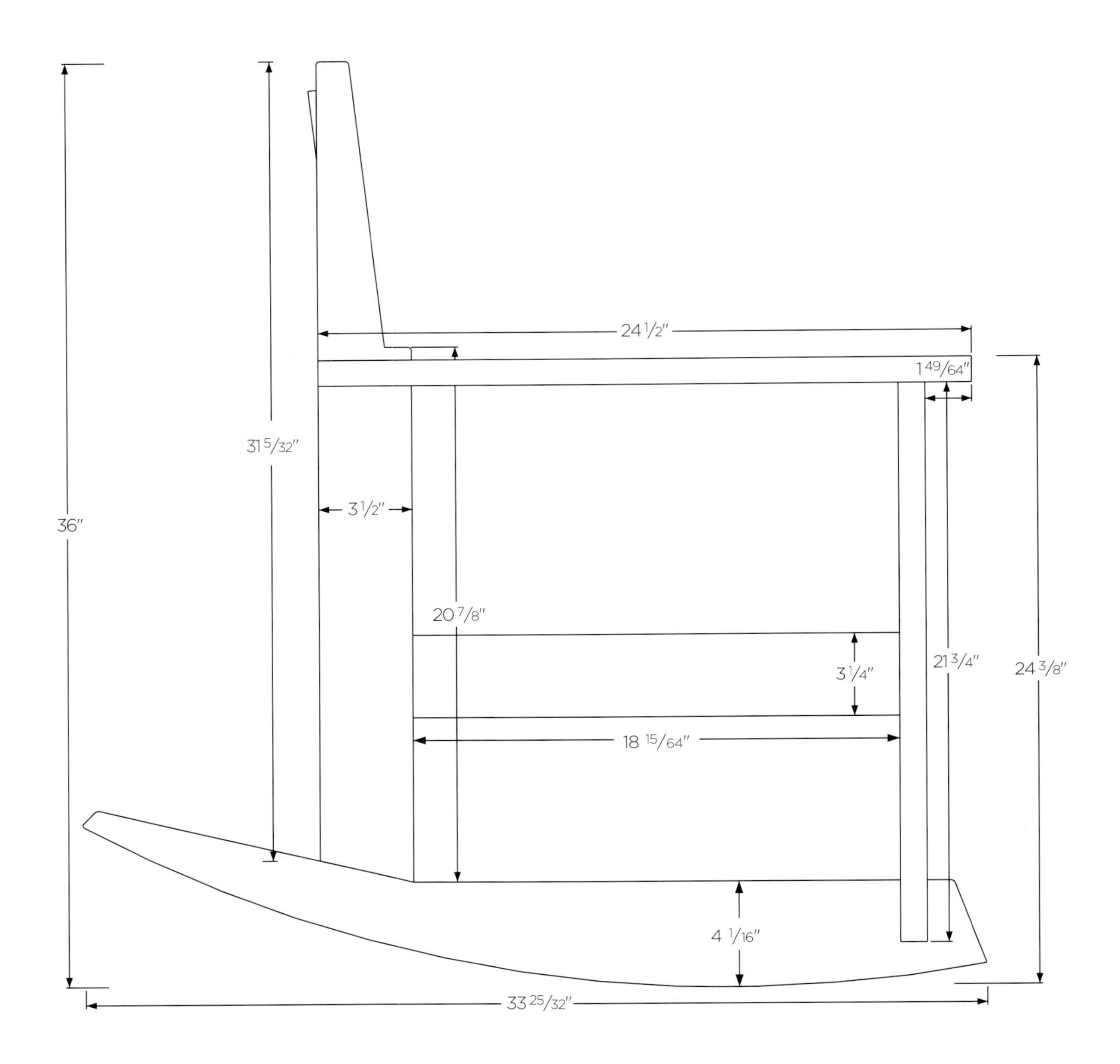

24 1/2"
1 49/64"
31 5/32"
36"
3 1/2"
20 7/8"
3 1/4"
21 3/4"
24 3/8"
18 15/64"
4 1/16"
33 25/32"

TOP VIEW

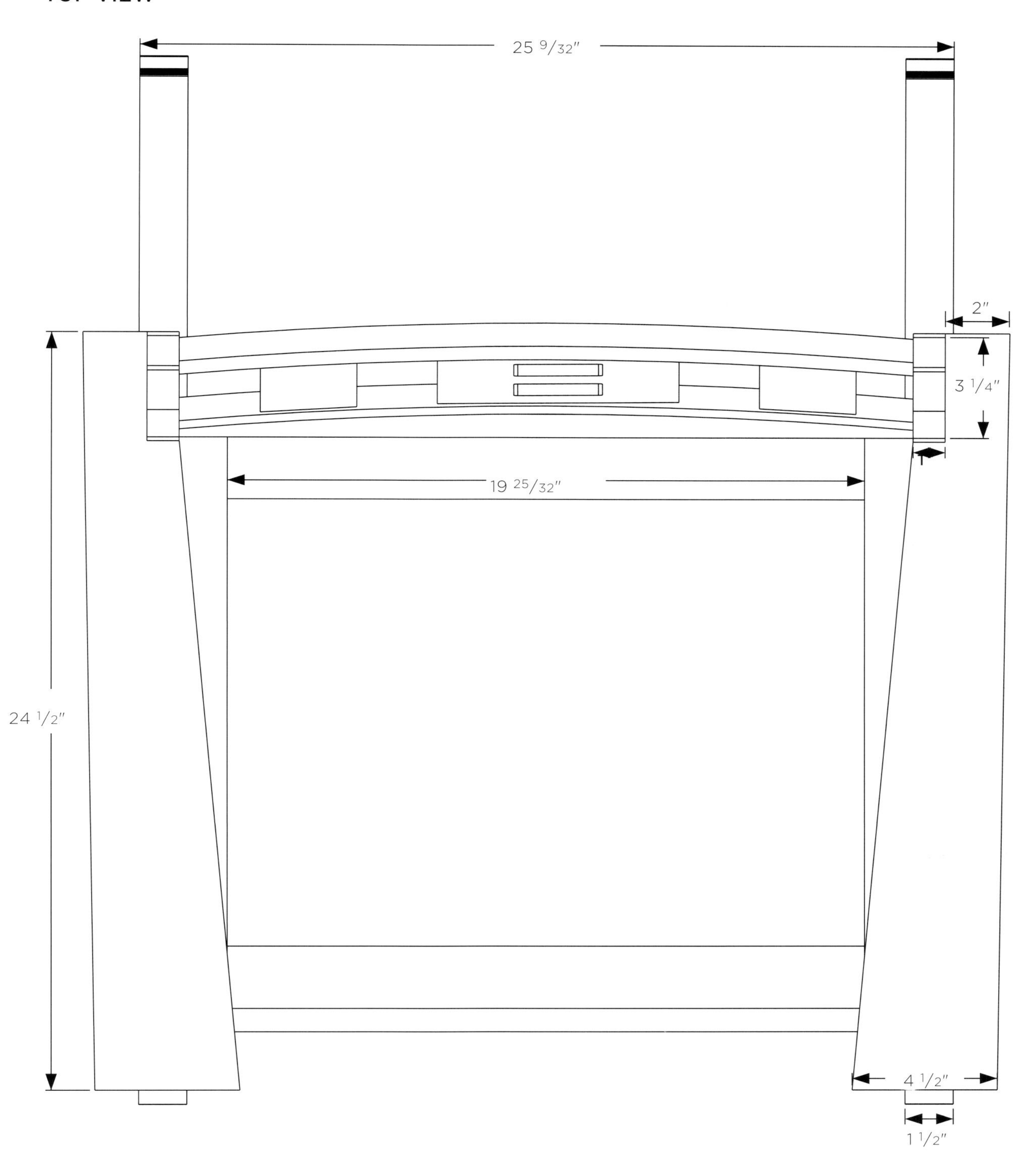

25 9/32"
2"
3 1/4"
19 25/32"
24 1/2"
4 1/2"
1 1/2"

DETAILED SECTION VIEW

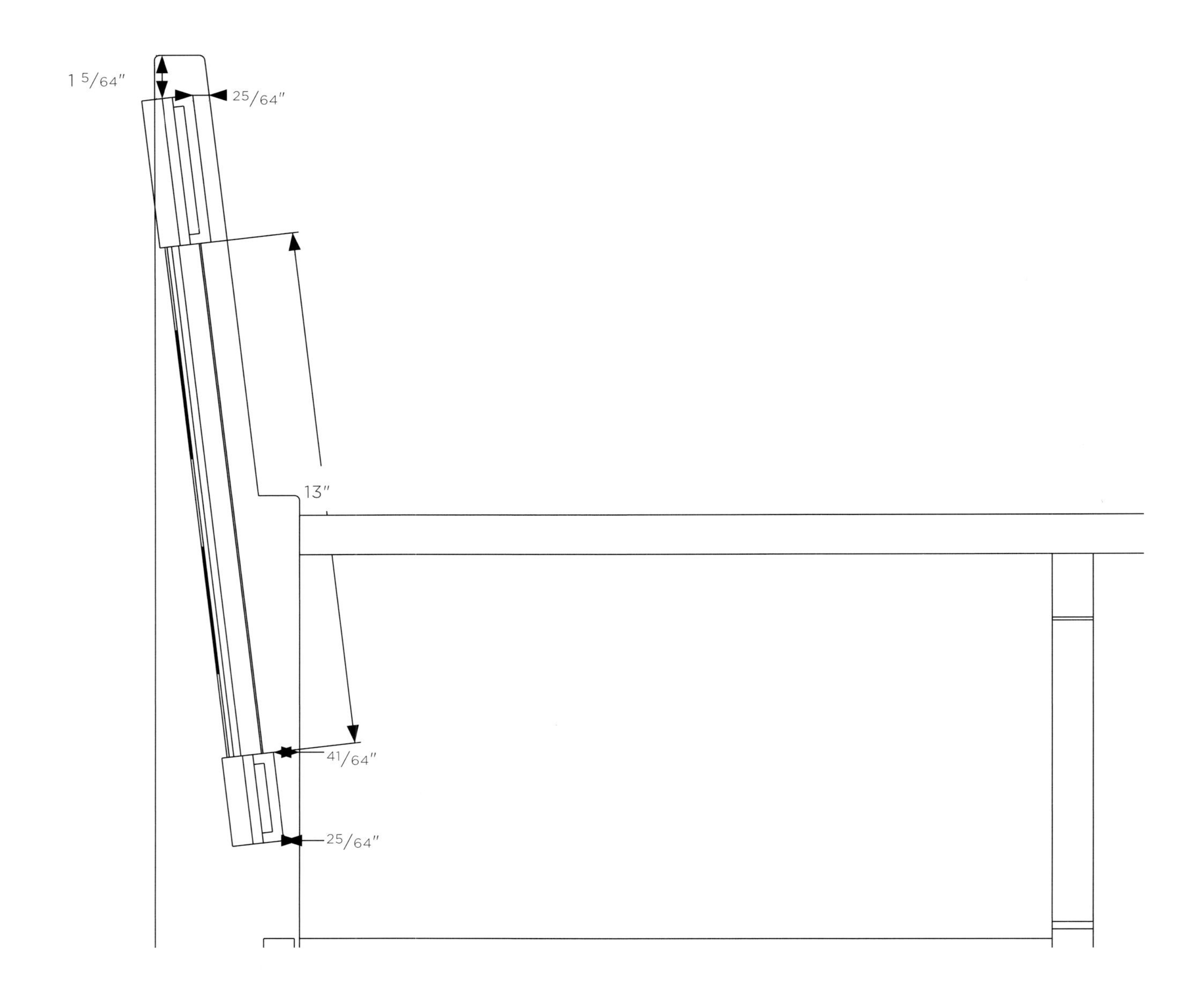

SEAT BACK RAIL TOP VIEW

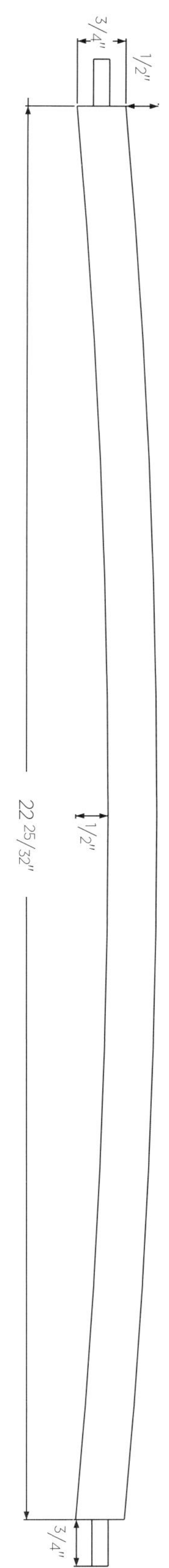

ROCKER RUNNER DETAILED SIDE VIEW

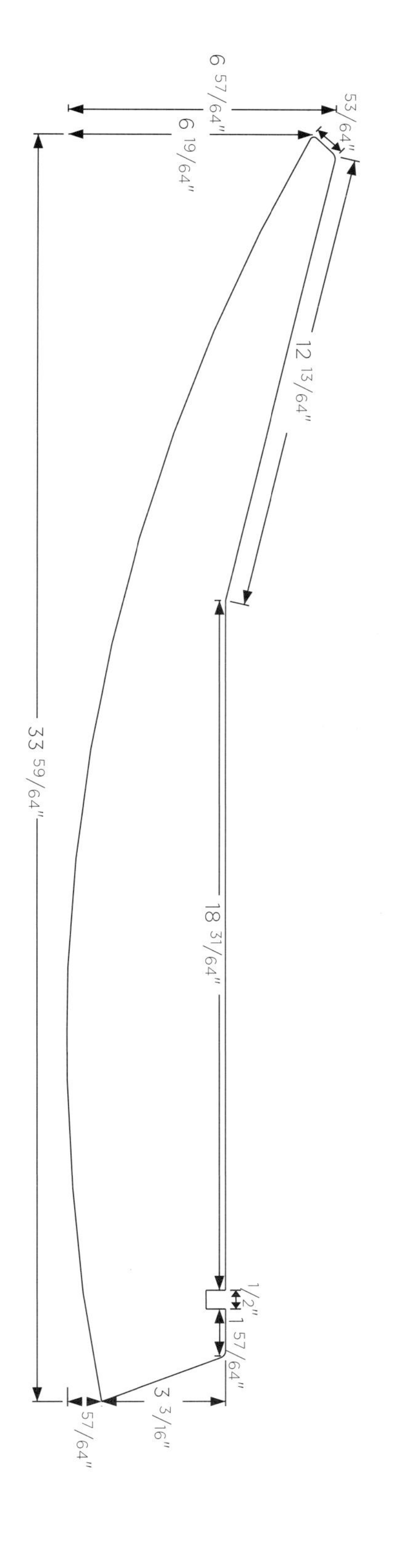

REAR LEG DETAIL VIEW

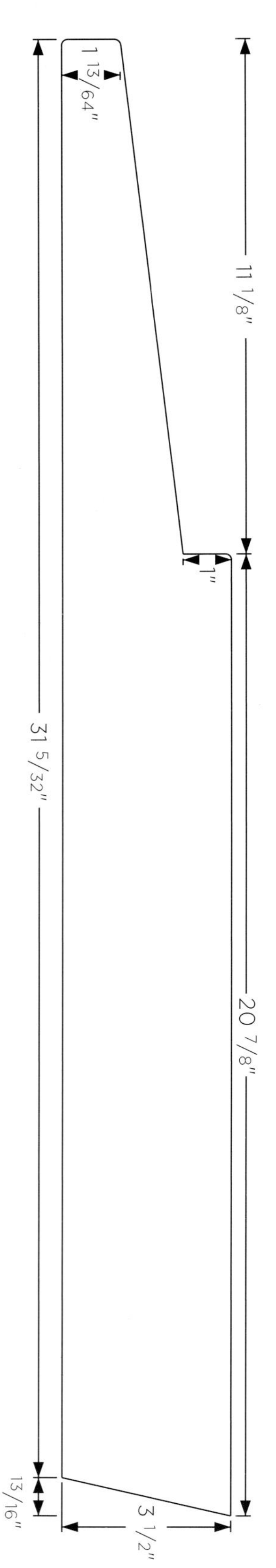

ARM DETAIL TOP VIEW

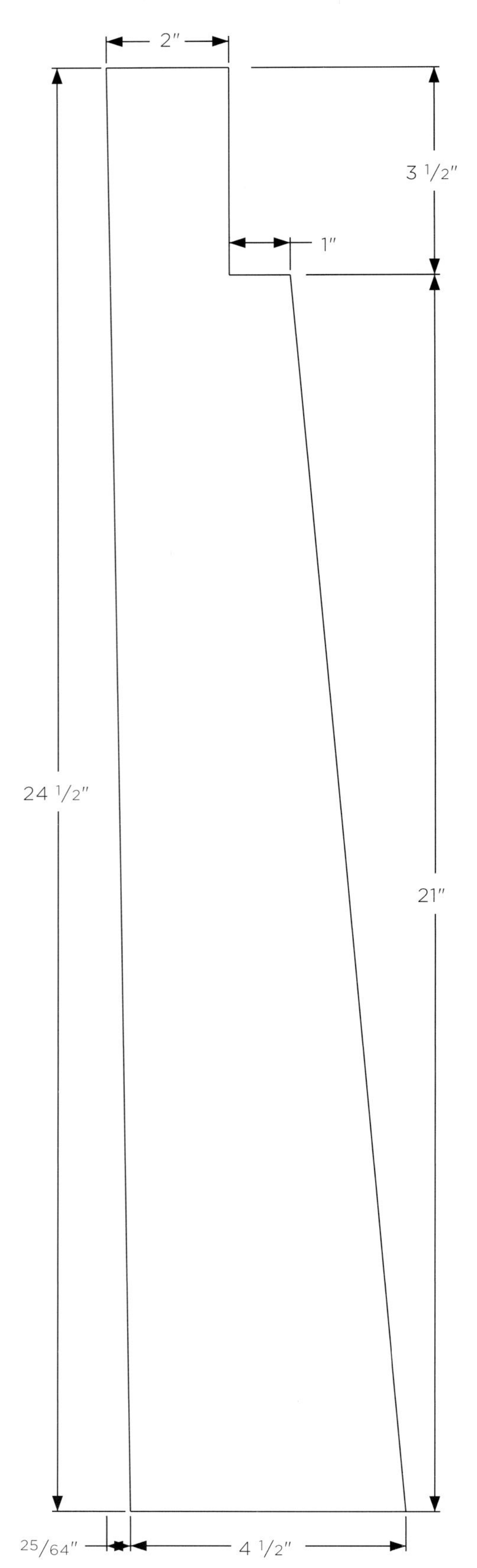

No. 700

STANDING DESK

45″ high x 38″ wide x 15″ deep — $11.00 (1903)

The dropfront desktop and shallow depth might make for a less-than-ideal desk, but the Japanese influence — the legs and overhanging top evoke a *torii* gate — make it a conversation piece. Nor does the distinctive form require complicated construction. The original was screwed together through plugged holes in the sides, possibly to allow for flat shipping from the factory. To increase utility, pigeonholes or shallow drawers could be substituted for the slats in the center compartment.

EXPLODED VIEW

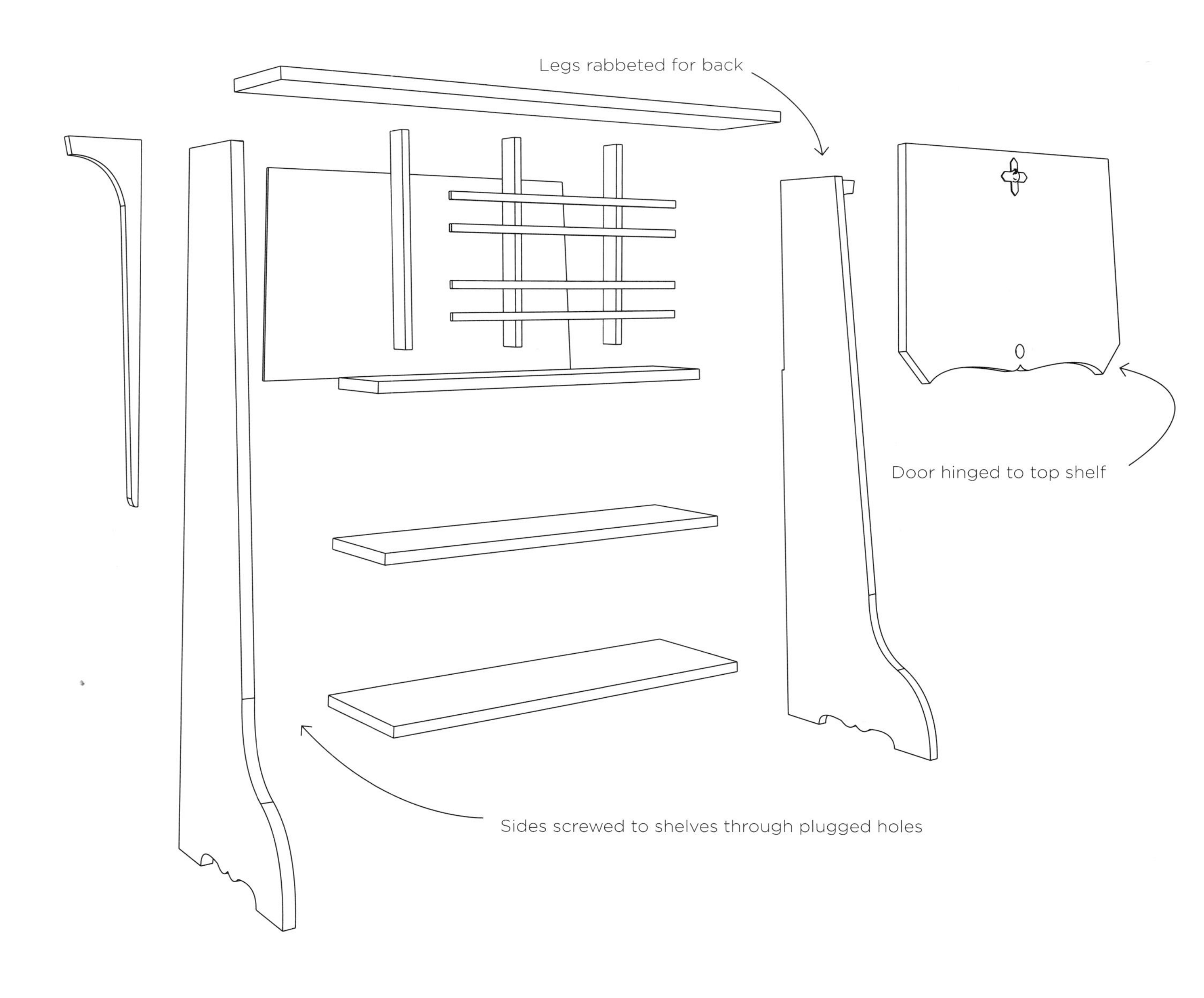

PART LIST

Qty	Description	Length	Width	Thickness
1	back panel	25 15/16"	15"	1/4"
1	bottom shelf *	27 11/16"	8 3/4"	3/4"
2	corbel	21 7/32"	4"	3/4"
1	middle shelf *	26 9/16"	7"	3/4"
4	pigeonhole rail	17 23/64"	1/2"	1/4"
3	pigeonhole stile	14 1/4"	1 1/2"	1/2"
2	side	44 1/4"	15"	3/4"
1	top	38"	6 1/2"	3/4"
1	top shelf *	25 7/16"	5 1/4"	3/4"

* shelf ends are cut at 3° angles

WITHOUT DOOR FRONT VIEW

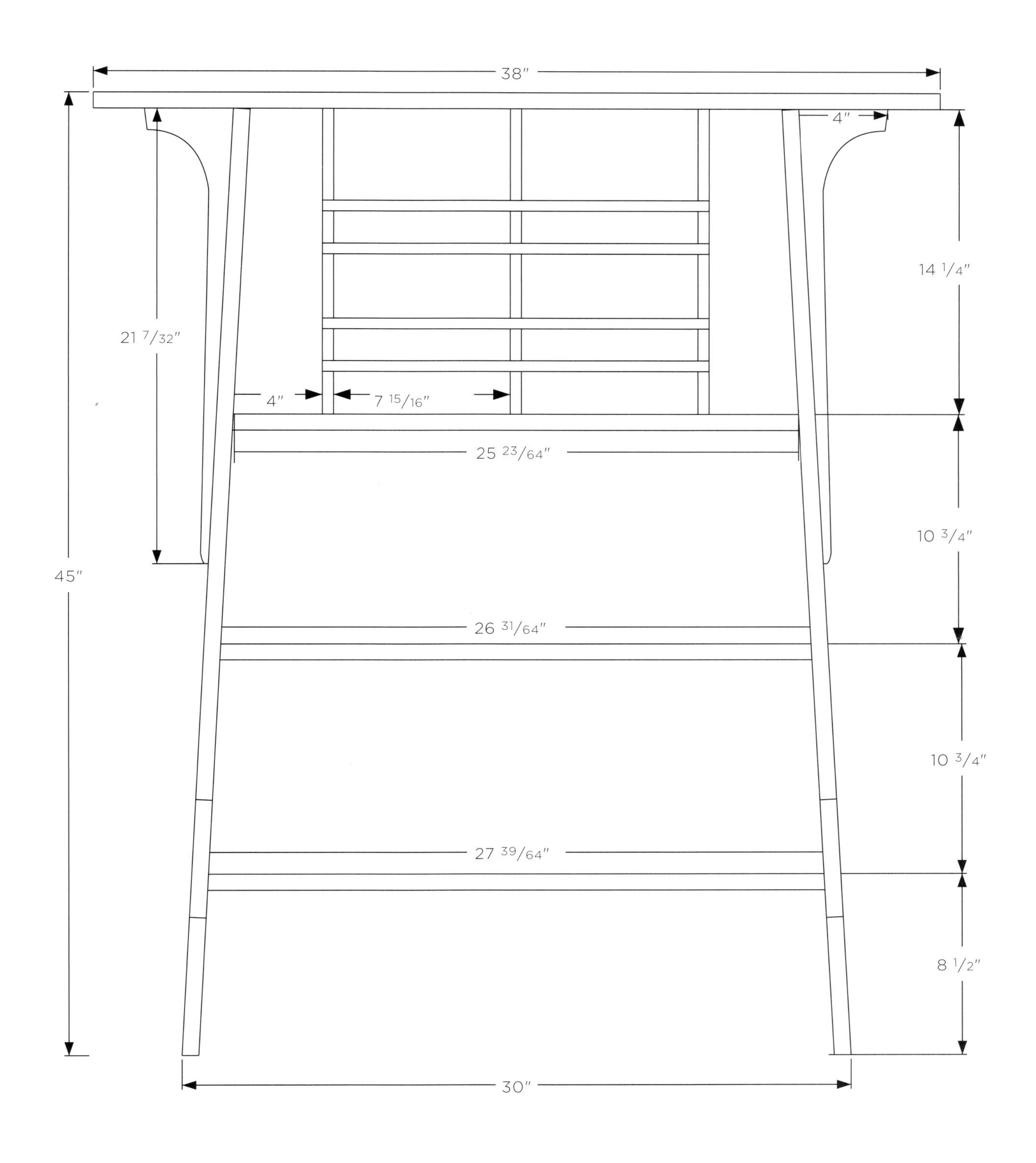

FRONT VIEW

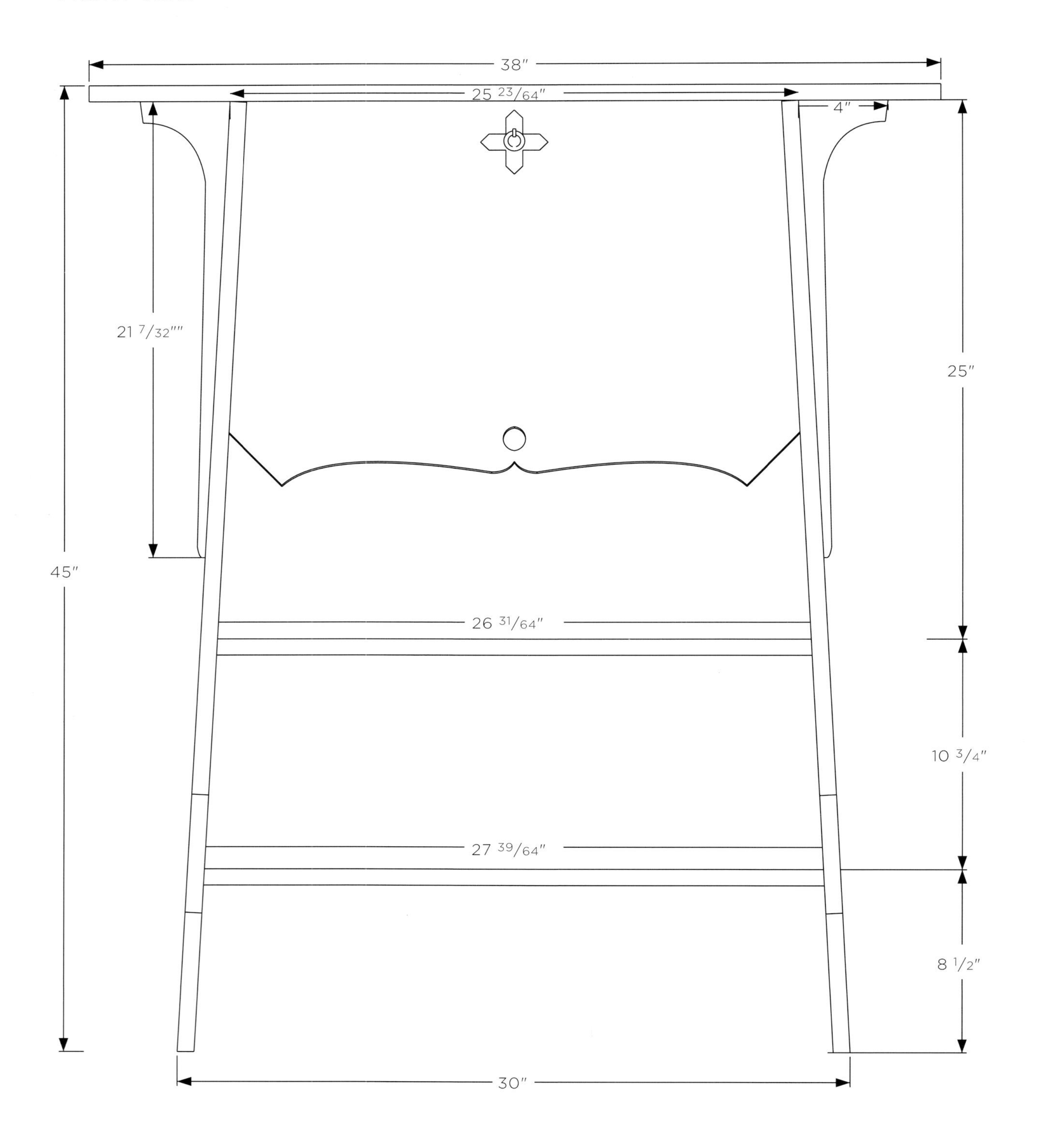

38″
25 23/64″
4″
21 7/32″″
25″
45″
26 31/64″
10 3/4″
27 39/64″
8 1/2″
30″

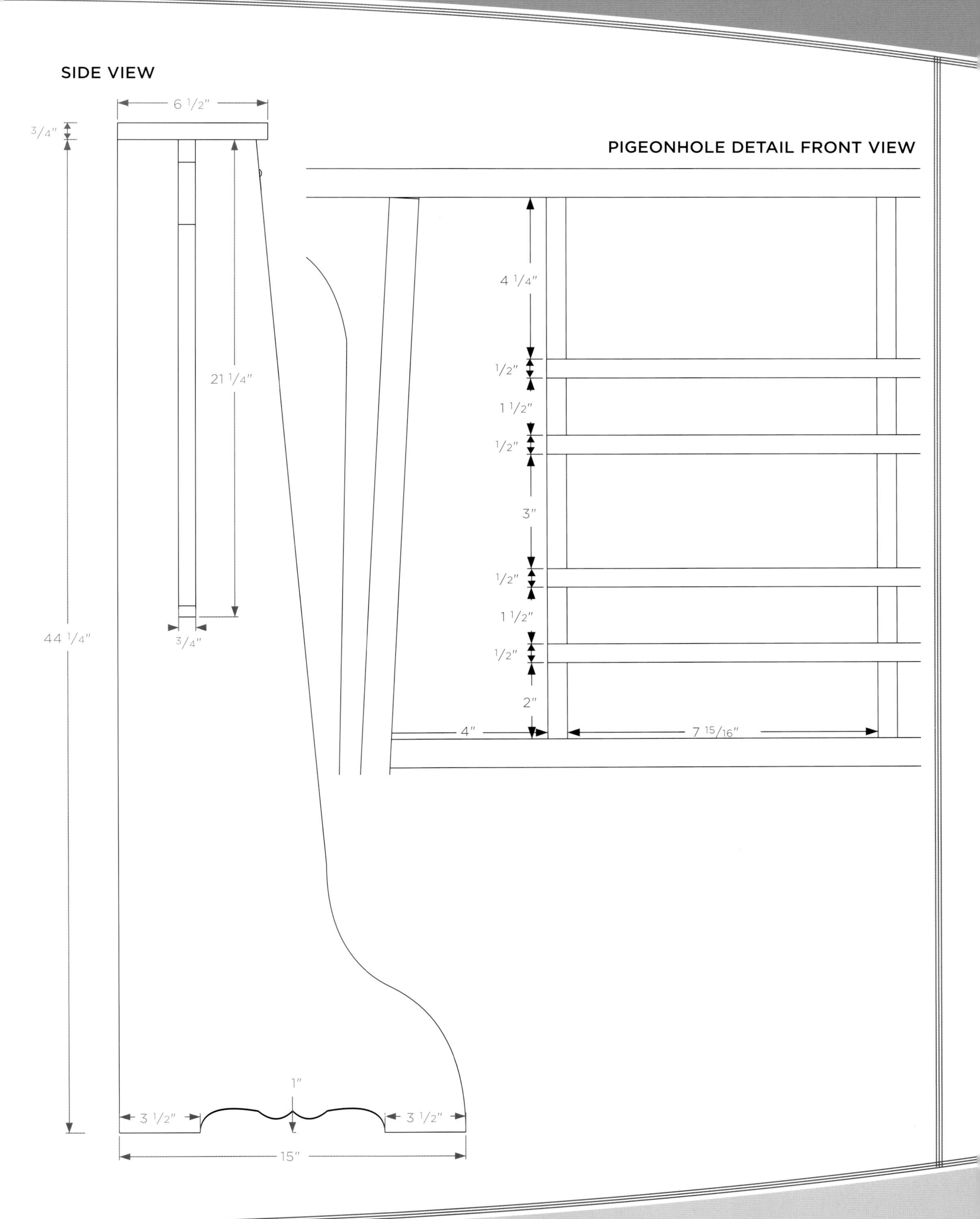

SIDE VIEW
6 1/2"
3/4"
21 1/4"
3/4"
44 1/4"
1"
3 1/2"
3 1/2"
15"
PIGEONHOLE DETAIL FRONT VIEW
4 1/4"
1/2"
1 1/2"
1/2"
3"
1/2"
1 1/2"
1/2"
2"
4"
7 15/16"

No. 736

DESK

38 1/2" high x 3" wide x 2" deep

This desk exhibits a strong Mission influence. The small footprint includes a surprising amount of storage, and small drawers substituted for the pigeonholes would make that space more usable.

EXPLODED VIEW

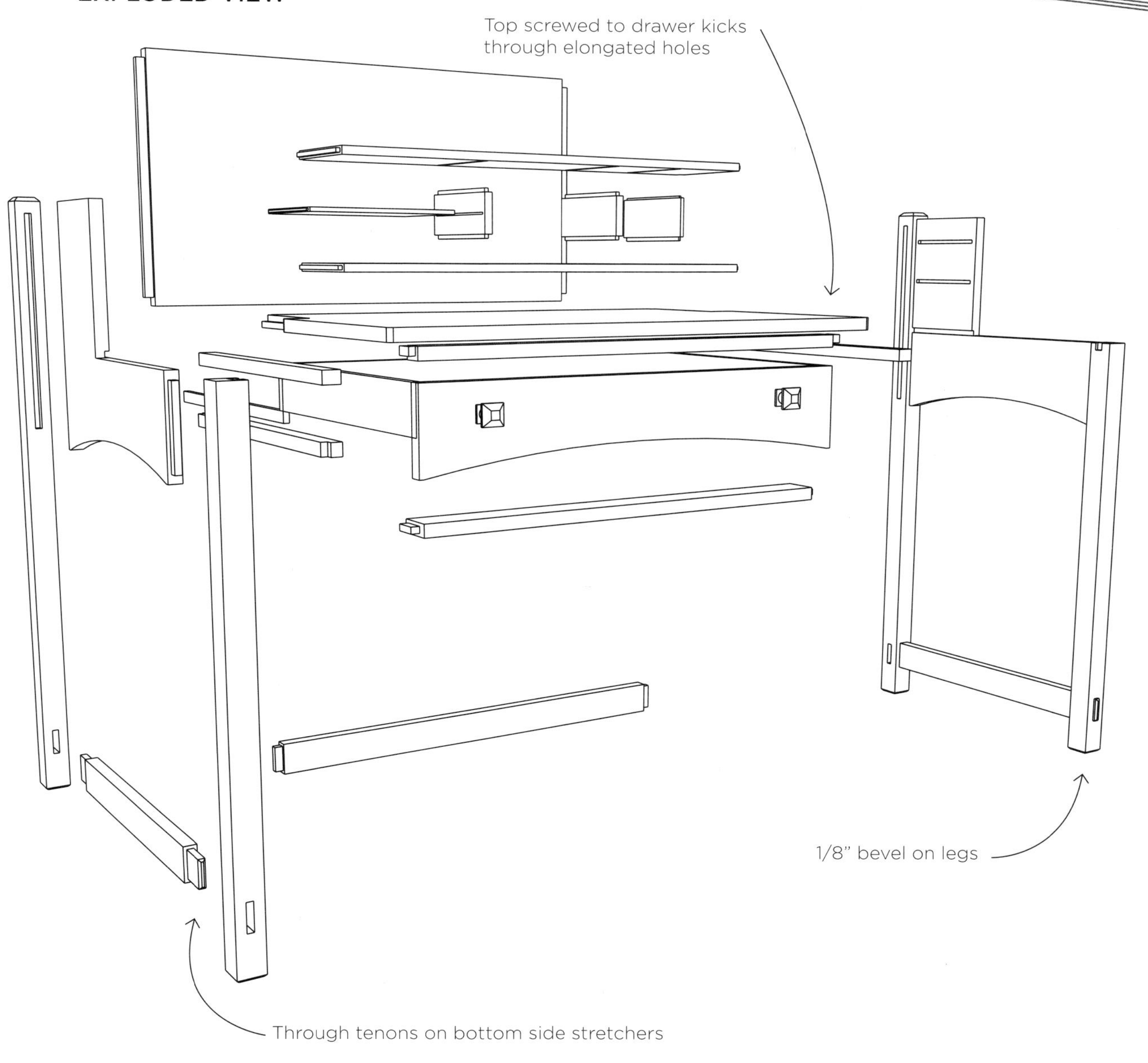

PART LIST

Qty	Description	Length	Width	Thickness
1	back	28"	14 1/2"	3/4"
2	divider	6 1/4"	3"	1/2"
1	drawer bottom	26 1/2"	17 3/8"	1/4"
1	drawer front	27"	2 7/8"	1/2"
1	drawer face	27"	5"	3/4"
2	drawer guide	17"	3/4"	3/8"
2	drawer kick	17"	1"	3/4"
2	drawer side	17 3/8"	2 7/8"	1/2"
2	drawer runner	17 3/4"	1"	3/4"
2	front leg	29 1/4"	1 1/2"	1 1/2"
1	front stretcher	28"	1 1/8"	3/4"
2	rear leg	38 1/2"	1 1/2"	1 1/2"
1	rear stretcher	28"	2"	3/4"
2	shelf	28 1/4"	6 1/4"	1/2"
2	side	18"	14 1/2"	3/4"
2	side stretcher	20 1/2"	2"	3/4"
1	small divider	6 1/4"	2 7/8"	1/4"
1	small shelf	9 7/32"	6 1/4"	1/4"
1	top	31"	19 3/8"	3/4"
1	webframe rail	26 3/4"	2"	3/4"

FRONT VIEW

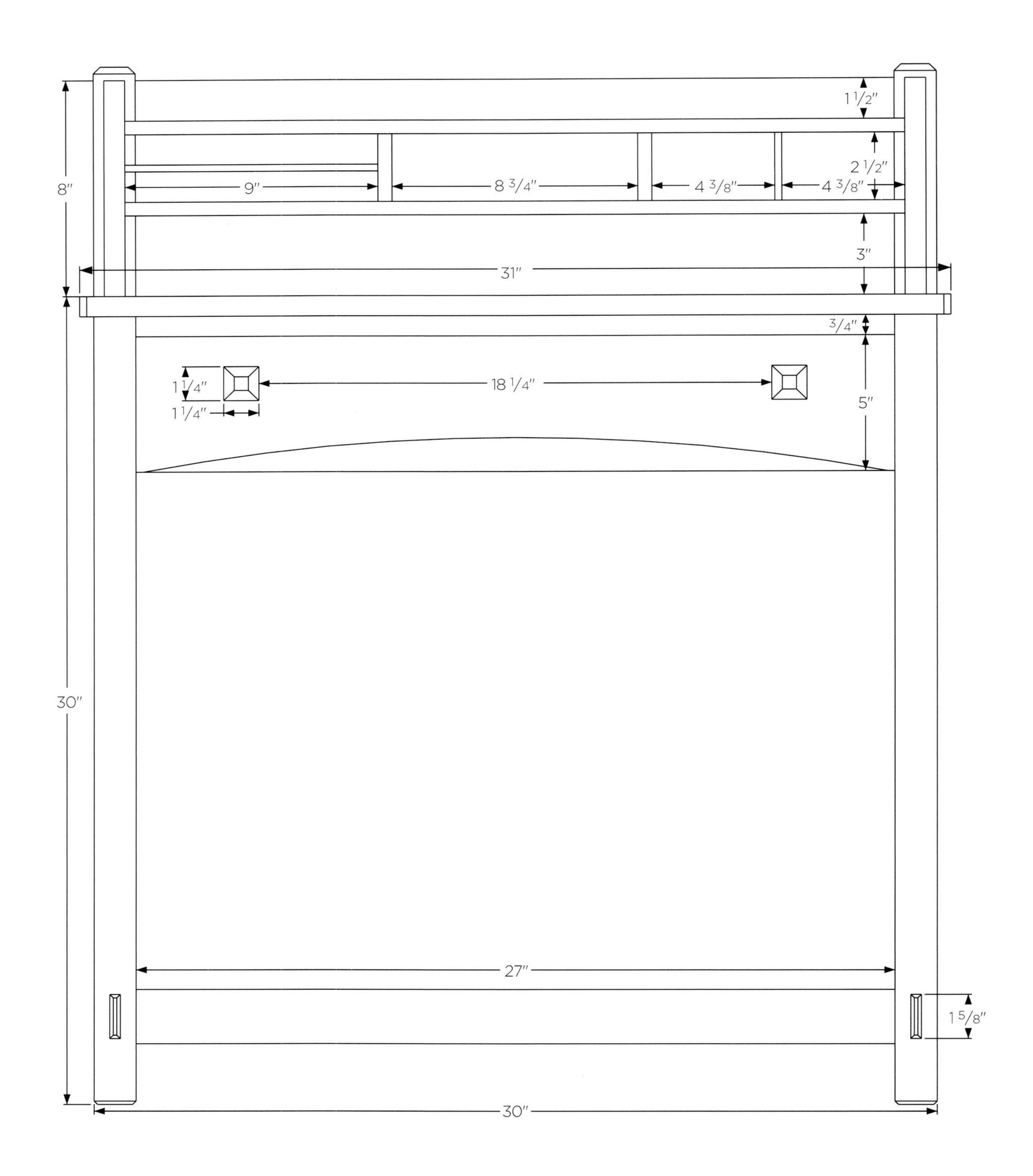

SIDE VIEW

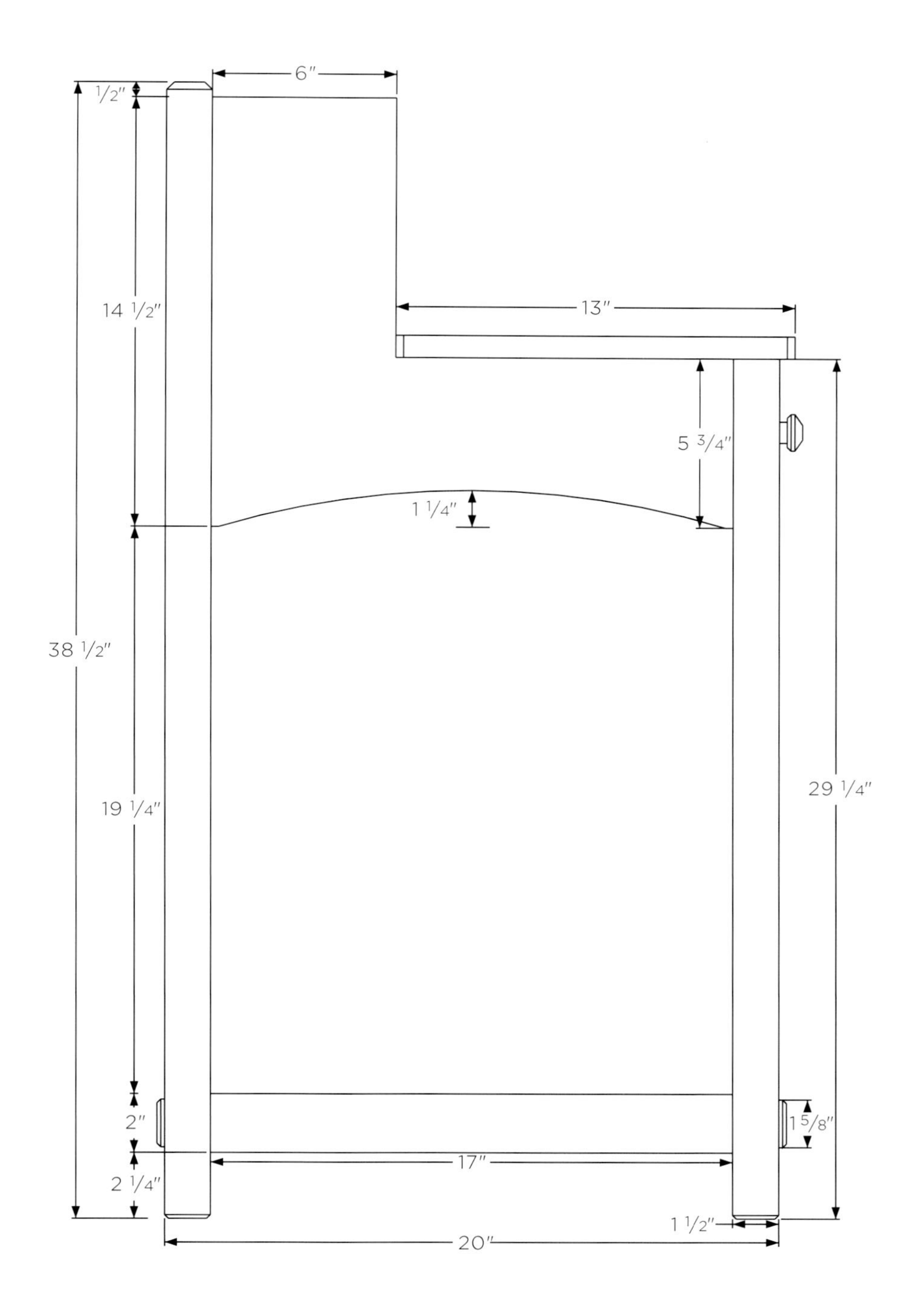

TOP VIEW

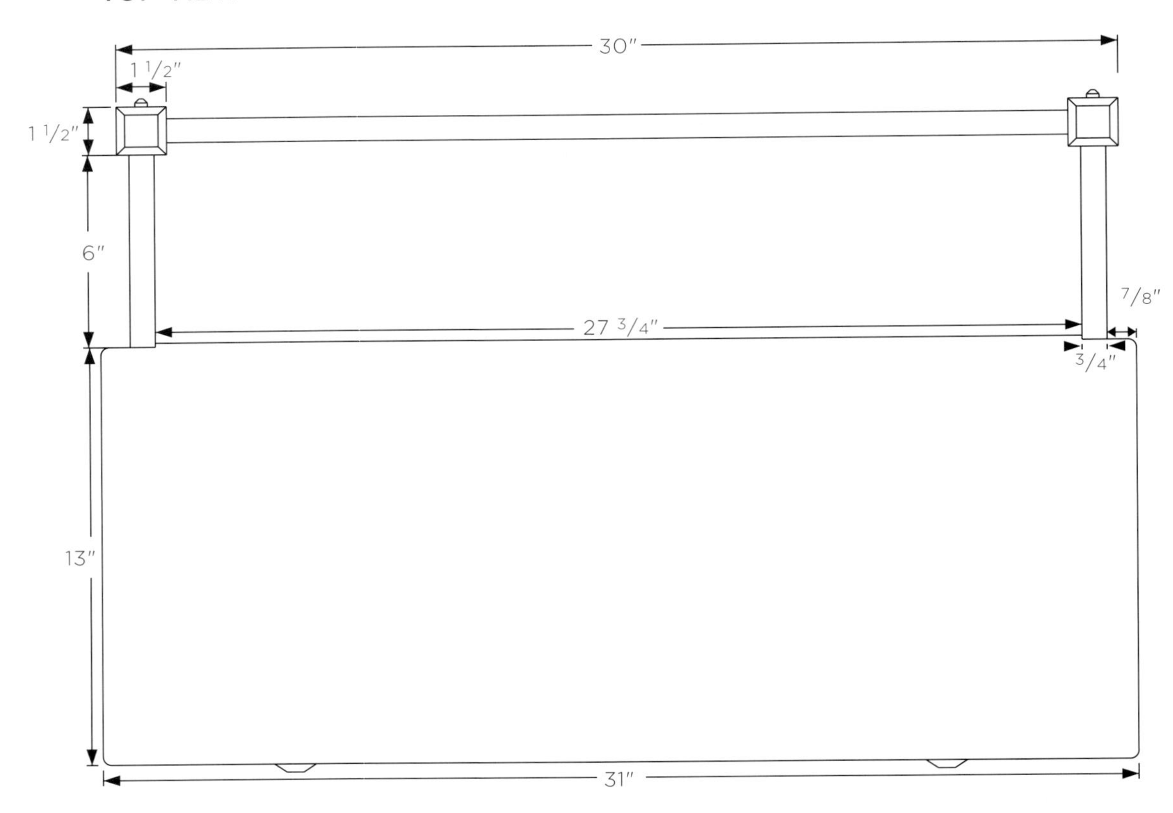

TOP SECTION VIEW

No. 1162

LIBRARY TABLE

29″ high x 42″ wide x 28 1/2″ deep

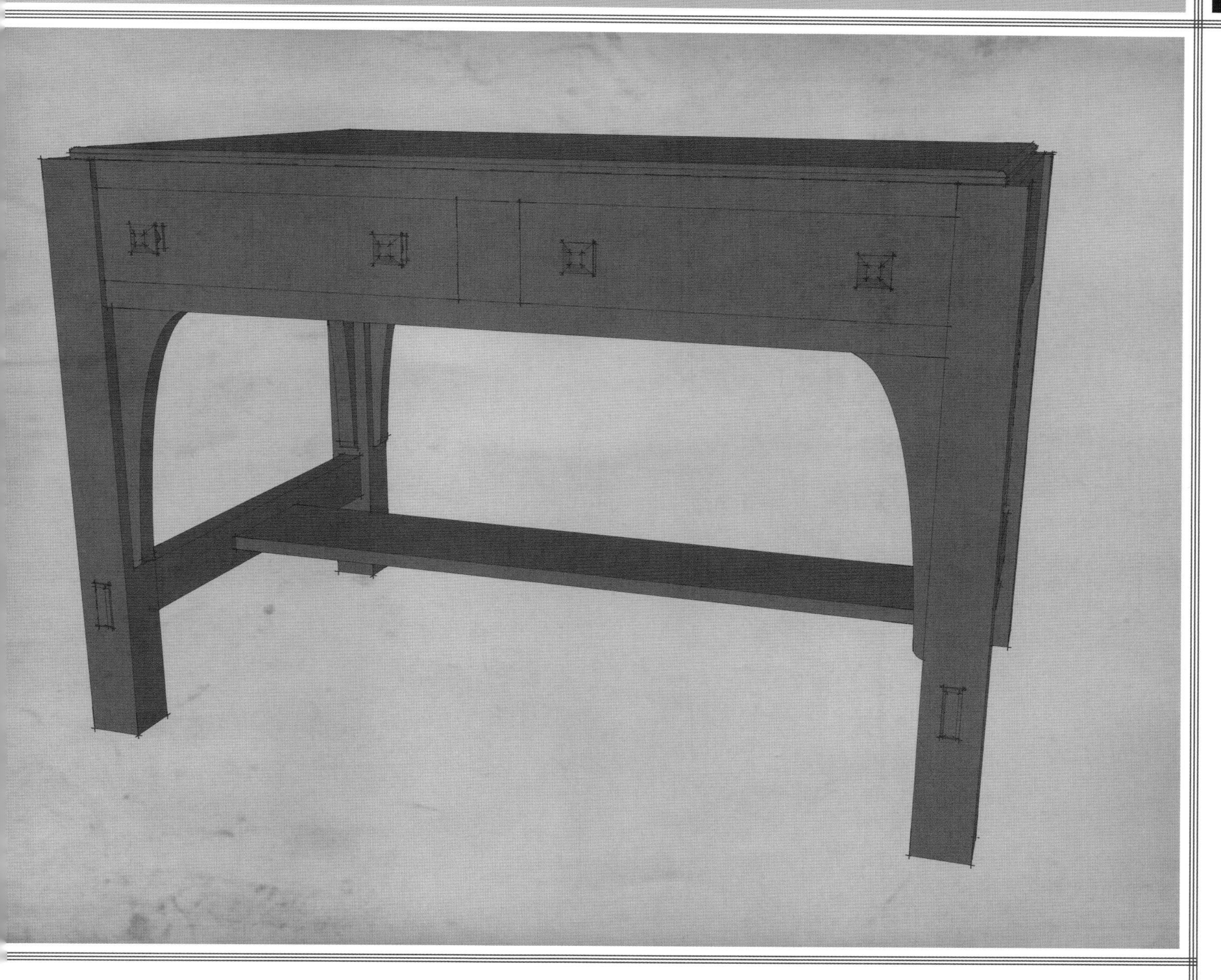

Corbels and the rounded edges of the inset top help lighten the heavy lines of the No. 1162, but this is still a massive form more suited for larger spaces. Despite the desk's size, the long stretcher restricts legroom, and could be eliminated.

EXPLODED VIEW

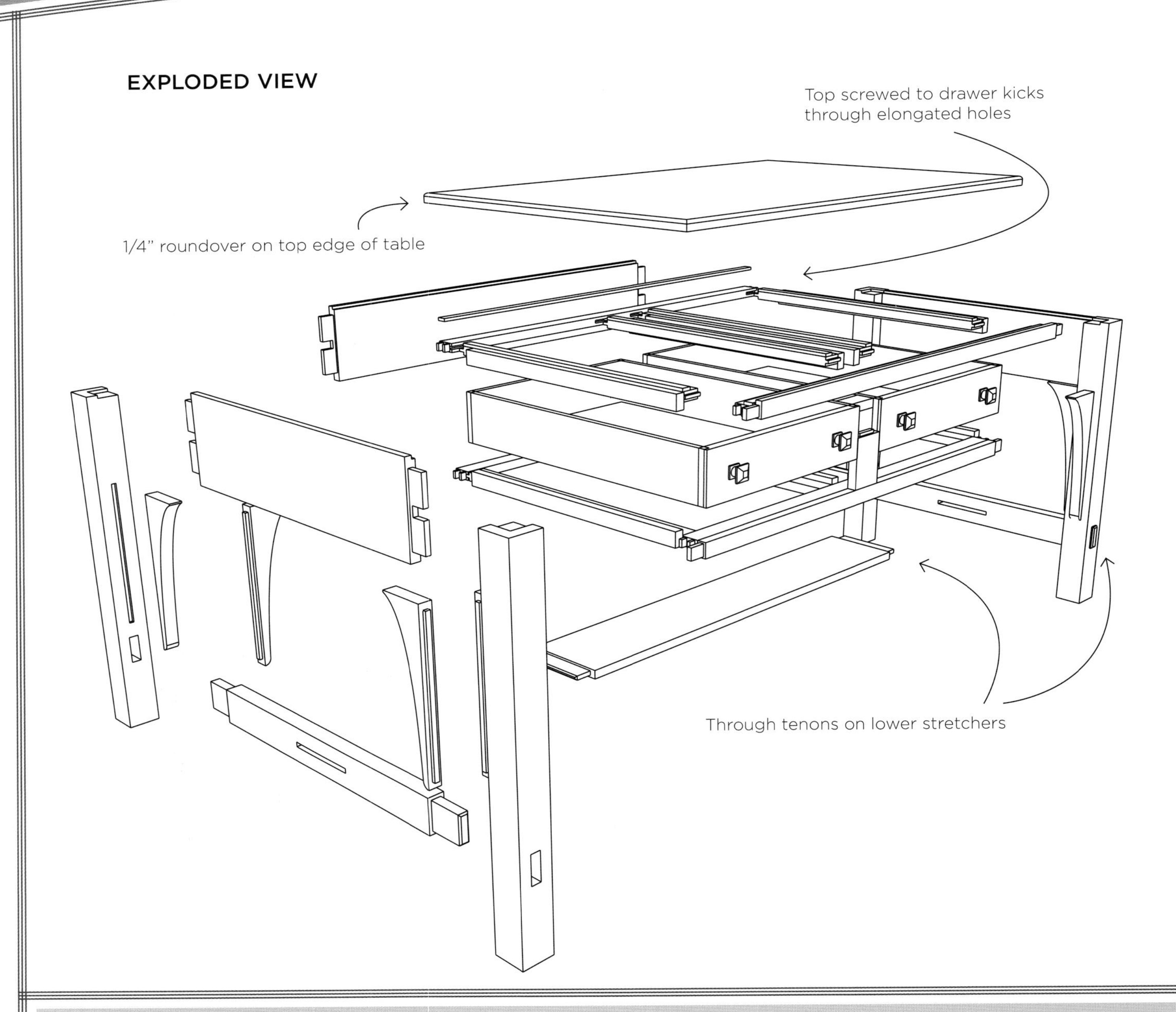

PART LIST

Qty	Description	Length	Width	Thickness
1	back apron	39 1/2"	6 3/4"	3/4"
8	corbel	13"	3 3/4"	1"
2	drawer back	17 1/8"	4 1/4"	1/2"
1	drawer block	2 3/4"	1 1/2"	3/4"
2	drawer bottom	24 1/4"	16 5/8"	1/4"
1	drawer divider	4 3/4"	2 3/4"	3/4"
2	drawer front	17 1/8"	4 1/4"	3/4"
8	drawer guide	22"	1 1/4"	3/4"
4	drawer side	25"	4 1/4"	1/2"
1	lower front apron	39 1/2"	1 1/4"	3/4"
1	upper apron	39 1/2"	1 1/4"	3/4"

Qty	Description	Length	Width	Thickness
4	knob	1 1/4"	1 1/4"	1 1/8"
4	leg	28 1/2"	2 1/2"	2 1/2"
2	long fill strip	37"	3/4"	1/4"
1	long stretcher	41 1/4"	6 3/4"	3/4"
4	short fill strip	23 1/8"	3/4"	1/4"
2	side apron	26"	6 3/4"	3/4"
2	side stretcher	29"	2 3/4"	1 1/4"
1	top	40 1/4"	26 3/4"	3/4"
4	web frame rail	38"	1 1/2"	3/4"
8	web frame stile	23 7/8"	1 1/2"	3/4"

FRONT VIEW

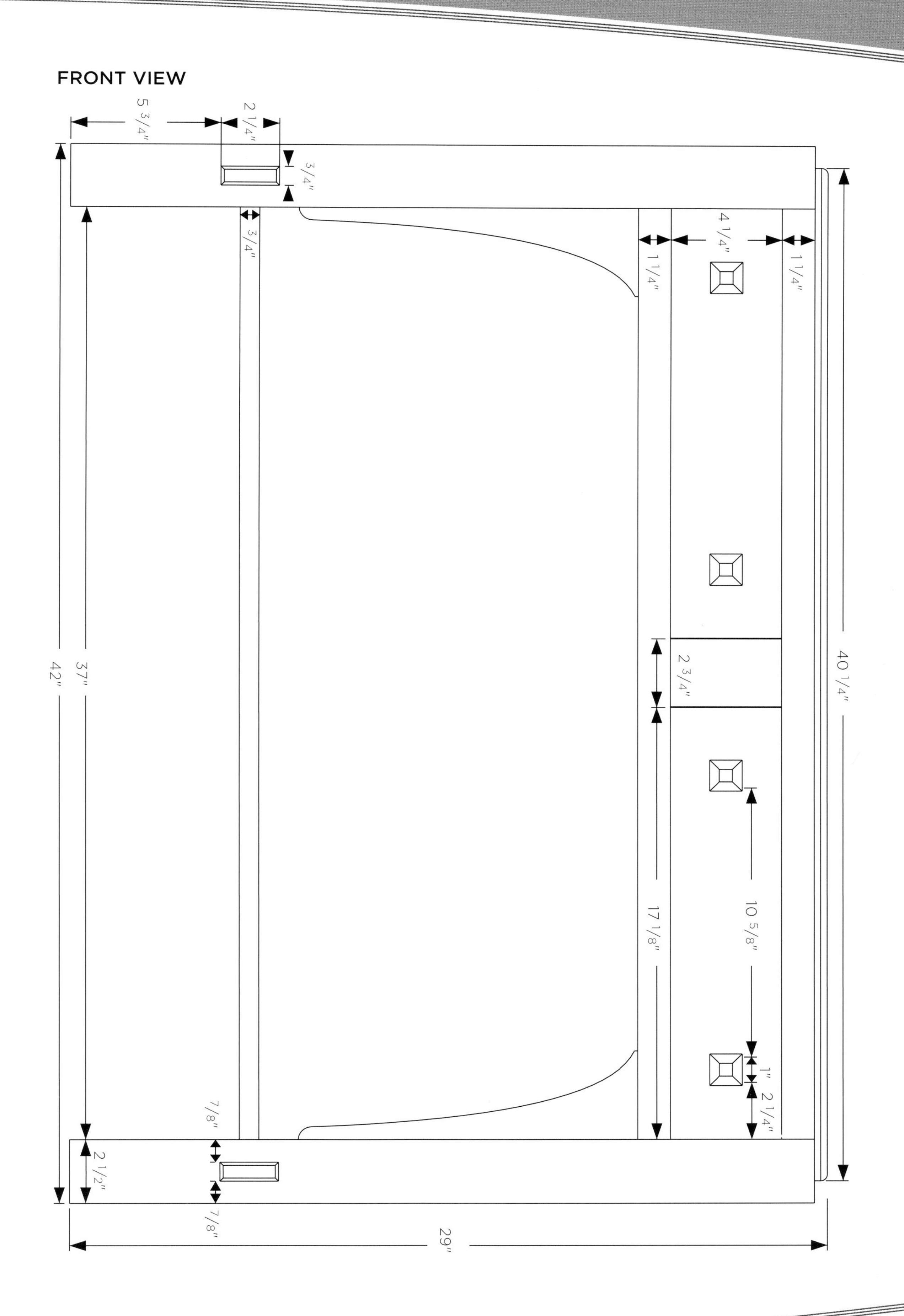
5 3/4"
2 1/4"
3/4"
3/4"
4 1/4"
1 1/4"
1 1/4"
42"
37"
2 3/4"
40 1/4"
17 1/8"
10 5/8"
1"
2 1/4"
7/8"
2 1/2"
7/8"
29"

TOP SECTION VIEW

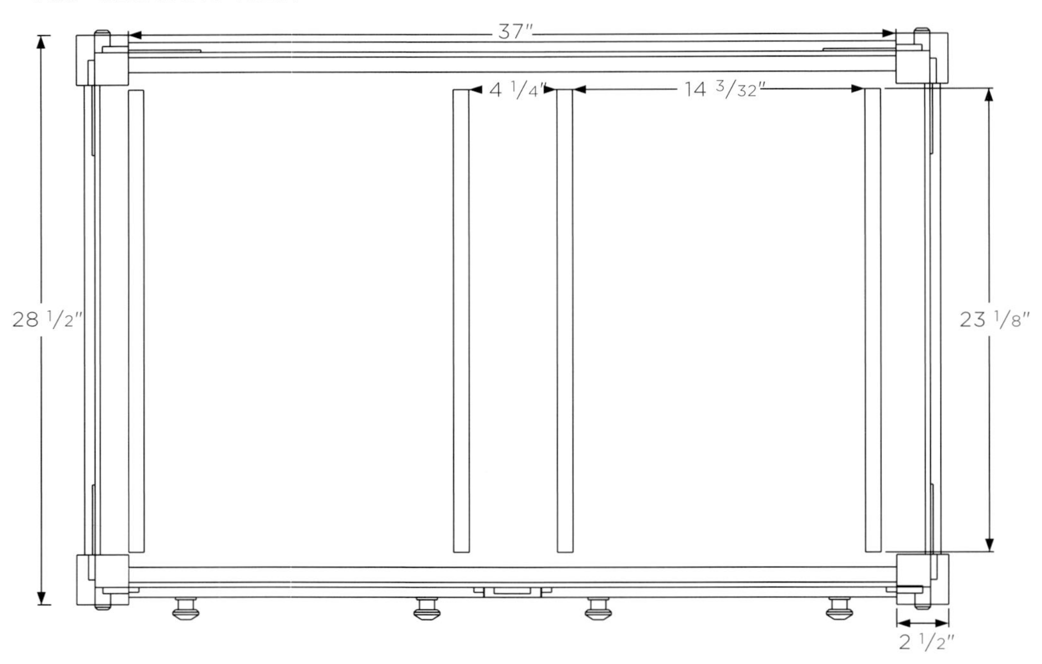

SIDE VIEW

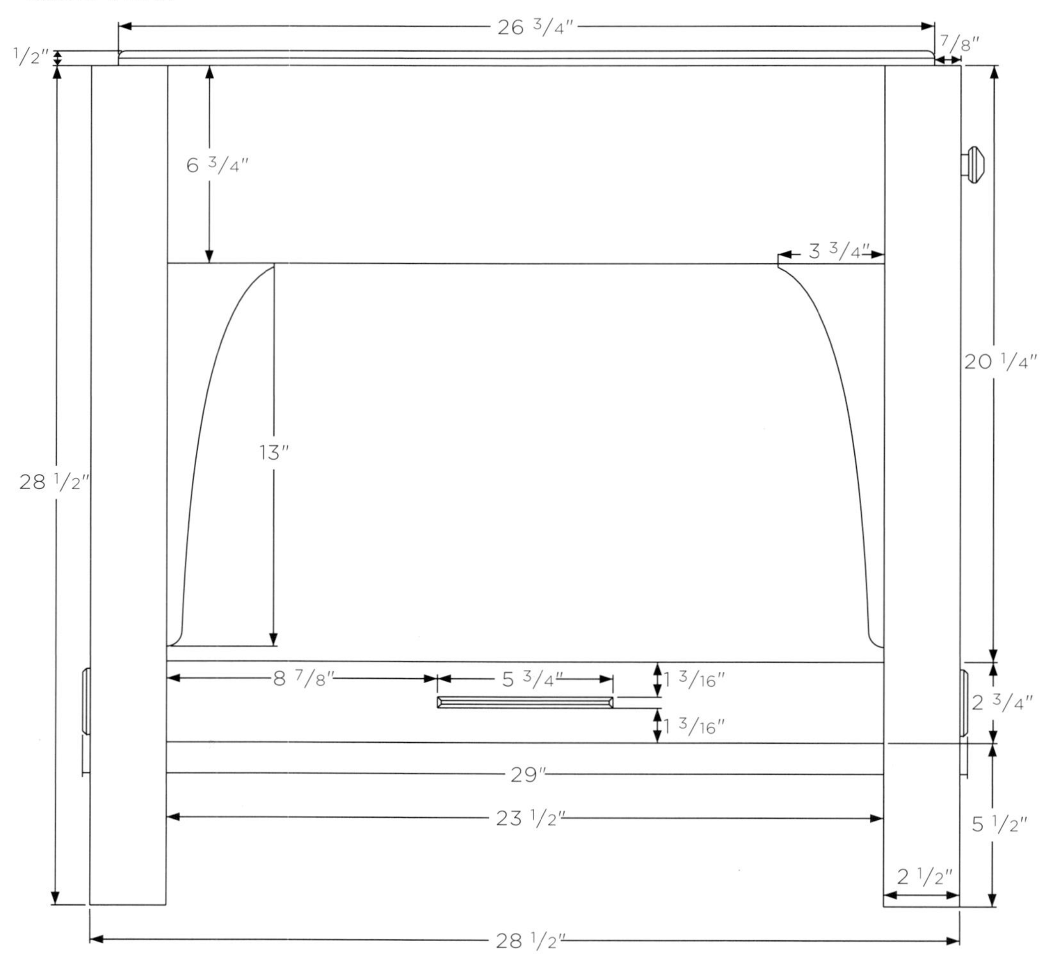

No. 243-1/2

BENCH

24″ high x 24″ wide x 18″ deep — $14.00 (1905)

This bench makes a convenient seat at the foot of a bed and is easily sized to match different bed sizes by altering the length of the front and back rails. If a cushion will be used with the bench, consider replacing the solid seat with a frame and webbing to support the cushion.

EXPLODED VIEW

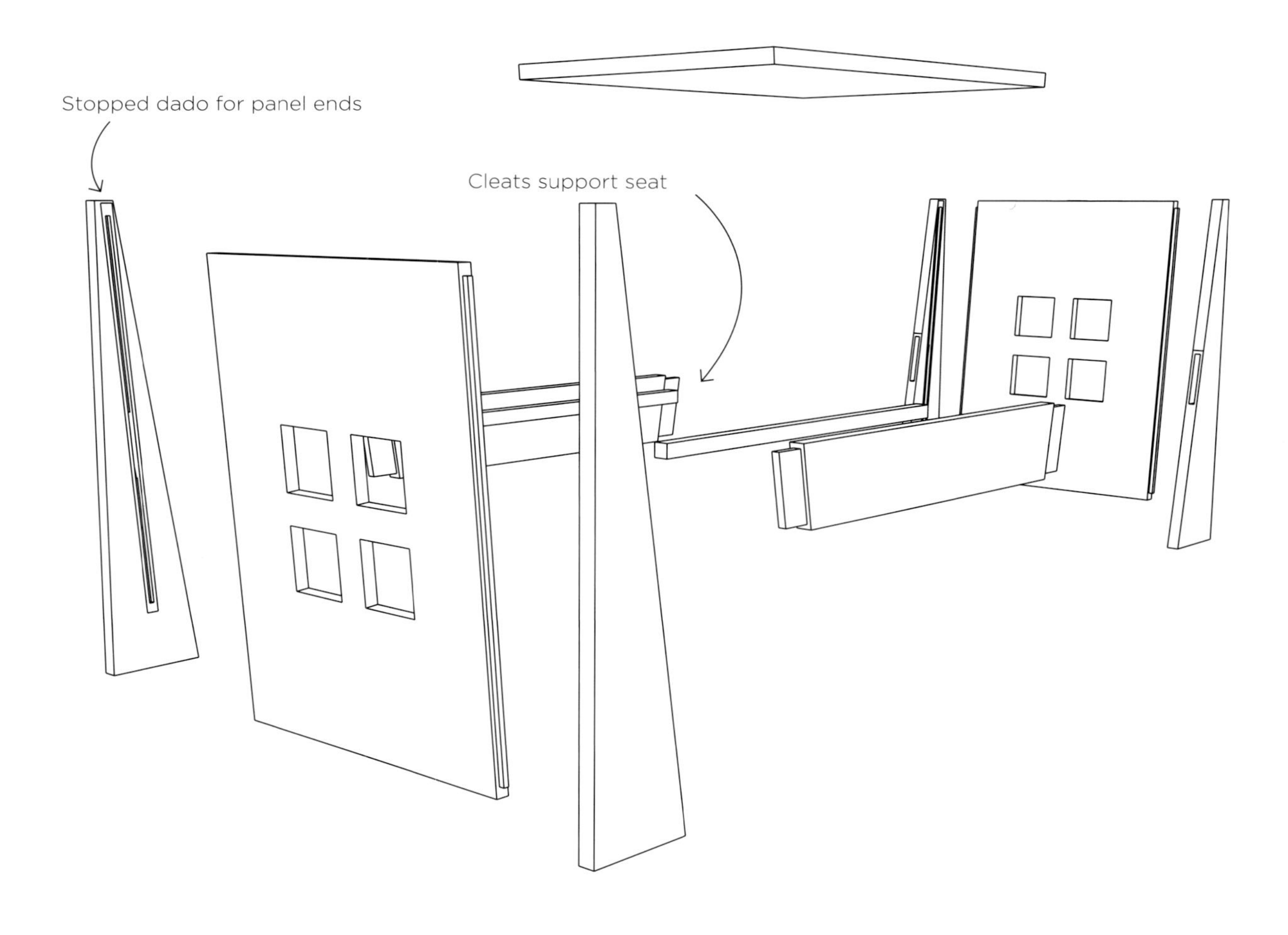

PART LIST

Qty	Description	Length	Width	Thickness
4	leg	24 1/2"	5"	3/4"
2	seat cleat	21 19/32"	3/4"	3/4"
2	panel	21 9/16"	16"	5/8"
1	seat	22 53/64"	15 1/2"	3/4"
2	stretcher	24"	4"	3/4"

FRONT SECTION VIEW

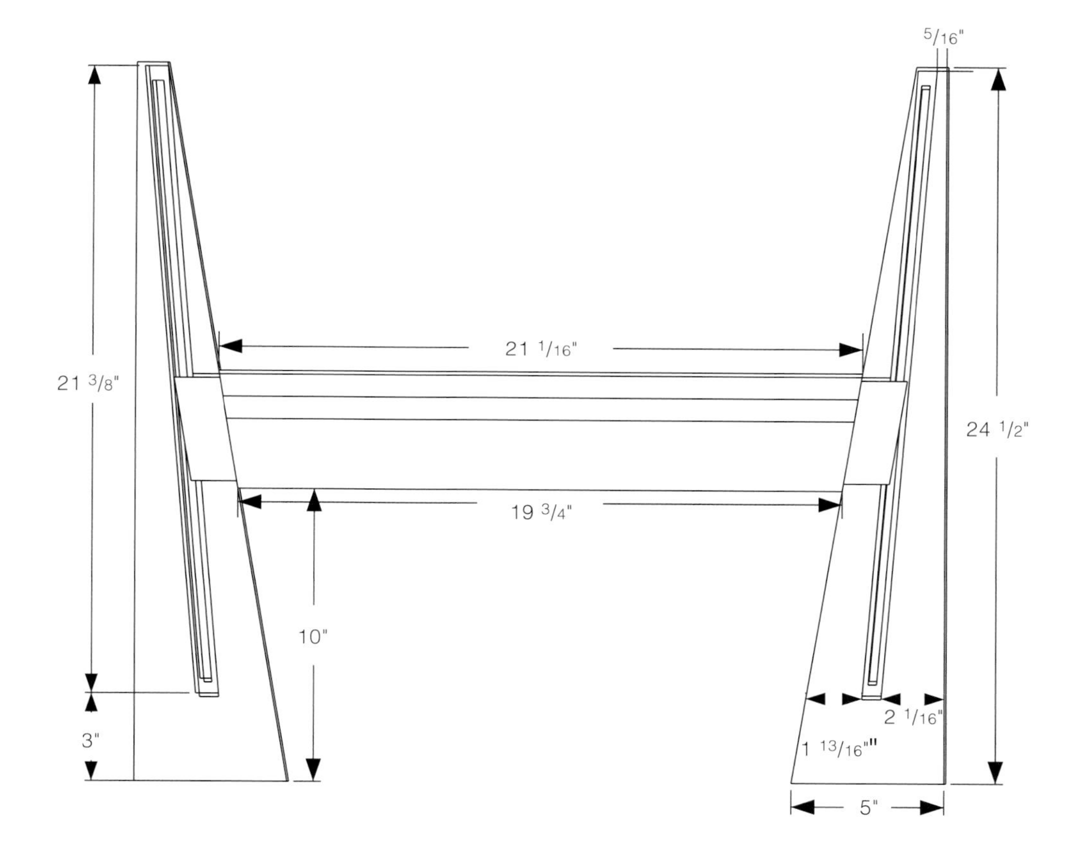

SIDE VIEW

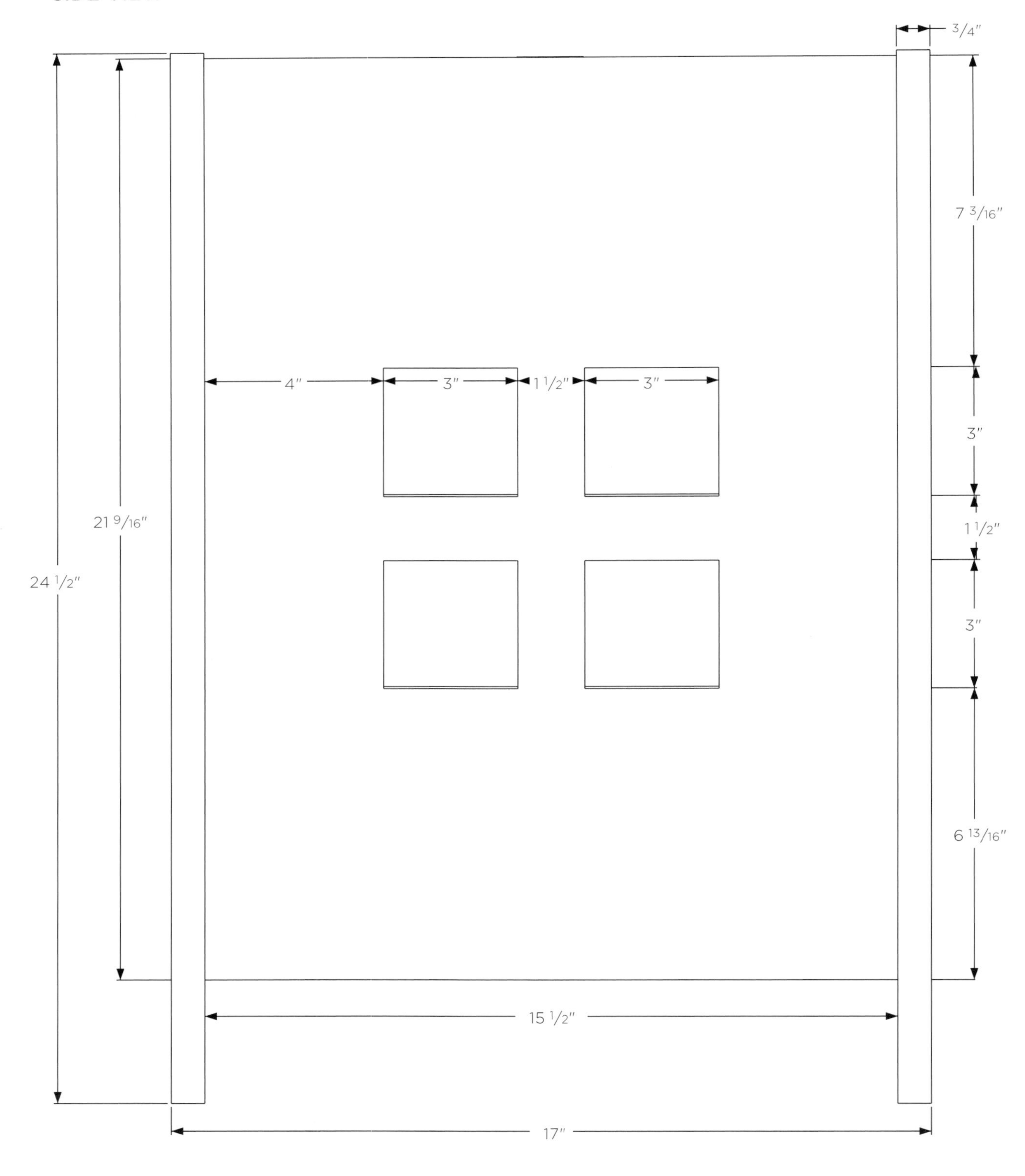

No. 470

BED

52″ high x 64.5″ wide x 86″ deep

Limbert bedroom pieces tend to be less distinctive than the furniture the company produced for more public spaces. At first glance, the No. 470 seems to follow this trend, but closer inspection reveals the subtle variation in thickness in the different frame members and the through tenons at the frame top and sides. As drawn here, the bed has been sized to accommodate a queen-sized matress by slightly extending the width of the center slats. The choice for bed irons or slats to support the box spring and mattress is left to the builder's discretion, as is whether to use bed bolts or other hardware to connect rails to footboard and headboard. Depending on the hardware used to attach the footboard and headboard to bedrails, the bedrails may need to be cut longer to accommodate tenons.

EXPLODED VIEW

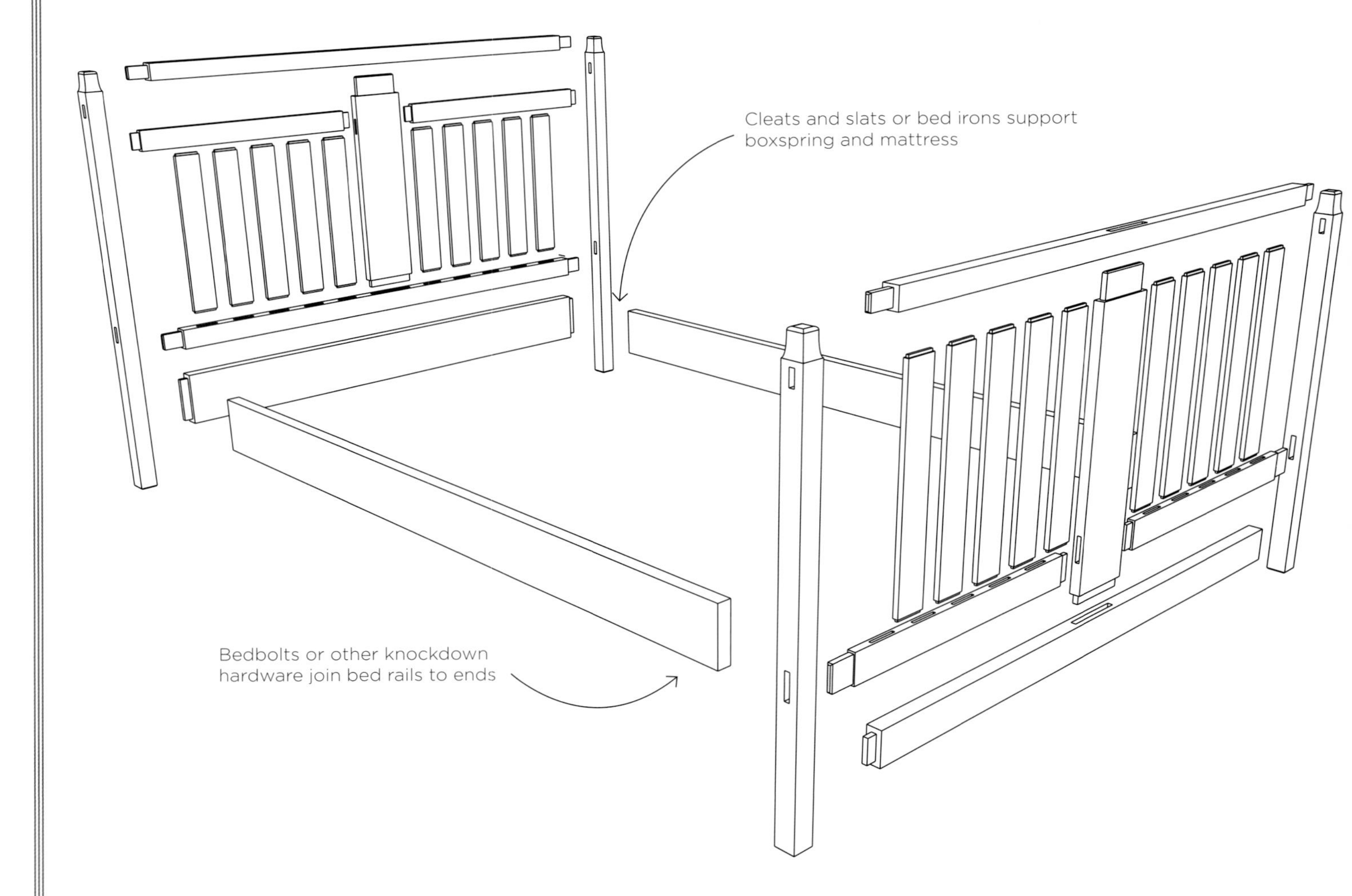

Cleats and slats or bed irons support boxspring and mattress
Bedbolts or other knockdown hardware join bed rails to ends

PART LIST

Qty	Description	Length	Width	Thickness
2	bedrail	82"	6 1/2"	1 1/2"
1	footboard bottom rail	62 1/2"	3 1/2"	1 1/2"
1	footboard center slat	31"	6 1/2"	1"
2	footboard leg	42"	2"	2"
2	footboard middle rail	30 1/2"	3"	3/4"
10	footboard slat	22"	3"	1/2"
1	footboard top rail	65 1/2"	2"	1 1/2"
1	headboard bottom rail	62 1/2"	6 1/2"	1 1/2"
2	headboard leg	52"	2"	2"
1	headboard lower middle rail	65 1/2"	2 1/2"	1 1/2"
10	headboard slat	20 1/4"	3"	1/2"
1	headboard center slat	28 1/2"	6 1/2"	1"
2	headboard upper middle rail	29"	2 1/2"	3/4"
1	headboard upper rail	65 1/2"	2"	1 1/2"

HEADBOARD FRONT VIEW

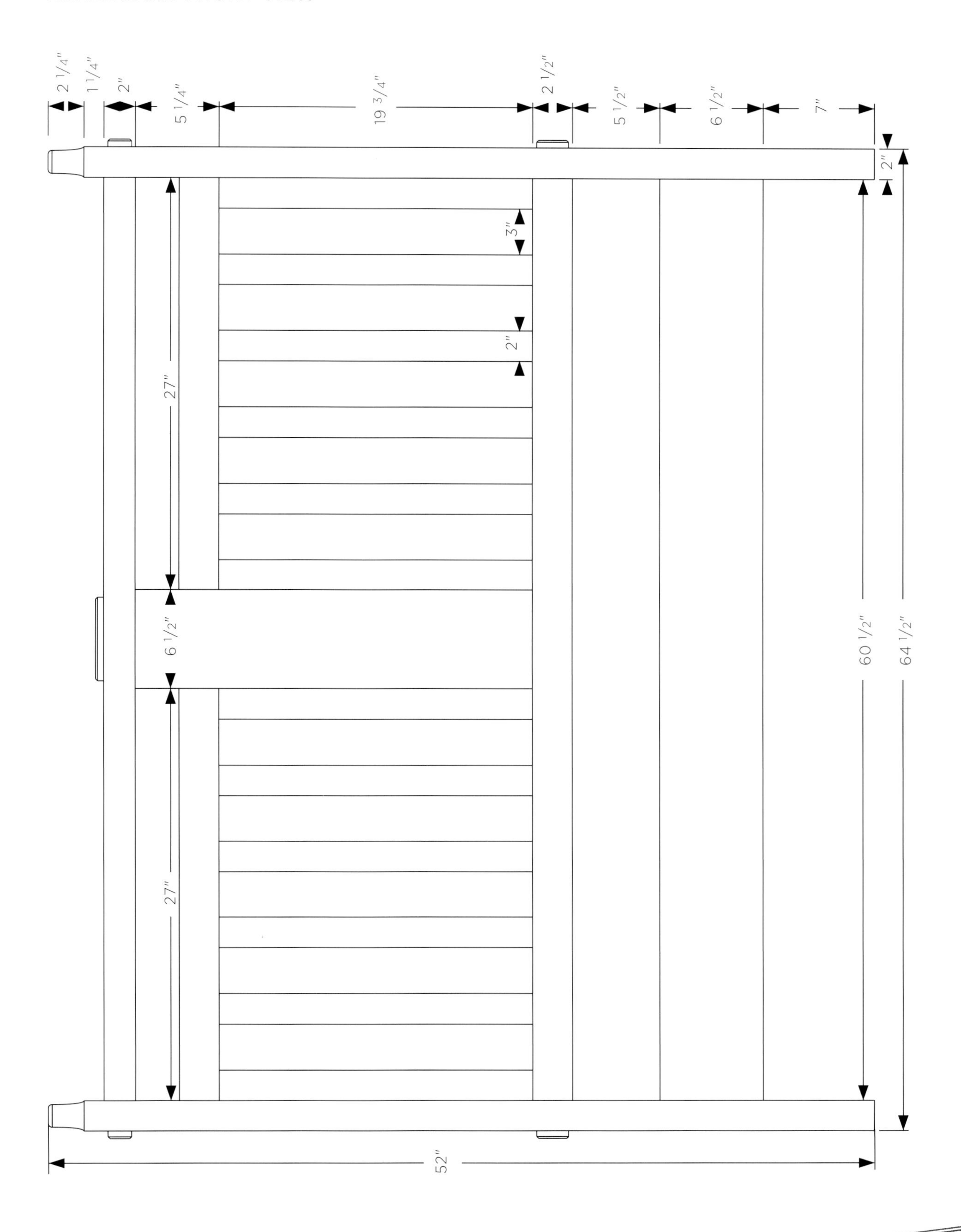

FOOTBOARD FRONT VIEW

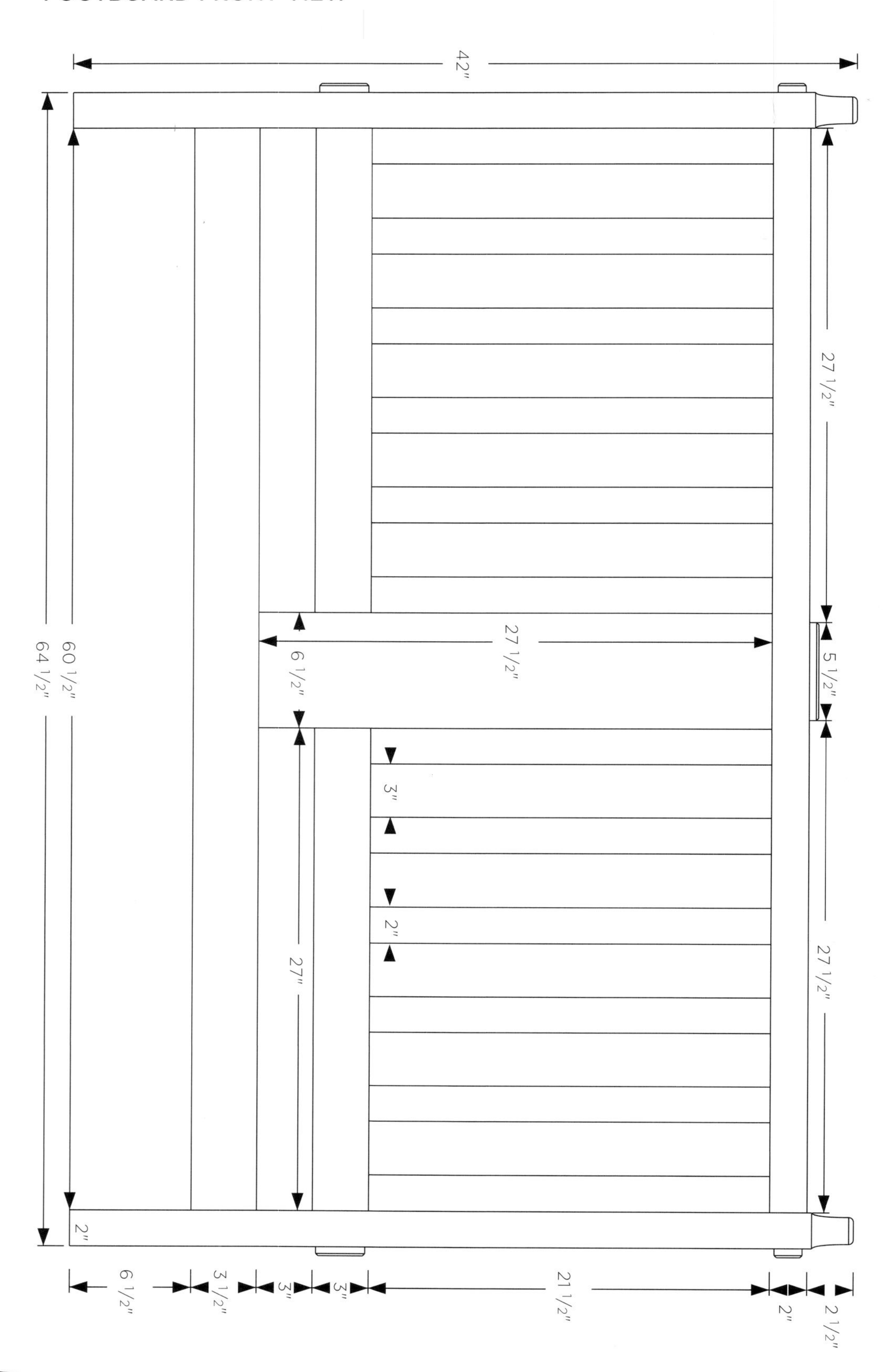

SIDE VIEW

19 1/4"
2"
25 1/2"
1 1/2"
1 1/2"
2 1/4"
2"
82"
7"
6 1/2"
2"
13 3/16"
2 5/8"
21 15/16"
1 1/2"
2 1/4"

No. 491

WARDROBE

69″ high x 50″ wide x 24″ deep

As thoughtful as Craftsman home designs can be, adequate closet space often seems to slip the architect's mind, so a wardrobe can be a convenient piece. The No. 491 shares inset top and through tenons common to much of Limbert's bedroom furniture (see also the No. 499 Somnoe in this chapter). The asymmetrical layout calls to mind Japanese *tansu*, and substituting different hardware would strenghten that connection. The original featured a rack for an umbrella in the large door and a slide-out hanger bar mounted front to back as well as a mirror hung on the small cupboard door. A bar mounted from side to side doesn't yield much additional hanging space, but it does make it easier to mount the bar.

EXPLODED VIEW

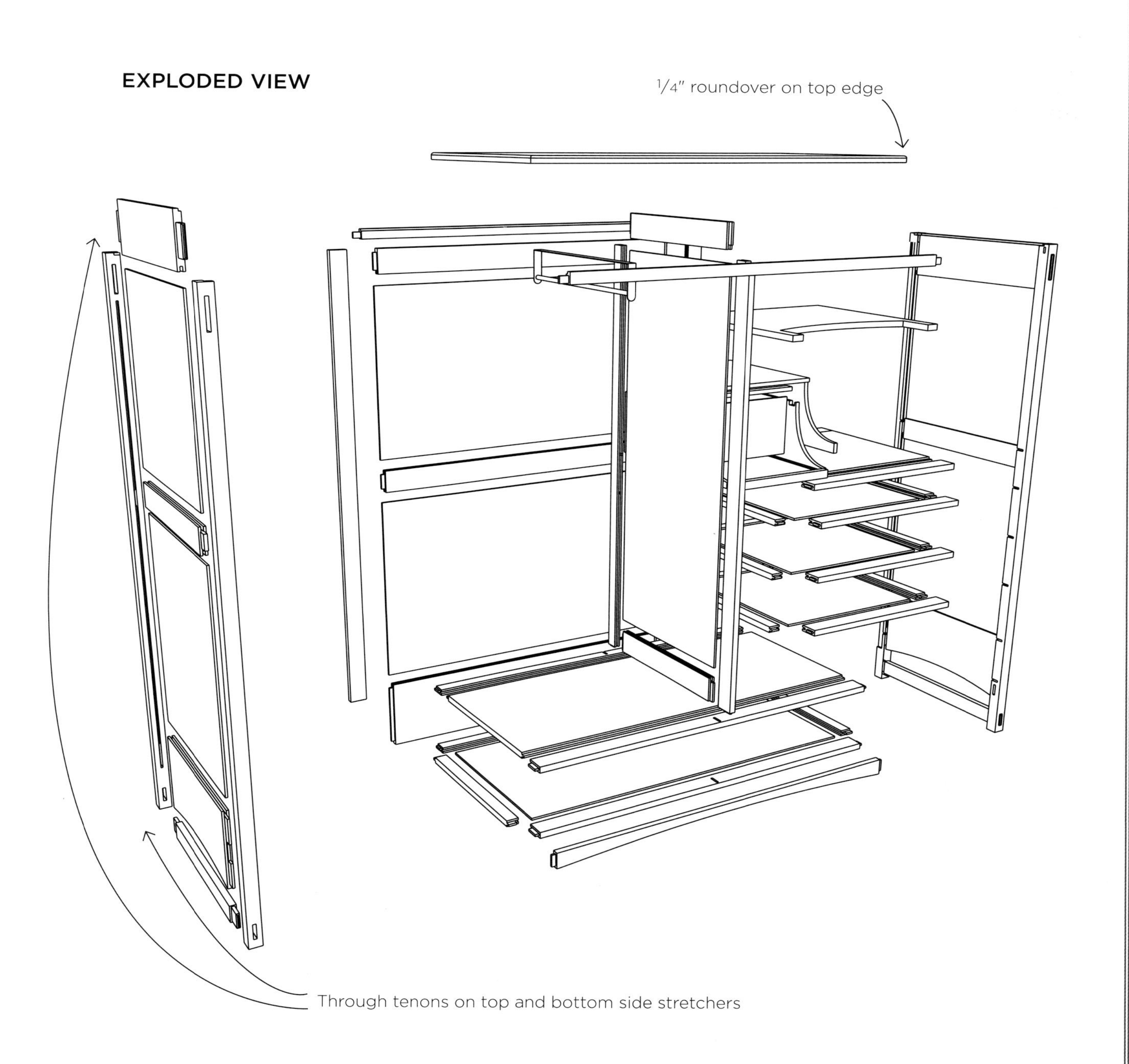

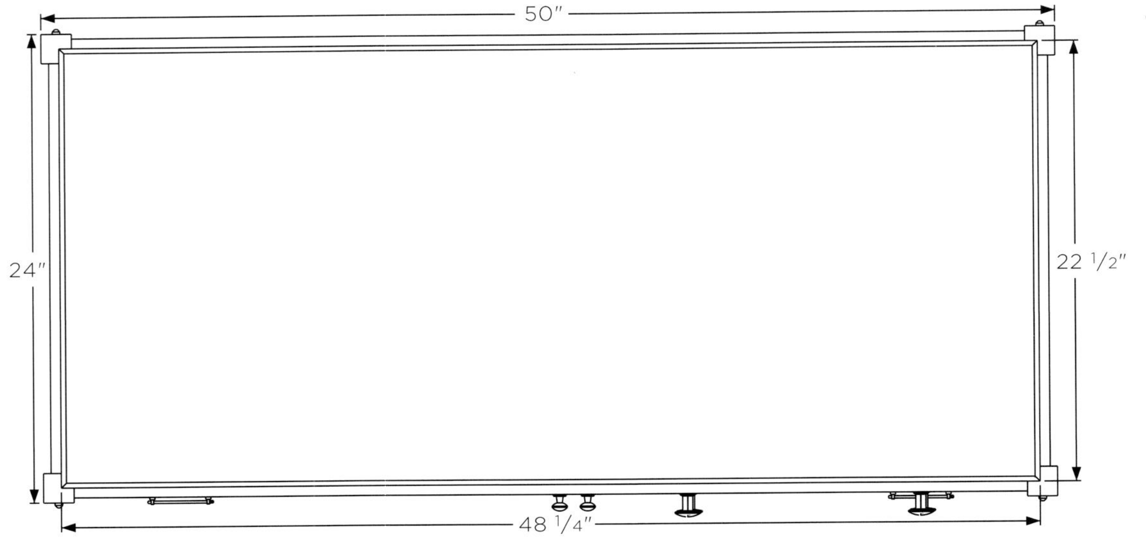

TOP VIEW

PART LIST

Qty	Description	Length	Width	Thickness
1	back lower panel	44 1/2"	25 1/2"	1/4"
1	back lower rail	44"	9 1/4"	3/4"
1	back middle rail	44"	3"	3/4"
2	back stile	62 1/4"	2 1/4"	3/4"
1	back upper panel	44 1/2"	23 1/4"	1/4"
1	back upper rail	44"	3 1/4"	3/4"
1	back top stretcher	48"	1 1/4"	3/4"
1	bottom dust panel	45"	20"	1/4"
1	bottom shelf	47"	20"	3/4"
1	center divider panel	49"	20"	1/4"
2	center divider rail	20"	3"	3/4"
1	center divider stile	54 1/4"	1 1/2"	3/4"
1	closet door lower rail	19 1/4"	4"	3/4"
1	closet door panel	46 3/4"	18 1/4"	1/4"
2	closet door stile	53"	4 1/4"	1 1/2"
1	closet door upper rail	19 1/4"	3 1/4"	3/4"
1	cupboard door panel	20"	16"	1/4"
2	cupboard door rail	17"	3 1/4"	3/4"
2	cupboard door stile	25 1/2"	3 1/2"	3/4"
1	cupboard shelf	22"	21 7/8"	3/4"
1	drawer 1 back	22"	4 1/2"	1/2"
1	drawer 1 front	22"	4 1/2"	3/4"
2	drawer 1 side	21 1/2"	4 1/2"	1/2"
2	drawer 2 back	22"	6 1/4"	1/2"
2	drawer 2 front	22"	6 1/4"	3/4"
4	drawer 2 side	21 1/2"	6 1/4"	1/2"
1	drawer 3 back	22"	7 1/2"	1/2"
1	drawer 3 front	22"	7 1/2"	3/4"
2	drawer 3 side	21 1/2"	7 1/2"	1/2"
1	drawer 4 back	47"	5 1/2"	1/2"
1	drawer 4 bottom	46 1/2"	21 1/4"	1/4"
1	drawer 4 front	47"	5 1/2"	3/4"
2	drawer 4 side	21 1/2"	5 1/2"	1/2"
1	front bottom stretcher	48"	2"	3/4"
5	front drawer divider	22 1/2"	2 1/4"	3/4"
1	front top stretcher	49"	1 1/4"	3/4"
2	front webframe crosspiece	48"	2 1/4"	3/4"
4	leg	68 1/2"	1 1/2"	1 1/2"
2	side bottom rail	23"	9 1/4"	3/4"
2	side lower panel	25 3/4"	22"	1/4"
2	side middle rail	23"	3"	3/4"
2	side stretcher	24 1/2"	2"	3/4"
2	side top rail	24 1/2"	5 3/4"	3/4"
2	side upper panel	22"	22"	1/4"
4	small drawer bottom	21 1/2"	21 1/4"	1/4"
3	small dust panel	20"	20"	1/4"
1	top	48 1/4"	22 1/2"	3/4"
1	top shelf panel	22"	19 1/4"	3/4"
1	umbrella bar	19 1/2"	3 1/8"	3/4"
1	umbrella shelf	2 49/64"	20"	3/4"
1	valet drawer back	13 1/2"	8"	1/2"
1	valet drawer bottom	20 1/4"	13"	1/4"
1	valet drawer divider	12 1/2"	7 1/4"	1/4"
1	valet drawer divider top piece	13 1/2"	10"	1/2"
1	valet drawer front	13 1/2"	10"	3/4"
2	valet drawer side	2 1/2"	8"	1/2"
1	valet side	21 7/8"	8"	1/2"
1	valet top	16"	14 3/8"	1/2"
1	vertical divider	54 1/4"	2 1/4"	3/4"
3	webfram rear stile	22 1/2"	1 1/2"	3/4"
2	webframe long stile	47 1/2"	1 1/2"	3/4"
8	webframe rail	2"	1 1/2"	3/4"

FRONT VIEW

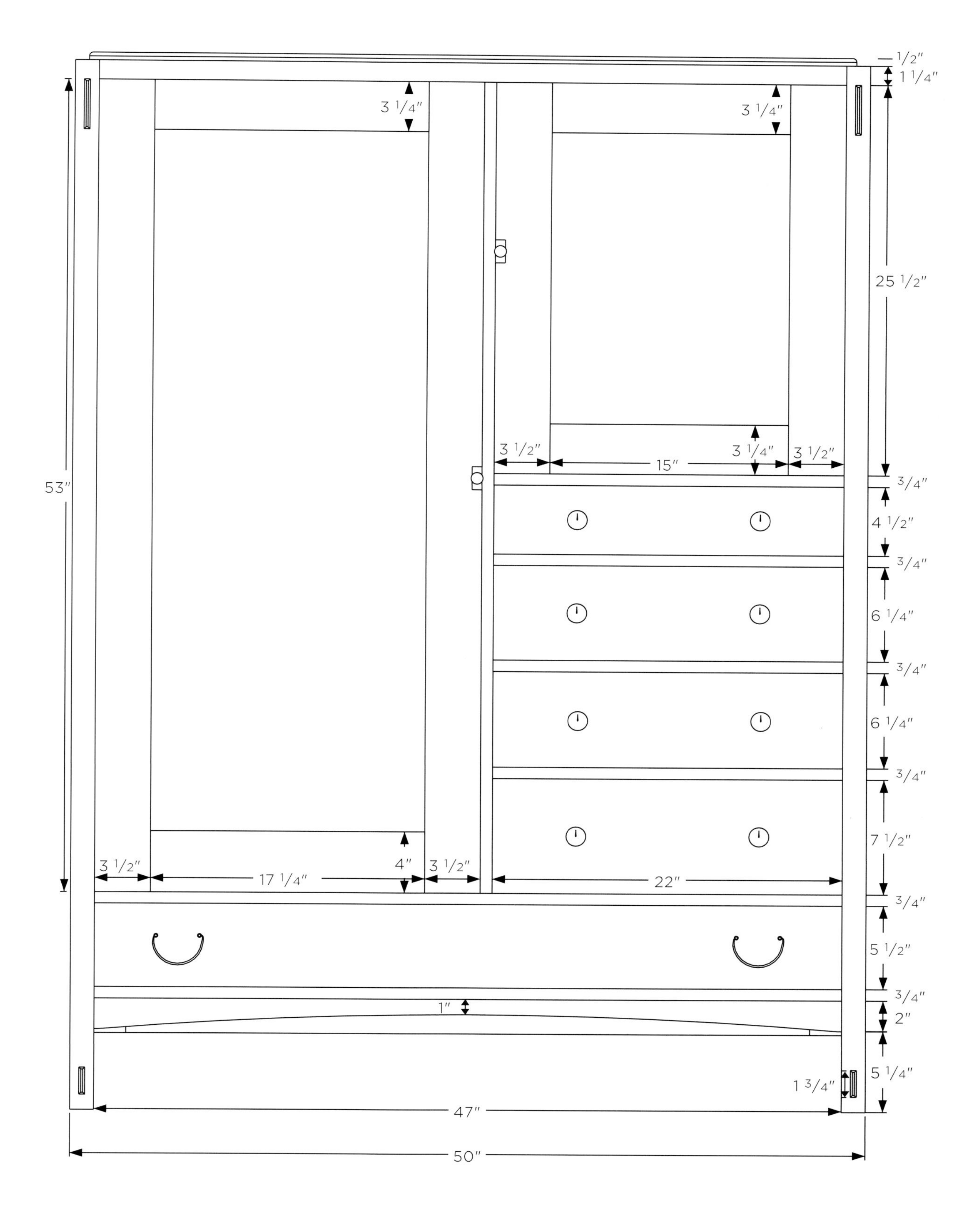

1/2"
1 1/4"
3 1/4"
3 1/4"
25 1/2"
53"
3 1/2"
15"
3 1/4"
3 1/2"
3/4"
4 1/2"
3/4"
6 1/4"
3/4"
6 1/4"
3/4"
7 1/2"
3 1/2"
17 1/4"
4"
3 1/2"
22"
3/4"
5 1/2"
3/4"
1"
2"
5 1/4"
1 3/4"
47"
50"

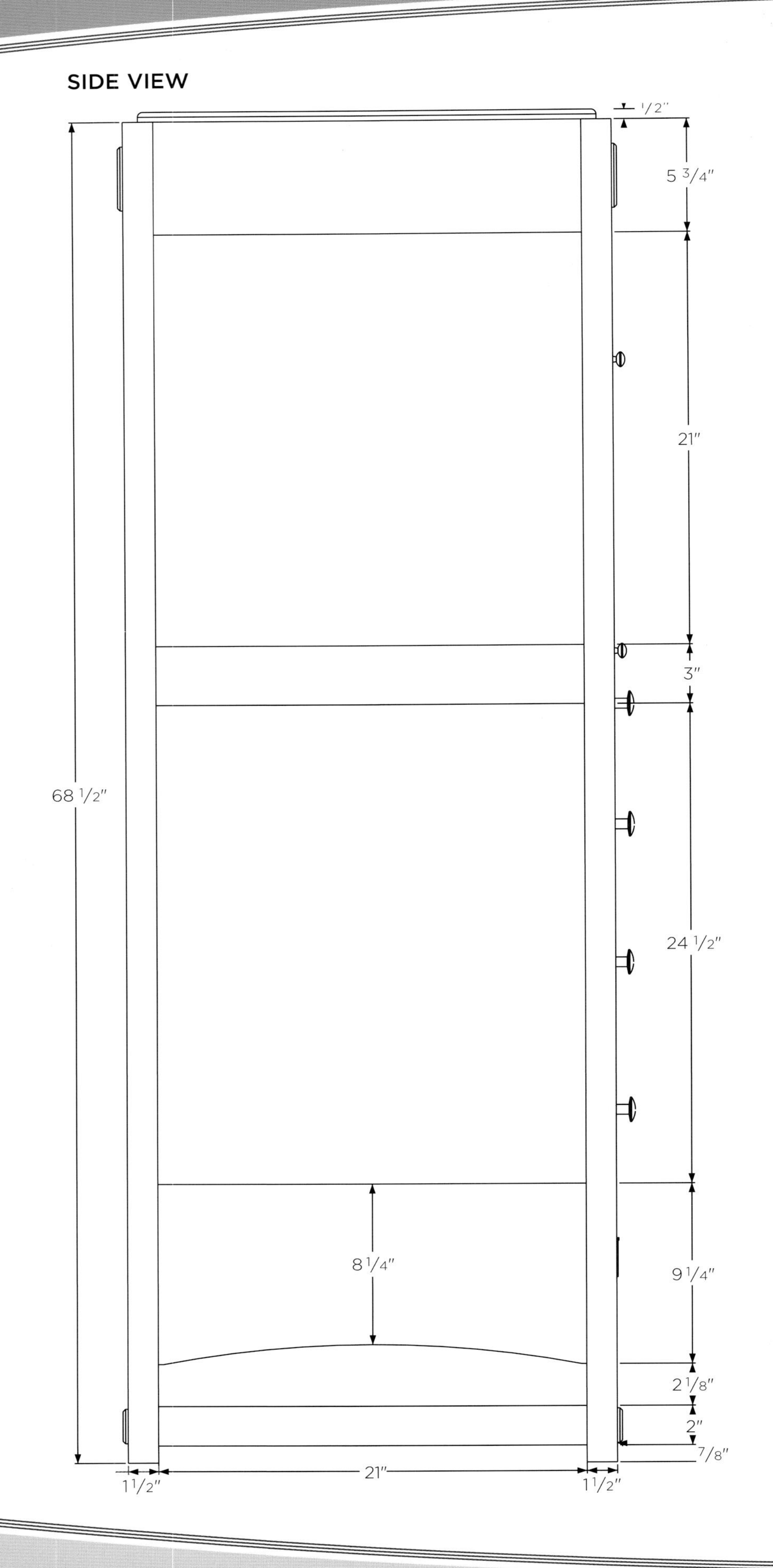
SIDE VIEW
1/2"
5 3/4"
21"
3"
68 1/2"
24 1/2"
8 1/4"
9 1/4"
2 1/8"
2"
7/8"
1 1/2"
21"
1 1/2"

No. 499

SOMNOE

30″ high x 16″ wide x 16″ deep

This small nightstand packs a surprising amount of complexity into its frame, so it provides a good introduction to joinery as well as a convenient place for a lamp. The inset top and through tenons, design motifs common to much Limbert bedroom furniture, share tight quarters with a frame-and-panel case, captive shelf, webframe and drawer.

EXPLODED VIEW

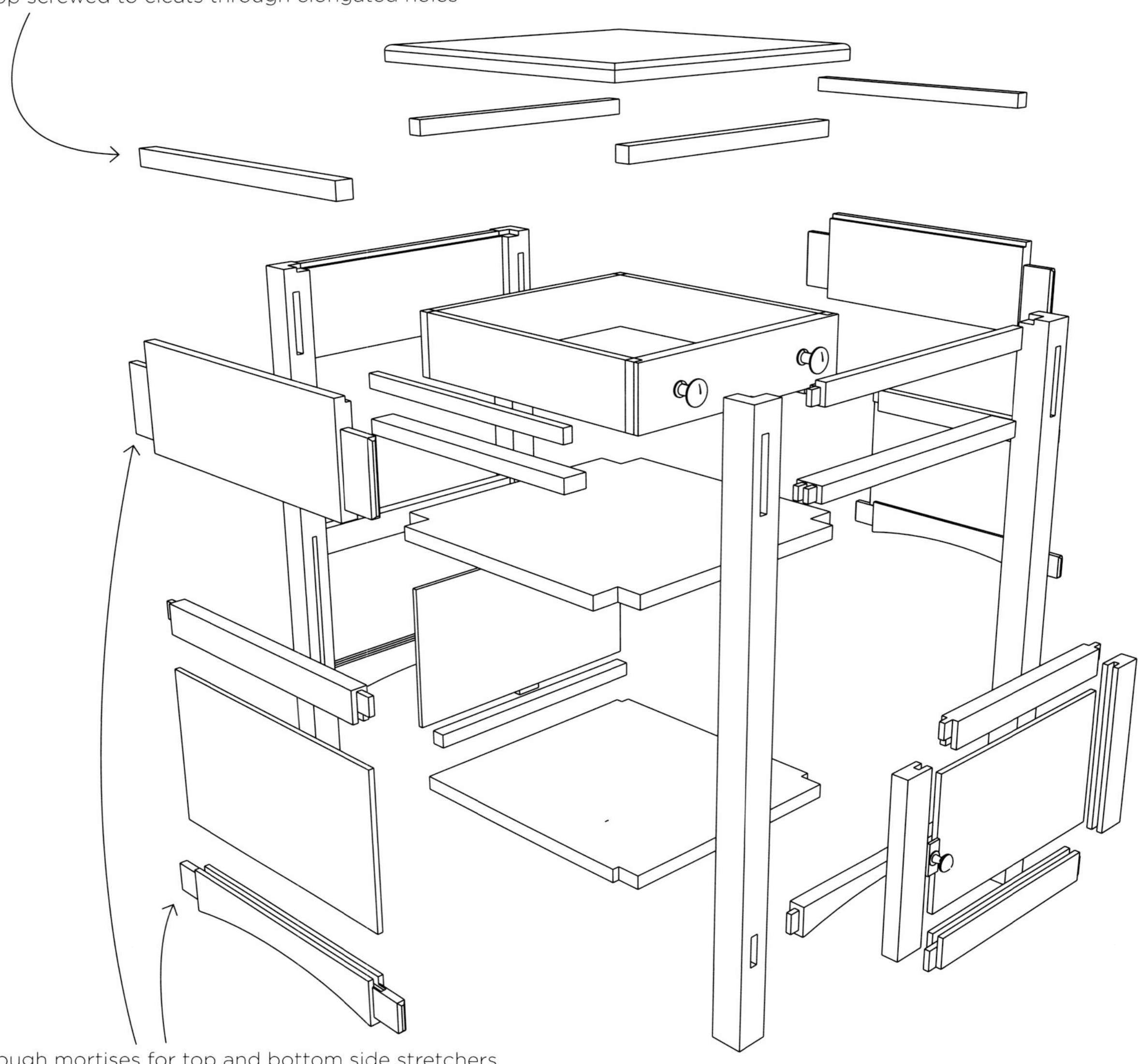

PART LIST

Qty	Description	Length	Width	Thickness
1	back stretcher	14 3/8"	5"	3/4"
1	bottom stretcher	14"	2 1/4"	3/4"
1	cabinet shelf	14 5/8"	13 7/8"	3/4"
3	cabinet side top stretcher	14 3/8"	1 1/2"	3/4"
1	cabinet top	16"	15 7/8"	3/4"
1	cleat	13"	3/4"	3/4"
1	door bottom rail	11"	1 1/2"	3/4"
1	door panel	11"	6 1/2"	1/4"
2	door stile	8 1/4"	1 1/2"	3/4"
1	door top rail	11"	1 1/4"	3/4"
1	drawer bottom	13 1/2"	12 1/2"	1/4"
1	drawer front	13"	3 1/4"	3/4"
2	drawer kick	13"	3/4"	3/4"

Qty	Description	Length	Width	Thickness
2	drawer runner	13"	1 1/4"	3/4"
2	drawer side	14"	3 1/4"	1/2"
2	drawer spacer	13"	3/4"	1/2"
1	front lower stretcher	14"	1 1/4"	3/4"
1	front stretcher	14"	1 1/2"	3/4"
1	front top apron	14"	1"	3/4"
4	leg	28 1/2"	1 1/2"	1 1/2"
2	lower side stretcher	16 1/2"	2 1/4"	3/4"
3	panel	14"	7 3/4"	1/4"
2	side stretcher	16 1/2"	5"	3/4"
1	top	14 1/2"	14 1/2"	3/4"
2	top cleat	12 1/2"	3/4"	3/4"

FRONT VIEW

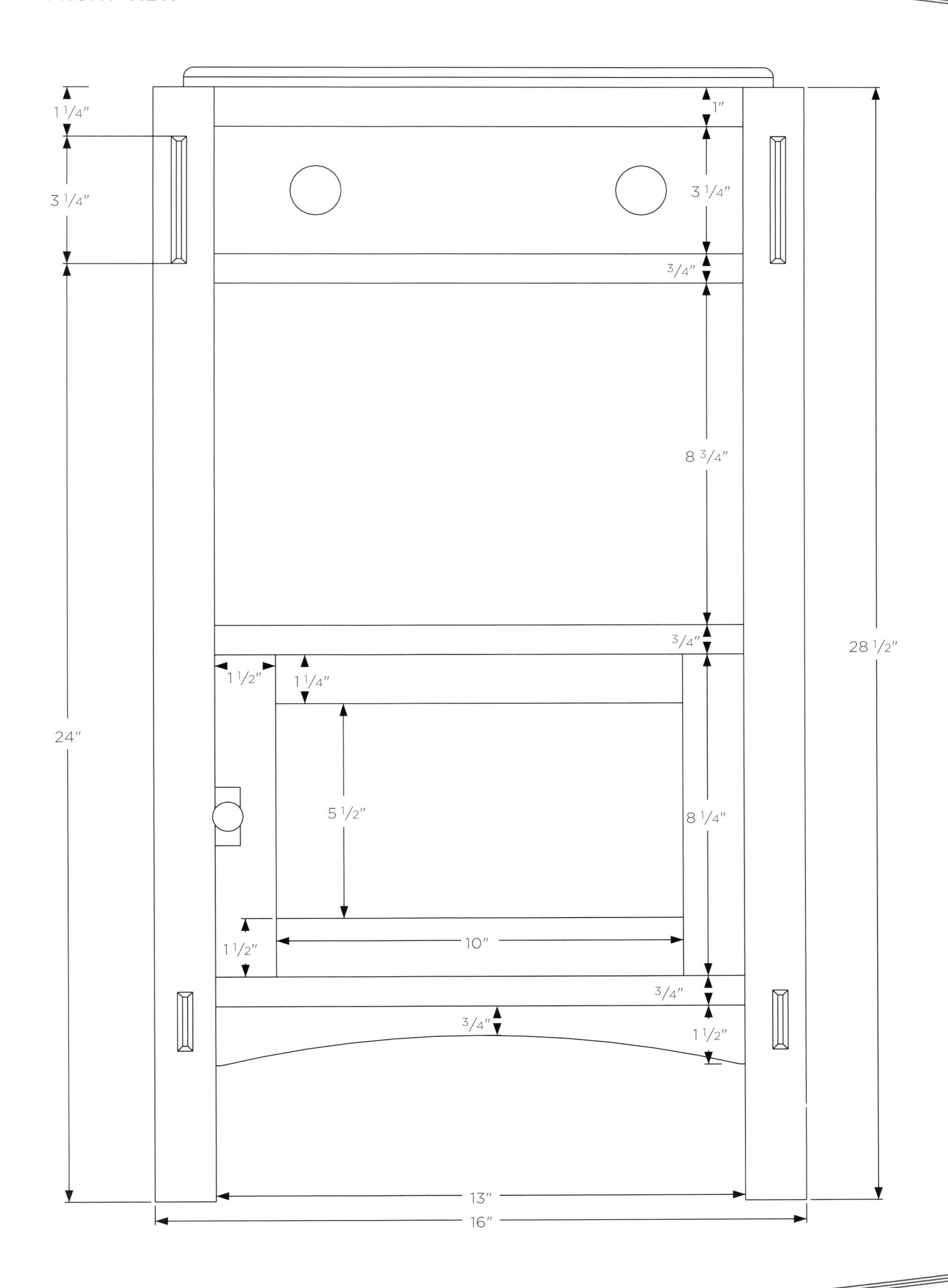
1 1/4″
3 1/4″
24″
1″
3 1/4″
3/4″
8 3/4″
3/4″
28 1/2″
1 1/2″
1 1/4″
5 1/2″
8 1/4″
1 1/2″
10″
3/4″
3/4″
1 1/2″
13″
16″

SIDE SECTION VIEW

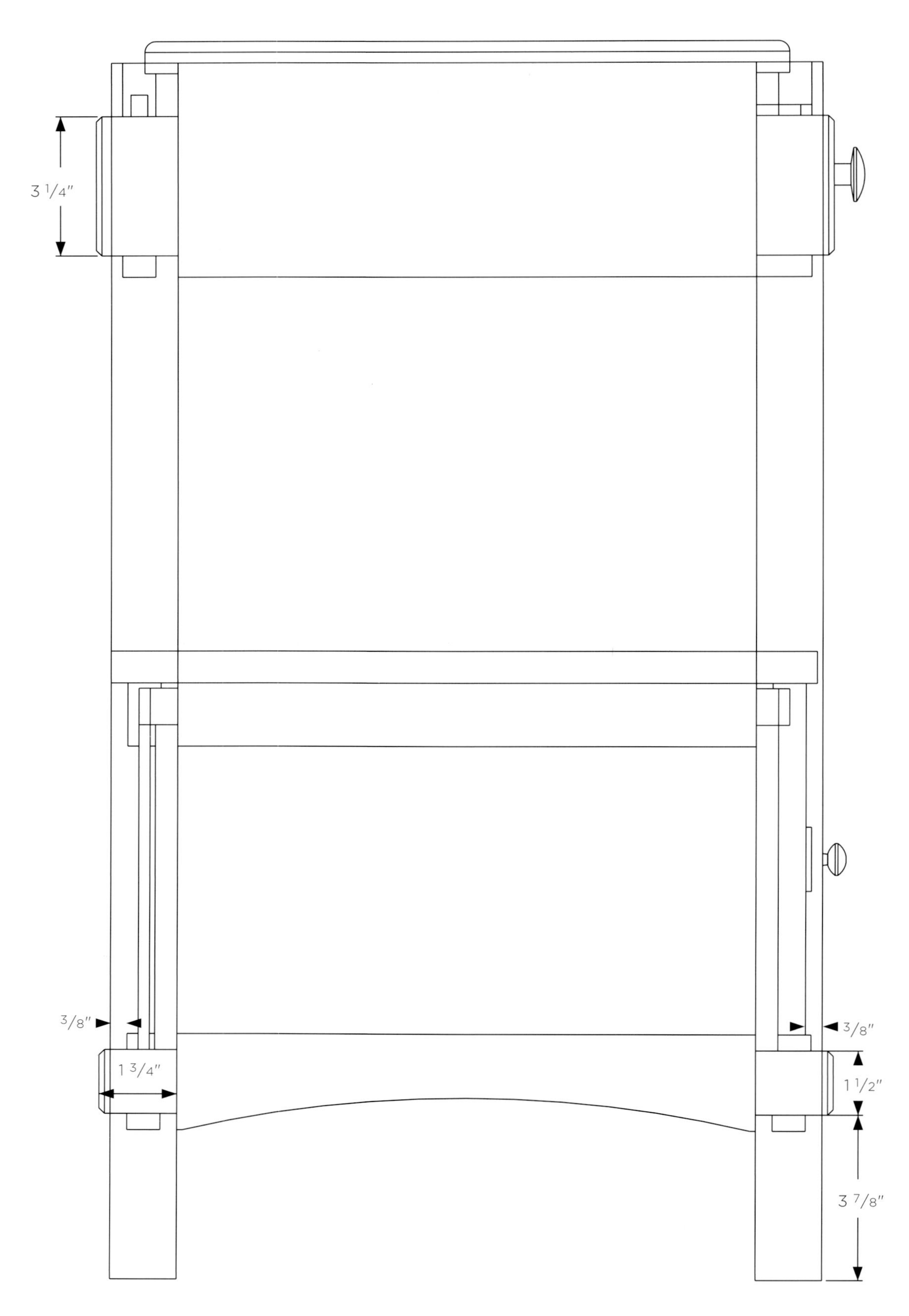

SIDE VIEW

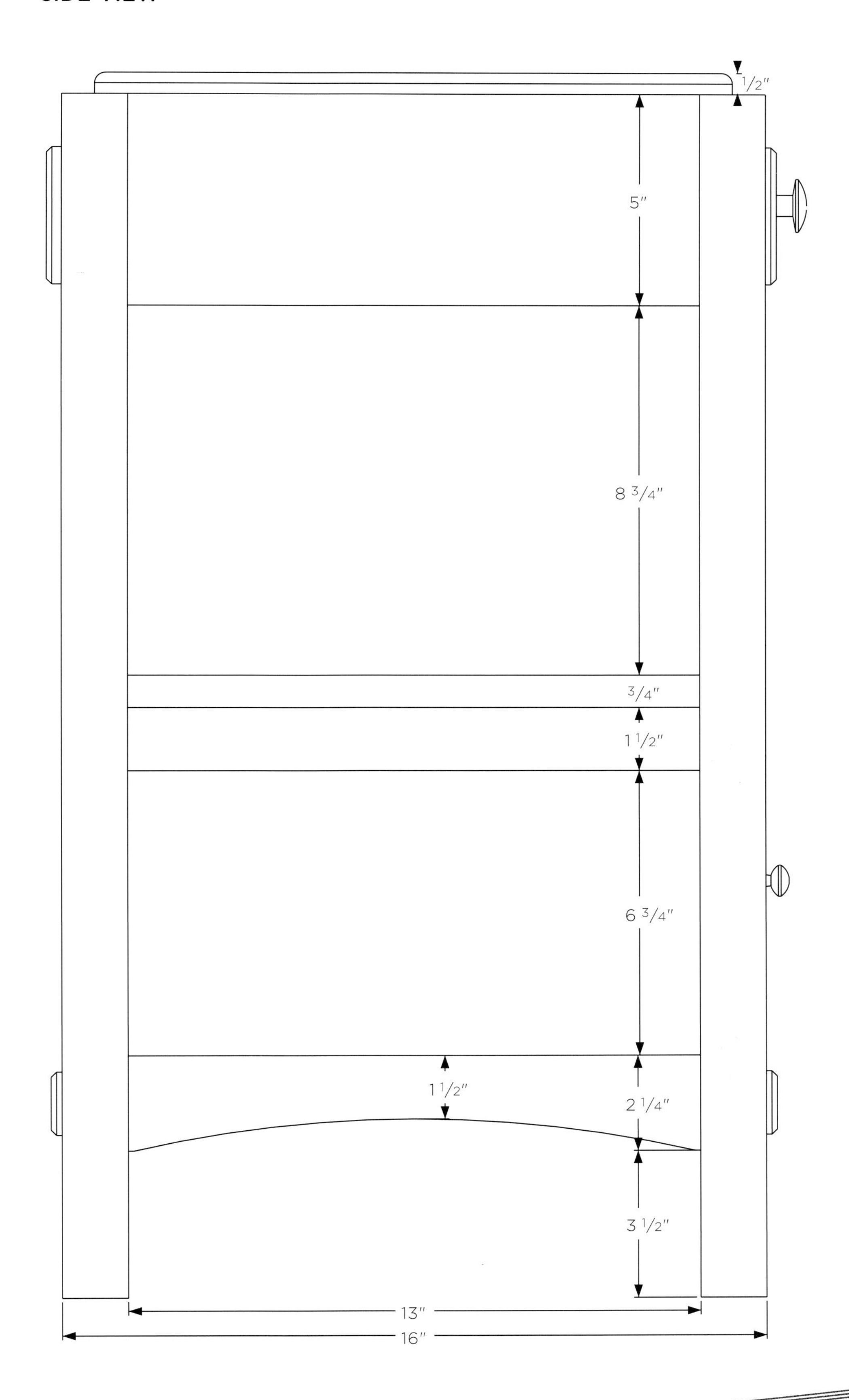

TOP VIEW

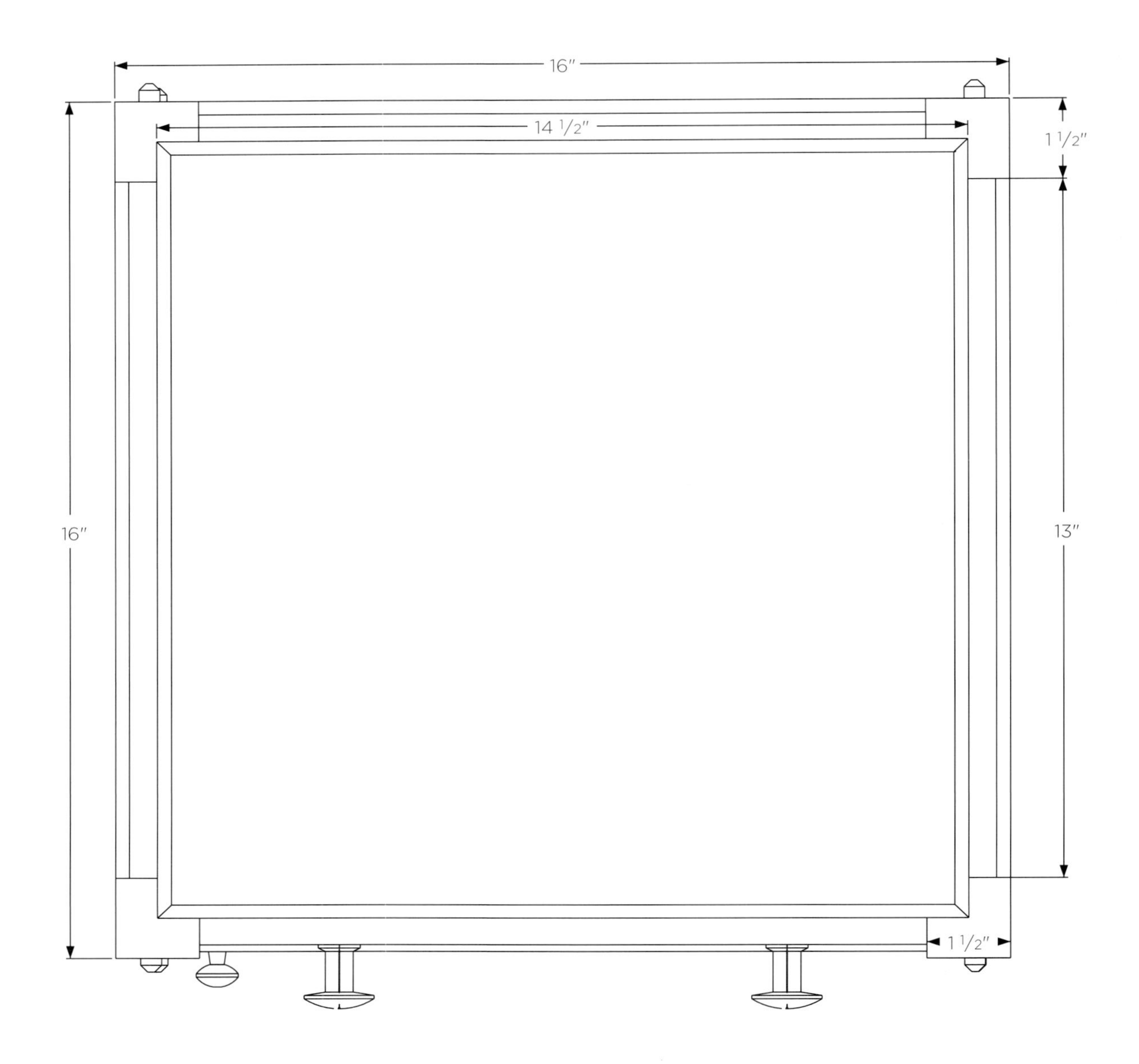

FURTHER READING

WORKS CONSULTED

The following titles have been invaluable in researching the life of Charles Limbert and the history of the Limbert Furniture Company.

Bartinique, Patricia. *Kindred Styles: The Arts and Crafts Furniture of Charles P. Limbert*
New York: Gallery 532 Soho, 1995. This now out of print exhibition catalog is the best single reference on Limbert and his furniture.

Edwards, Robert L., ed. *The Arts & Crafts Furniture of Charles P. Limbert: Two Catalogues* With an Introduction
Watkins Glen, NY: American Life Foundation, 1982.

Charles P. Limbert Co. Limbert Arts and Crafts Furniture: The Complete 1903 Catalog
Mineola, NY: Dover, 1992.

Charles P. Limbert Co. *Booklet 114*
Grand Rapids MI, circa 1910. A holding of the Internet Archive at:
www.archive.org/details/limbertsholla00char.

Gray, Stephen, ed. *Limbert's Holland Dutch Arts and Crafts Furniture, 3rd Ed*
Philmont, NY: Turn of the Century Editions, 1997.

Rago, David, Suzanne Sliker, and David Rudd. *The Arts & Crafts Collector's Guide*
Layton, UT: Gibbs Smith, 2005

Stott, Annette. *Holland Mania: the Unknown Dutch Period in American Art & Culture*
New York: Overlook Press, 1998

PREVIOUSLY PUBLISHED LIMBERT DESIGNS

The following sources, arranged by Limbert catalog number, contain either plans or instructions for producing select Limbert pieces.

Unnumbered Console Table. Lang, Robert. More Shop Drawings for Craftsman Furniture.
Bethel, CT: Cambium Press, 2002. 53-55.

492 1/2 Dressing Table.
Lang, Robert. More Shop Drawings for Craftsman Furniture. Bethel, CT: Cambium Press, 2002. 108-112.

139 Octagonal Dining Table.
Lang, Robert. Shop Drawings for Craftsman Furniture. Bethel, CT: Cambium Press, 2001. 119-121.

158 Library Table. Paolini, Gregory. "Make a Limbert-style Coffee Table" Fine Woodworking 215 (2010):
28-35.

238 Tabourette. Schwarz, Christopher. "Limbert Bookcase" Popular Woodworking's Arts& Crafts Furniture Projects. Ed.
Thiel, David. Cincinatti, OH: Popular Woodworking Books, 2008. 46-51.

240 Lamp Table. "Limbert-style Arts & Crafts. Wood Magazine #192.
September 2009. Available as a paid download at: www.woodstore.net/liarcrta.html.

255 Waste Paper Box.
Shwarz, Christopher. Popular Woodworking Magazine. Available as a free download at: www.popularwoodworking.com/wp-content/uploads/2010/10//Wastebox.pdf.

300 Magazine Stand.
Thiel, David. Arts & Crafts Furniture Anyone Can Make. Popular Woodworking Books. 2010. 142-149.

340 Book Case.
Schwarz, Christopher. "Limbert Bookcase" Popular Woodworking's Arts& Crafts Furniture Projects. Ed. Thiel, David. Cincinatti, OH: Popular Woodworking Books, 2008. 40-51.

353 Magazine Shelf.
Howard, Blair. Arts & Crafts Furniture: Projects You Can Build for the Home. Fresno, CA: Linden Publishing, 1999. 94-99.

500 Café Chair.
Thiel, David. Arts & Crafts Furniture Anyone Can Make. Popular Woodworking Books. 2010. 74-85.

FURNITURE CONSTRUCTION AND FINISHING

New woodworkers will find the following sources helpful as they build their skills.

I Can Do That.
Collects Popular Woodworking Magazine articles designed to introduce new woodworkers to the craft. They also publish a manual of a basic tool set. Available for free at: www.popularwoodworking.com/projects/icandothat.

Jewitt, Jeffrey The Complete Illustrated Guide to Finishing.
Taunton, 2004. A useful introduction to applying a range of finishes.

Lang, Robert. "Composing With Wood Grain." Woodworking Magazine Spring (2009):
18-23. A thorough primer on wood selection.

Rae, Andy. The Complete Illustrated Guide to Furniture and Cabinet Construction.
Taunton, 2001. Introduces standard construction techniques.

Rogowski, Gary. The Complete Illustrated Guide to Joinery.
Taunton, 2002. A comprehensive survey of cutting joints using hand and power tools.

Rodel, Kevin. "Fuming With Ammonia." Fine Woodworking 126 (1997):
46-49. Provides a concise introduction to using ammonia to color wood.

METRIC CONVERSION CHART

To convert	To	Multiply by
Inches	Centimeters	2.54
Centimeters	Inches	0.4
Feet	Centimeters	30.5
Centimeters	Feet	0.03
Yards	Meters	0.9
Meters	Yards	1.1

ABOUT THE AUTHOR

Michael is an amateur woodworker with a special interest in the inspired minimalism of Shaker and Arts and Crafts furniture. He can often be found working on his Craftsman bungalow or building furniture for it. Follow his work at www.1910craftsman.com.

DEDICATION

In addition to tolerating my bad behavior in antique stores and furniture showrooms as I crawled under and manhandled furniture to see how it was put together, my wife Katherine prompted me to go from the vague idea of a potential book to a concrete proposal, then entertained countless conversations on Charles Limbert and his furniture over the last year. Without her encouragement and comments, this book would not exist, so this is for her.

ACKNOWLEDGEMENTS

My sincere thanks to the following people.

Heather Edwards at the Grand Rapids Public Library, Catherine Jung at the Holland Museum and Lauri Perkins at Winterthur Library helped source the archival images.

The Editorial Staff at Popular Woodworking Books.

Read This Important Safety Notice

To prevent accidents, keep safety in mind while you work. Use the safety guards installed on power equipment; they are for your protection.

When working on power equipment, keep fingers away from saw blades, wear safety goggles to prevent injuries from flying wood chips and sawdust, wear hearing protection and consider installing a dust vacuum to reduce the amount of airborne sawdust in your woodshop.

Don't wear loose clothing, such as neckties or shirts with loose sleeves, or jewelry, such as rings, necklaces or bracelets, when working on power equipment. Tie back long hair to prevent it from getting caught in your equipment.

People who are sensitive to certain chemicals should check the chemical content of any product before using it.

Due to the variability of local conditions, construction materials, skill levels, etc., neither the author nor Popular Woodworking Books assumes any responsibility for any accidents, injuries, damages or other losses incurred resulting from the material presented in this book.

The authors and editors who compiled this book have tried to make the contents as accurate and correct as possible. Plans, illustrations, photographs and text have been carefully checked. All instructions, plans and projects should be carefully read, studied and understood before beginning construction.

Prices listed for supplies and equipment were current at the time of publication and are subject to change.

 Published by Popular Woodworking Books, an imprint of F+W Media, Inc., 10151 Carver Rd., Suite 200, Blue Ash, Ohio, 45236. (800) 289-0963 First edition.

Distributed in Canada by Fraser Direct
100 Armstrong Avenue
Georgetown, Ontario L7G 5S4
Canada

Distributed in the U.K. and Europe by
F&W Media International, LTD
Brunel House, Ford Close
Newton Abbot
TQ12 4PU, UK
Tel: (+44) 1626 323200
Fax: (+44) 1626 323319
E-mail: enquiries@fwmedia.com

Distributed in Australia by Capricorn Link
P.O. Box 704, Windsor, NSW 2756 Australia
Tel: (02) 4560 1600; Fax: (02) 4577 5288
Email: books@capricornlink.com.au

17 16 15 14 13 5 4 3 2 1

Acquisitions editor: David Thiel
Designer: Bethany Rainbolt
Production coordinator: Debbie Thomas

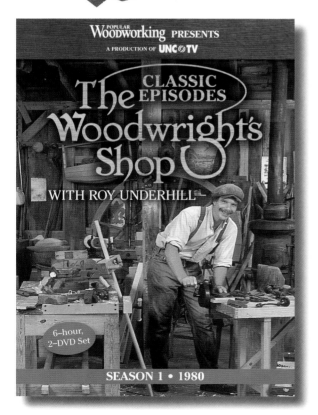

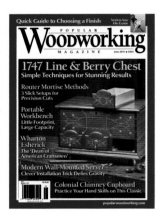

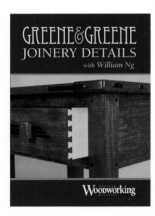